linked

NAVPRESS

Discipleship Inside Out®

NavPress is the publishing ministry of The Navigators, an international Christian organization and leader in personal spiritual development. NavPress is committed to helping people grow spiritually and enjoy lives of meaning and hope through personal and group resources that are biblically rooted, culturally relevant, and highly practical.

**For a free catalog go to www.NavPress.com
or call 1.800.366.7788 in the United States or 1.800.839.4769 in Canada.**

Linked: Connections Between God, Each Other, and Us
©2009 The Navigators

All rights reserved. No part of this publication may be reproduced, stored in a retrieval system, or transmitted in any form or by any means, electronic, mechanical, photocopying, recording, or otherwise, without the prior permission from NavPress, P.O. Box 35001, Colorado Springs, CO 80935

www.navpress.com
www.studentlifebiblestudy.com

NAVPRESS, Student Life, and the Student Life logo are registered trademarks. Absence of ® in connection with these trademarks does not indicate an absence of registration of those marks.

Unless otherwise indicated, all Scripture quotations are taken from the Holy Bible: New International Version (North American Edition), copyright ©1973, 1978, 1984, by International Bible Society. Used by permission of Zondervan Publishing House.

Some Scripture passages were taken from *The Message*, copyright ©1993, 1994, 1995, 1996, 2000, 2001, 2002. Used by permission of NavPress Publishing Group.

Inside images © jupiterimages, BananaStock, Comstock, Photodisc, istockphoto, Ruth Tinsley, and Student Life

ISBN-13: 978-193504-083-5

Printed in the United States of America

2 3 4 5 6 / 16 15 14 13 12

linked
CONNECTIONS BETWEEN GOD, EACH OTHER, AND US

NAVPRESS
Discipleship Inside Out®

studentlife**bible**study

TABLE OF CONTENTS

How To Use | Teachers i
How To Use | Students iii
Introduction v

JUSTICE: The Rightness And Fairness Of God 12
Lesson 1: Just God 14
Lesson 2: God Cares 20
Lesson 3: God Judges 26
Lesson 4: God Delivers 32
Lesson 5: The Injustice Problem 38
Lesson 6: Do Justice 44

NEXUS: God's Covenant With Us 50
Lesson 1: Created For A Relationship 52
Lesson 2: Different From The Rest 58
Lesson 3: What's Love Got To Do With It? 64
Lesson 4: Jesus Enters The Picture 70
Lesson 5: All Things New 76
Lesson 6: Relationship With A Purpose 82

BRIDGING THE GAP: A Look At Isaiah 88
Lesson 1: Reason Together 90
Lesson 2: Righteous Wrath 96
Lesson 3: Quick Grace 102
Lesson 4: Safe And Secure 108
Lesson 5: Suffering Servant 114
Lesson 6: Free Future 120

THE MEANS: The Grace Of God 126
Lesson 1: Why Grace? 128
Lesson 2: Grace On Display 134
Lesson 3: Grace We Need 140
Lesson 4: Life-Giving Grace 146
Lesson 5: Life-Changing Grace 152
Lesson 6: How Does God's Grace Change How We See Others? 158

TOGETHER: How We Relate To Others 164
Lesson 1: Made for Each Other 166
Lesson 2: Love One Another 172
Lesson 3: Established Relationships 178
Lesson 4: Lasting Relationships 184
Lesson 5: Unified Together 190
Lesson 6: Mutual Respect 196

CHOSEN: A Study On The Peoples Of God 202
Lesson 1: What If? 204
Lesson 2: The Need To Be Needy 210
Lesson 3: True Community 216
Lesson 4: Give Yourself Away 222
Lesson 5: Swimming Upstream 228
Lesson 6: Carry Each Other's Burdens 234

ALL ABOUT YOU: Living A Life Of Worship 240
Lesson 1: Knowing The One We Worship 242
Lesson 2: Worship – It's His Call To Make 248
Lesson 3: An Audience of One 254
Lesson 4: Not Confined To A Place 260
Lesson 5: Sacrifice – A Primary Ingredient 266
Lesson 6: Worship Is A Forever Thing 272

NEXT: God's Promise For The Future 278
Lesson 1: The God Of The Future 280
Lesson 2: His vs. Mine 286
Lesson 3: Living In Today 292
Lesson 4: What Is To Come? 298
Lesson 5: What Is God Waiting For? 304
Lesson 6: Be Ready 310

Closing 316
Acknowledgments 319

HOW TO USE | Teachers

THE *LINKED* STUDENT BOOK is an amazing **supplemental** component for the *Linked* Curriculum. This highly interactive and experiential resource will change the way your students approach their personal time of devotion. Every aspect is meant to make your students' study of relationships with God and people both informative and entertaining. Your students will actually enjoy picking up this book and discovering what the next page holds.

Now that you've purchased it, the question is, "How does it work?"

Glad you asked.

The *Linked* Student Book is designed for your students to work through outside of class, on their own. The book consists of content that supports each of the lessons in the year-long study. As you teach each *Linked* lesson, the student book will deliver a week's worth of interactive content to reinforce the big picture truths of the lesson.

Linked consists of eight, six-week courses. The *Linked* Student Book has eight sections that correspond with each of the *Linked* courses. *Linked* is designed to allow you to work through the eight courses in whatever order you choose. The student book functions the same way; each of the eight sections of the book stand alone, allowing your students to experience the book in the same order they experience your lessons.

Each *Linked* lesson features an optional *Linked* Student Book activity. This activity is a way of providing an intersection between the in-class lesson content and the out-of-class student book content. Not only do the activities help remind and encourage your students to spend time in their books each week, but it allows teachers to focus on a specific activity in the book that ties in with the in-class lesson.

Finally, the *Linked* Student Book is an invaluable prayer guide. During the week, you will be able to follow along with your students' devotional content. Pray for each day's biblical truth to take root in your students' lives, growing to full spiritual maturity.

Use the *Linked* Student Book as a springboard into converstions with your students outside of the classroom environment. Maximize your opportunities for ongoing discipleship throughout each week of the year.

HOW TO USE | Students

THE BOOK YOU'RE HOLDING IN YOUR HANDS MAY BE DIFFERENT THAN ANY BOOK YOU'VE EVER HELD.

It is less of a book and more of an experience.

This book will take you on a journey of discovery—a journey that will lead you to answer two very important questions:

What does it mean to be in relationship with God, and how does that impact everything else in your life?

You will begin to formulate your answers to these questions as you begin to work through the chapters of this book. Each chapter corresponds with a specific six-week course of StudentLife**Bible**Study's *Linked* study. These chapters are designed for you to work through at your own pace, just one page per day. From time to time, your teacher might encourage you to work on specific activities. But for the most part, this book is designed for you to work through on your own.

Told you this book was different.

You see, every aspect of this book was designed with **you** in mind.

It is unique. After all, you're unique too.

There are a lot of different sides to you. The same is true with this book.
There are sections in this book that will challenge you. There are sections that will entertain.

There are activities that will ask you to write down your thoughts, your fears, and your dreams. There are many sections that will ask you to merely think.

The way you encounter this book will depend on the order in which your leader decides to teach you. Some of you will begin this book at the beginning and end at the end. Some of you will start in the middle and jump around. The order you are led to engage it in doesn't matter as much as your attitude does.

Your challenge is to commit to reading this book with a teachable spirit. Allow the Holy Spirit to teach and lead you as you are led to encounter Him. If you approach this book with this attitude, you will find that God will dramatically transform your understanding of Him. He will take you deeper into His presence and begin to use your life in ways you might not be able to imagine right now.

ONE LAST THING AND THIS IS IMPORTANT: Because this book is unique and made just for you, it works differently than other books. Some pages have activities and instructions. Some pages are thought-provoking devotions. Some pages are just pictures meant to stir your mind and heart. The key to using this book is to take every page one at a time, soaking in the content and letting the Spirit work in your heart.

INTRODUCTION

Linked

You are not alone.

We all play a part in this string of events called life. So what's it all about? What holds it together? What matters?

People were created for relationship. Not only are we surrounded by other people in this world but we are designed to live in relationship with an eternal God. These relationships are connected to each other.

God's Word reveals that it is impossible to separate a love for God from a love for His people, so everyone you meet matters to God. Everything you do matters to God. It's all linked.

If you want to live wholeheartedly for the sake of something greater than yourself, a good start would be to keep reading this book. **Why should you read this book?** After all, it's big. And it's not necessarily something you chose for yourself. Some adult probably encouraged you to give it a shot.

So what's in it for you? Why is this book worth your time?

Well, believe it or not, this book was designed specifically with teenagers in mind. It was designed with *you* in mind.

What does this mean exactly? Glad you asked.

This book is **visual**. Quite simply it looks awesome. This was done on purpose. It was done for you. You know what you like. And you don't like dry, stuffy, boring books, so we made this one look really cool.

This book is **interactive**. It doesn't just tell you stuff; it asks you stuff. There are lots and lots of places for you to share your thoughts, to express yourself, and to sound off and give an opinion.

This book is **entertaining**. There are some things that are included only to make you smile. After all, you like to have fun, so a book designed for you should be fun too, right?

But, most importantly, this book is **transformative.** Well, maybe it's more like a vehicle of transformation. What does that mean? Well, this book exposes you to God's Word. It points you to His teachings. It introduces you in the most wonderful ways to God and His character.

This book looks cool. It is interactive. It is entertaining. But if it is only those things, it is no different than any magazine on the shelf at your favorite bookstore.

The most important thing about this book is that it brings you into the presence of God the Father, His Son, Jesus, and the Holy Spirit. And it accomplishes all of this by taking you deep into the Word of God, the Bible.

Intrigued? Interested? Curious? Good...

Keep reading.

This book is made of 8 sections that correspond with the 8, six-week studies you will be studying in class.

Here's a short description of the sessions and what you can expect to find in them.

Justice: The Rightness and Fairness of God—This unit explores the justice of God. He is just because He is holy and, therefore, is the only one able and worthy to judge all. Although completely just, God is also compassionate toward His people when they suffer and seeks to show grace to them. As a result, His people are also to show justice and compassion to the world.

Nexus: God's Covenant with Us—God created people for a relationship with Him. However, because of His holiness and justice, the sin of His people provided a barrier between themselves and God. Through His compassion, God sent His Son, Jesus, to provide the way to destroy the barrier while being true to His holy character. Now, within this covenant relationship, His people express God's just and holy character to the world.

Bridging the Gap: Isaiah—This unit provides a clear picture of God's justice and grace to His chosen people. God's people were sinful and rebellious, but His grace continued to seek them for His purposes and to turn them to Himself—ultimately through His Suffering Servant.

The Means: The Grace of God—The previous unit noted that God's people were unable to have a relationship with Him except for the grace of God. This unit goes deeper into God's grace and dives into the ultimate expression of His grace through the sacrifice of Christ. Because of this grace, His people are able to live for His purposes, representing His grace to the world.

Together: How We Relate to Others—God not only created people for a relationship with Himself, He created them to relate with other people. He did not create people for isolation. This unit explores how our relationship with God prepares us for and is reflected in our relationships with others.

Chosen: A Study on the Peoples of God—This unit focuses on the people of God as a community. As the body of Christ, the people of God are identified by their actions.

All About You: Living a Life of Worship—God's character is deserving of all of our praise and glory. As the people of God, we are called to worship God with our lives and will do so for all of eternity.

Next: God's Promise for the Future—God has promised that His people will live eternally with Him. This unit studies that promise and what it means in our lives today and for the future.

JUSTICE

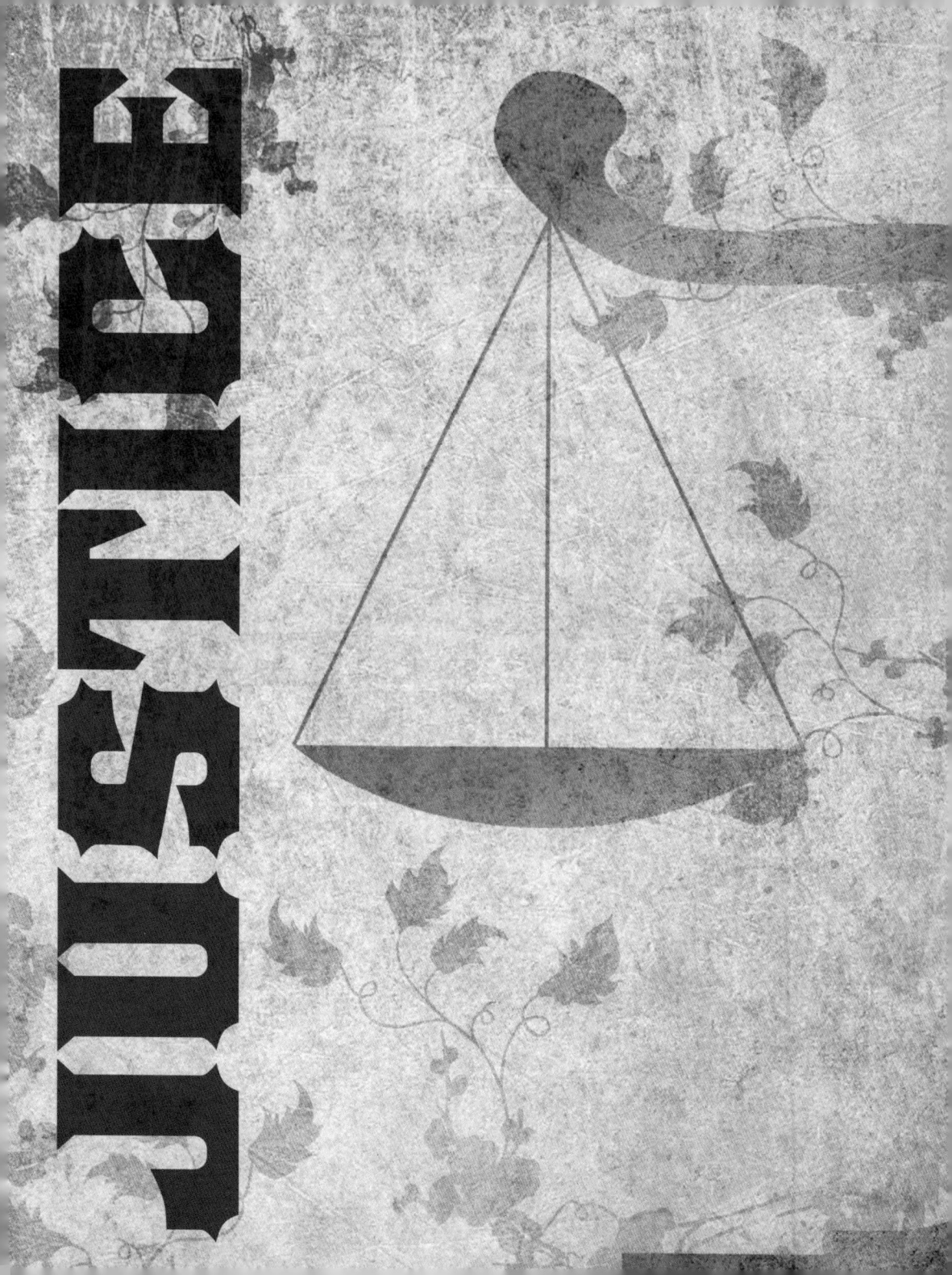

The world is a crazy place. Injustice seems to be the norm. Life isn't fair. This is often a major barrier in relationships with God and with other people. If so many bad things happen, how can anybody be trusted and how can a loving God exist?

Over the next several weeks, you'll see that not only does God care about justice, but also that a right perspective on justice will draw you closer to God as you trust in His love, power, wisdom, and timing in the midst of a world gone mad.

Justice has become somewhat of a buzzword in our culture, associated with causes that people support. But what do we mean by justice? For starters, you'll learn that God is the very definition of justice. You'll learn that God cares deeply for those who suffer and see that God deals justly with those who cause people to suffer (in a way only God can). You'll learn that God actively seeks to rescue those who suffer from injustice. But God doesn't want to act alone. He wants you to be a living, breathing agent of justice in this world as well. So, what are you waiting on?

LESSON 1: Just God –pg 14-19
LESSON 2: God Cares –pg 20-25
LESSON 3: God Judges –pg 26-31
LESSON 4: God Delivers –pg 32-37
LESSON 5: The Injustice Problem –pg 38-43
LESSON 6: Do Justice –pg 44-49

justice // lesson 1 day 1 // 14

GOD IS JUST.

WHERE DO YOU SEE INJUSTICE IN THE WORLD AROUND YOU? TODAY, THINK ABOUT HOW THE WORLD'S INJUSTICE IS EXACTLY OPPOSITE OF GOD'S JUSTICE.

Does injustice in the world cause you to doubt God's love and power or trust his love and power?

ELEMENTAL NATURE

Think for a moment about the elemental nature of things. What is the elemental nature of water? It's wet. If you leave your windows open when it rains, your car gets wet. That's what happens when something encounters water. What is the elemental nature of fire? It's hot. If you were to stick your hand on a hot barbecue grill, what would happen? When you touch fire, you get burned. (Here's a fun one to consider… What is the elemental nature of your coach? Your parents? Your brother or sister?)

Read Psalm 9:7–20. Now, you know that Psalms is a collection of 150 poems—mostly songs—written by a few different guys. We think David wrote 75 of them, which is by far the most by one author. Other writers include Solomon (possibly two psalms), Moses (one psalm), the Sons of Korah (11 psalms), and Asaph (12 psalms). There are a few psalms for which no writer has ever been identified. The psalms express so many emotions: some positive, some not so much. They provide a great source of inspiration for all believers.

Psalm 9 is one written by David. In this psalm, David praised God, acknowledging God's character and works. In the beginning of this psalm, David revealed to us one aspect of God that we might define as part of God's "elemental nature." God is pretty complex, so His nature is too. It can't be described in one word. But part of His nature is this idea of justice.

Look at verses 7–8. God reigns on a throne. And that throne is established for one reason: judgment. God is the judge of all things. But look at verse 8. Look at how God judges. With justice! His judgment is not done on a whim, or out of spite. It is administered with perfect justice.

God, quite literally, is just.

How does it make you feel knowing that God judges the actions and hearts of all people?
What do you think of when you hear the word justice?
What does it mean to be just? What is the opposite of justice?

justice // lesson 1 day 3 //16

JUSTICE

FUNCTION: NOUN

PRONUNCIATION: ('JES-TES)

ORIGINS: MIDDLE ENGLISH, FROM ANGLO-FRENCH JUSTISE; FROM LATIN JUSTITIA; FROM JUSTUS[1]

First originated in the mid-12th century. From the French word justise, meaning "the exercise of authority in vindication of right by assigning reward or punishment." From Latin origins, justitia, meaning "righteousness, equity," from justus "upright, just." The original French word had multiple applications, including "uprightness, equity, vindication of right, court of justice, judge."

The word first appeared in English around 1200 as a title for some sort of judge or court officer. The English meaning, "the administration of law," began to appear around 1300.

There is evidence from 1382 of the word being used to imply, "righteous in the eyes of God, upright and impartial."

What does the word justice mean to you?
What images does it bring to mind?
How do you see the concept played out in the world around you?

justice // lesson 1 day 4 // 17

★★★ **Instructions: Read these verses and meditate on God as the very definition of justice.** ★★★

FOR I, THE LORD, LOVE JUSTICE; I HATE ROBBERY AND INIQUITY. IN MY FAITHFULNESS I WILL REWARD THEM AND MAKE AN EVERLASTING COVENANT WITH THEM. -ISAIAH 61:8 ★★★★★★★★★★★★★★

Evil men do not understand justice, but those who seek the LORD understand it fully. -Proverbs 28:5

IT IS UNTHINKABLE THAT GOD WOULD DO WRONG, THAT THE ALMIGHTY WOULD PERVERT JUSTICE. -JOB 34:12

FOR THE LORD IS RIGHTEOUS, HE LOVES JUSTICE; UPRIGHT MEN WILL SEE HIS FACE. (PSALM 11:7)

I get my knowledge from afar; I will ascribe justice to my Maker. -Job 36:3

But the LORD Almighty will be exalted by his justice, and the holy God will show himself holy by his righteousness. -Isaiah 5:16

YOUR RIGHTEOUSNESS IS LIKE THE MIGHTY MOUNTAINS, YOUR JUSTICE LIKE THE GREAT DEEP -PSALM 36:6

He will judge the world in righteousness; he will govern the peoples with justice. -Psalm 9:8

Righteousness and justice are the foundation of your throne; love and faithfulness go before you. -Psalm 89:14

justice // **lesson 1 day 5** // 18

LOOK AT THE IMAGES ON THIS PAGE.
WHAT IDEAS OF JUSTICE COME TO MIND WHEN YOU LOOK AT EACH OF THESE PICTURES?

GOD

revenge

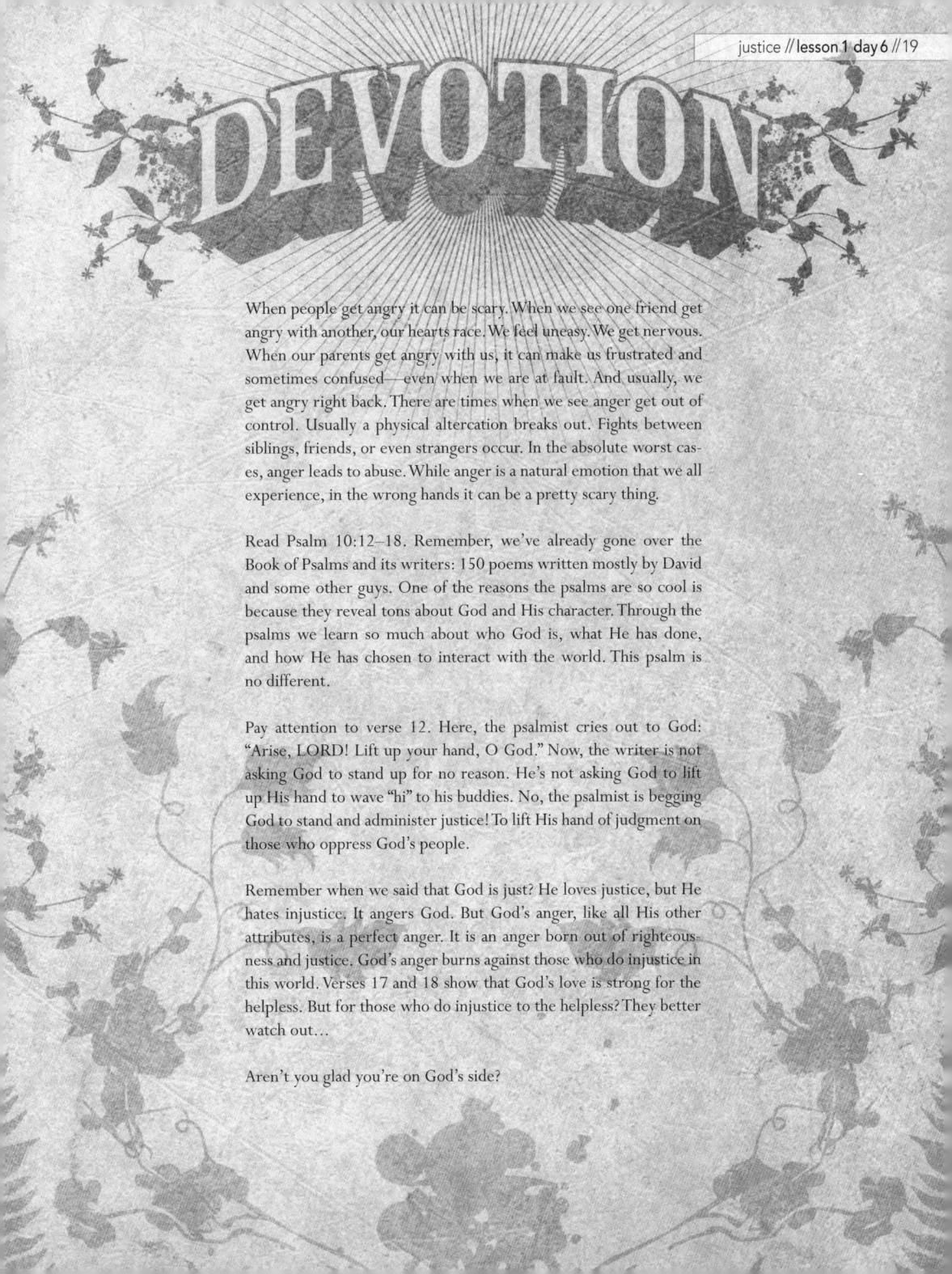

DEVOTION

When people get angry it can be scary. When we see one friend get angry with another, our hearts race. We feel uneasy. We get nervous. When our parents get angry with us, it can make us frustrated and sometimes confused—even when we are at fault. And, usually, we get angry right back. There are times when we see anger get out of control. Usually a physical altercation breaks out. Fights between siblings, friends, or even strangers occur. In the absolute worst cases, anger leads to abuse. While anger is a natural emotion that we all experience, in the wrong hands it can be a pretty scary thing.

Read Psalm 10:12–18. Remember, we've already gone over the Book of Psalms and its writers: 150 poems written mostly by David and some other guys. One of the reasons the psalms are so cool is because they reveal tons about God and His character. Through the psalms we learn so much about who God is, what He has done, and how He has chosen to interact with the world. This psalm is no different.

Pay attention to verse 12. Here, the psalmist cries out to God: "Arise, LORD! Lift up your hand, O God." Now, the writer is not asking God to stand up for no reason. He's not asking God to lift up His hand to wave "hi" to his buddies. No, the psalmist is begging God to stand and administer justice! To lift His hand of judgment on those who oppress God's people.

Remember when we said that God is just? He loves justice, but He hates injustice. It angers God. But God's anger, like all His other attributes, is a perfect anger. It is an anger born out of righteousness and justice. God's anger burns against those who do injustice in this world. Verses 17 and 18 show that God's love is strong for the helpless. But for those who do injustice to the helpless? They better watch out…

Aren't you glad you're on God's side?

justice // lesson 2 day 1 // 20

THEN I CALLED ON THE NAME OF THE LORD, O LORD SAVE ME!

Are you facing anything you might consider an injustice? Take a moment and voice a prayer to God. And while you're at it, voice a prayer for those who suffer injustice all around the world, each day.

SUFFERING

Where do you see suffering?

Do you see it in the faces of the hungry children on TV? Children in third world countries with hard-to-pronounce names?

Do you see it on the faces of the homeless in your city?

Maybe you see it on the faces of those who are mentally ill, trapped in a body and a mind that have betrayed them.

Do you see it on the faces of the addicts? The people in your town or on TV who have been taken captive by their addictions to meth, alcohol, cocaine, prescription meds… and so on…

Or maybe you see suffering on the face of the girl you know who has given herself over to feeding her sexual desires: multiple partners… living the party lifestyle…

Where do you see suffering? And what does it do to you? Does it make you uncomfortable? When you interact with the mentally ill, are you unsure what to say? When a homeless guy asks you for a dollar, is it hard to make eye contact? When the meth or coke or sex addict crosses your path, do you judge?

Do you see the hungry children and question God?

Psalm 116:1–11 tells us about God's reaction toward those who suffer. Verses 5–6 say, "The LORD is gracious and righteous; our God is full of compassion. The LORD protects the simplehearted; when I was in great need, he saved me."

God has compassion on those who suffer. God hears their cries. And while God chooses to respond to suffering in a way that only He knows and understands, Scripture is clear: God is compassionate toward those who suffer.

But are you?

justice // lesson 2 day 3 // 22

GOD CARES
ABOUT ALL KINDS OF INJUSTICE.

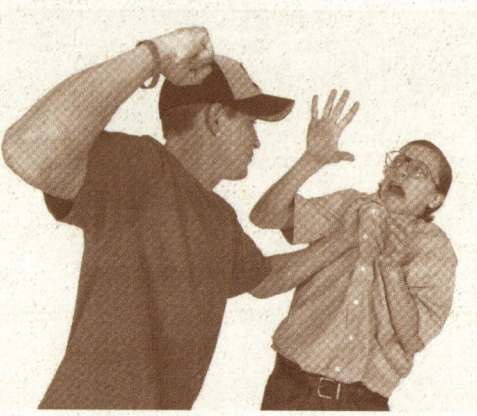

Do you see yourself in any of these images? If so, take a moment and say a prayer to God,

giving Him your

FEAR
ANGER
FRUSTRATION

...or whatever you feel as a result of the injustice in your life.

DEVOTION

What troubles do you face? What in your life would you consider as injustices committed against you? Now, you may have a pretty carefree life. Things may go well for you most of the time. But even the most happy-go-lucky teenager like you has some days when things aren't fair. Right?

OK, let's be honest. For most of you reading this, things are pretty good. Most of you aren't worried about whether you will eat today. Most of you will not worry about whether you will get attacked walking to school through the slums. Most of you reading this do not feel endangered because of your faith in God.

But for many people in the world, these are all very real concerns... and we can never forget that. Some of you reading this might face these troubles today as well. But for most reading this book, your troubles aren't that troubling.

But... they're all still real. And the battles you face in this life still hurt. And they still matter to God.

Read Psalm 103:1–6. David was a guy who understood trouble. He understood injustice. He understood that sometimes when you do the right thing, bad things still happen—through no fault of your own. David had some real unfair trials in his life. And if you read through the Psalms, you see David calling out to God in the midst of these trials. Some of David's words are brutally honest, and from his writings we can learn a lot about how to seek God in times of trouble. But in this particular passage, David did something a little different.

In Psalm 103:1-6, David praised God for all His good works. (This from a guy who knew what it was like to be kicked when he was already down.) In particular, verse 6 should speak to you as you consider the injustices that sometimes come your way: "The LORD works righteousness and justice for all the oppressed." So, next time you feel like the world has unfairly singled you out for ridicule, punishment, or other forms of mistreatment, remember this promise...

God does indeed work for righteousness and justice... and He works it for you!

justice // lesson 2 day 5 // 24

COMPASSION

Webster's defines compassion as "a sympathetic consciousness of others' distress together with a desire to alleviate it."

COMPASSION

An awareness of other's stress and a desire to do something to make it go away...

COMPASSION

God has it...

"As a father has compassion on his children, so the Lord has compassion on those who fear him."
Psalm 103:13

"I will have mercy on whom I will have mercy, and I will have compassion on whom I will have compassion."
Exodus 33:19

"Have mercy on me, O God, according to your unfailing love; according to your great compassion blot out my transgressions."
Psalm 51:1

Not that any of us deserve it...

But he gives it anyway...

"But you are a forgiving God, gracious and compassionate, slow to anger and abounding in love."
Nehemiah 9:17

Never forget this... God is compassion. When times get tough, he is there. His word assures us of this.

"The Lord is good to all; he has compassion on all he has made."
Psalm 145:9

justice // lesson 3 day 2 // 25

GENOCIDE
PHYSICAL ABUSE
POVERTY
OPPRESSIVE GOVERNMENT
BROKEN LEGAL SYSTEMS
UNTRUE GOSSIP
MURDER
WRONGFUL IMPRISONMENT
RELIGIOUS PERSECUTION
CHILD SEX TRADE
VERBAL ABUSE
AGE DISCRIMINATION
RACISM
DISHONEST GAIN
BULLYING
GENDER DISCRIMINATION

Look at this list of words. (It's a pretty harsh list, don't you think?) This is a list of injustices that go on in the world around you. Which of these do you think are the worst injustices? Why? Now identify the "smaller" injustices. Do these injustices hurt less because they aren't as "big" as the worst examples of injustice on this list?

Psalm 116:5 says that "God is full of compassion." God has compassion on those who suffer. Knowing God the way you do, do you think He has less compassion on those who suffer the "smaller" injustices? (Here's a hint: of course not.) Do you need God's compassion today?

justice // **lesson 3 day 1** // 26

GOD
WILL NOT ALLOW
INJUSTICE
TO GO
UNANSWERED

Think about this for a second:
How does it feel to see injustice?
To see people treated unfairly and to watch the bad guys go unpunished?
How does it make you feel knowing that God, in the end, is the final judge for all injustice?

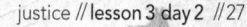

DEVOTION

Imagine you are sitting in your room, doing whatever you do in your spare time. Maybe you're playing a video game. Maybe you're killing time on Facebook. Maybe you're talking to a friend on the phone. Then suddenly, the door bursts open and in walks a bunch of big, official-looking guys in dark suits. One of them moves to the front of the group, shows you some sort of badge, and says: "My name is Agent #32457. You have been chosen by the Global Government Authority to be the final word in all disputes. You will be the sole judge of right and wrong in all matters—everywhere. Let's go."

Next, you are whisked away and taken to a secret bunker where it's your job to hear every single disagreement… every single case brought against another person… every single instance of reported wrongdoing in the world. It is your job to judge rightly in each case: who was wronged, who perpetrated the wrong, and what are the consequences?

Now, think for a moment: Could you do this? Of course not. How could anyone do this? First of all, who would ever qualify? And what would be the standard of right and wrong? It is a ridiculous scenario… .

Except that God does this every day—for all eternity.

Read Psalm 82:1–8. Pay special attention to verse 8: "Rise up, O God, judge the earth, for all the nations are your inheritance." That means the nations and all the people in them (for all of time) belong to God. He is the judge of the people. He judges people's thoughts and actions. And He does it according to His character. He alone is worthy to judge. He alone is worthy to stand as the sole standard of right and wrong. And God promises to judge the unjust.

Why is it such a good deal that God alone is the one to judge humans? Why is He uniquely suited to do that?

Why must God judge people? Why couldn't He just give people a break?

WHY DO BAD THINGS HAPPEN?

There's a saying that you hear from time to time, usually when a particular tragedy befalls someone who is likeable or of particularly high character. A terrible thing happens, and someone will inevitably ask, "Why do bad things happen to good people?" This is a reasonable emotion. It's somewhat normal to believe if we are good, good things will happen. Unfortunately, this doesn't always work out.

While the question, "Why do bad things happen to good people?" is interesting to ponder, even more perplexing might be the opposite: "Why do good things happen to bad people?" Doesn't this question cause us to doubt the way things work?

If you're honest, you've thought this before. We all know those one or two people who seem to live the charmed life. The guy that gets good grades, but who cheats on his tests. The girl that is class president, but who cheats on her boyfriend. The youth group star who never passes up the opportunity to talk about people behind their backs. You know these people. Maybe you're even one of them.

So, why does it happen? Why does God allow bad people to prosper? Well… not so fast. Read Jeremiah 5:26–29. Now, stop and reread verse 29: "Should I not punish them for this?" declares the LORD. "Should I not avenge myself on such a nation as this?" This is a rhetorical question; meaning, God already knows the answer. And the answer is "yes." God should and will punish those who are evil.

Now, God's sense of time is different than ours. To God a day is a year and a year a day. We see people succeeding who may act the worst possible. We cry, "Where is justice? Where is God?" But God says that justice is coming. It may not come in this life, but it is coming. God will have the last word. They may be successful in this life, but this life is merely a moment in time.

The evil will be judged. And for them, it will not end pretty.

GOD ALONE IS WORTHY AND ABLE TO JUDGE HUMANKIND

For the LORD is our judge, the LORD is our lawgiver, the LORD is our king; it is he who will save us. —Isaiah 33:22

Against you, you only, have I sinned and done what is evil in your sight, so that you are proved right when you speak and justified when you judge. —Psalm 51:4

But it is God who judges: He brings one down, he exalts another. —Psalm 75:7

He will judge your people in righteousness, your afflicted ones with justice. —Psalm 72:2

This will take place on the day when God will judge men's secrets through Jesus Christ, as my gospel declares. —Romans 2:16

The sea gave up the dead that were in it, and death and Hades gave up the dead that were in them, and each person was judged according to what he had done. —Revelation 20:13

Say among the nations, "The LORD reigns." The world is firmly established, it cannot be moved; he will judge the peoples with equity. —Psalm 96:10

There is only one Lawgiver and Judge, the one who is able to save and destroy. But you—who are you to judge your neighbor? —James 4:12

Rise up, O God, judge the earth, for all the nations are your inheritance. —Psalm 82:8

justice // lesson 3 day 5 // 30

RACISM
MURDER
POVERTY
PHYSICAL ABUSE

Psalm 9:8 says that God will "judge the world in righteousness." In God's eyes, sin is sin.

justice // lesson 3 day 6 // 31

SPREADING A LIE ABOUT A FRIEND

WHAT IS YOUR FIRST REACTION WHEN YOU SEE THE SCALE ABOVE? DO YOU WISH IT WERE DIFFERENT?

justice // lesson 4 day 1 // 32

GOD WILL RESCUE THE OPPRESSED

Scripture tells us that when oppressed people cry out to God, He answers them. He will rescue them. How does that change the way you view suffering in this world?

IT'S OK TO ASK QUESTIONS

We've talked a lot up to this point about God's sense of justice...

About His stand for righteousness . . .

About His desire to see the oppressed lifted up . . .

And about His desire to see oppressors brought down . . .

And, hopefully, you have done some real soul searching. By now, you have hopefully struggled with this idea of injustice and asked God some questions.

Maybe you've wondered why God allows injustice to happen. That's a fair question. And quite honestly, it's a tough one. It's hard to know the answer to it. Why does God allow suffering? We see hungry children and we ask, "What are you doing, God? Where are you?"

Two things you need to know: First, it's OK to ask God questions. In fact, it's part of growing in your faith. God isn't fragile. You can't hurt His feelings. You can seek Him with any questions you have. But here's the second thing. The answers to all of your questions are in His Word. That's right... all of them. The Bible contains what you need to know about God. Period.

So, you question why God allows suffering. You question why He does not seek out those who suffer and end their suffering. And those are good questions to ask. Just know that the answer is contained in His Word.

Try starting with Psalm 146:5–9. Look closely at verses 6–7. Verse 6 says God remains forever faithful. That means He has always and will always do what He says He will do. And in verse 7 says, "He upholds the cause of the oppressed and gives food to the hungry. The LORD sets prisoners free."

Maybe you've asked why God hasn't done something to free people from suffering. The Bible says He has and that He will. People still suffer, but we do not know what God is doing all around the world right at this moment. And no matter what happens in this world, the life of the believer is secured. Though there is suffering today, eternity holds joy, peace, and tranquility.

justice // lesson 4 day 3 // 34

GOD ACTIVELY SEEKS TO RESCUE VICTIMS OF INJUSTICE... ANY KIND OF INJUSTICE.

**HOW DOES THIS MAKE YOU FEEL?
HOW CAN YOU JOIN GOD ON THIS MISSION?**

justice // lesson 4 day 4 // 35

DO YOU REMEMBER JOB?

HE KNEW A LITTLE ABOUT SUFFERING, DIDN'T HE? IN THE MIDST OF HIS SUFFERING HE CRIED OUT TO GOD. WHY? BECAUSE JOB KNEW SOMETHING ABOUT GOD'S CHARACTER...

"But those who suffer he **delivers** in their suffering; he speaks to them in their affliction." -Job 36:15

GOD IS A DELIVERER. MEANING, THAT WHEN HIS PEOPLE ARE HURTING OR OPPRESSED, HE IS THERE TO DELIVER THEM FROM THEIR SUFFERING... TO SAVE THEM!

KING DAVID KNEW THIS TOO...

"From the LORD comes deliverance. May your blessing be on your people. Selah."
-Psalm 3:8

"Turn, O LORD, and deliver me; save me because of your unfailing love."
-Psalm 6:4

"Do not say, 'I'll pay you back for this wrong!' Wait for the LORD, and he will deliver you."
-Proverbs 20:22

SCRIPTURE ATTESTS TO GOD'S ABILITY TO DELIVER HIS PEOPLE...

"From the LORD comes deliverance. May your blessing be on your people. Selah." -Psalm 3:8

ARE YOU IN NEED OF DELIVERANCE? CRY OUT TO GOD... HE WILL HEAR YOU AND DELIVER YOU.

justice // lesson 4 day 5 // 36

SCRIPTURE TELLS US THAT GOD DESIRES TO AND PROMISES TO HELP THOSE WHO SUFFER.
WE CAN PUT CONFIDENCE IN THAT.
BUT HERE'S THE DEAL:
IF YOU'RE THE ONE SUFFERING, YOU MIGHT WONDER JUST WHEN GOD IS GOING TO STEP IN.
YOU MIGHT WONDER WHERE GOD IS.
YOU SEE, GOD DOESN'T EVER PROMISE TO RELIEVE OUR SUFFERING IMMEDIATELY.
HE JUST PROMISES THAT HE HEARS US.
AND THAT ULTIMATELY, HE WILL REDEEM US.
(AND PUNISH THOSE WHO OPPRESS.)
NOW, THIS REDEMPTION MIGHT NOT COME UNTIL WE REACH HEAVEN.
BUT IT WILL COME.
IN THE MEANTIME, WHAT DOES THE ONE SUFFERING NEED FROM GOD?
HOW DOES GOD SHOW THEM THAT HE DOES INDEED CARE FOR THEM?
THAT HE HEARS THEM AND WANTS TO EASE THEIR PAIN?
OH, HE HAS A LOT OF WAYS TO SHOW THOSE WHO SUFFER THAT HE CARES.
BUT ONE OF HIS FAVORITE WAYS IS THROUGH YOU.
THAT'S RIGHT: YOU.
YOU SEE, WHEN YOU REACH OUT TO THE SUFFERING IN THE NAME OF CHRIST AND LIGHTEN THEIR BURDEN,

THEY
SEE
GOD.

THEY SEE GOD IN YOU!
AND THEY UNDERSTAND THAT GOD TRULY WORKS THROUGH HIS CHILDREN.

DON'T EVER UNDERESTIMATE YOUR ROLE IN SHOWING THE WORLD THAT GOD TRULY CARES ABOUT THOSE WHO SUFFER.
YOU HAVE THE POWER TO MAKE A REAL DIFFERENCE
IT IS THE POWER OF
GOD IN YOU.

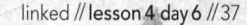

DEVOTION

Have you ever been in trouble for something you did wrong, only you thought you were doing it right? Maybe you tried to wash your dad's car but you grabbed the bottle of power steering fluid instead of the car soap. (It could happen. You might be surprised how similar the bottles look.) You thought you were doing what you were supposed to do… only to learn that you actually blew it.

In Matthew 25, Jesus is teaching in parables. You know what a parable is, right? It's a metaphorical or allegorical story that has a moral message. It's like a story used to teach a lesson. Jesus did a lot of His teaching in this way. It was a really useful way of relating to His audience. Remember, a lot of the people listening to Jesus were farmers and fishermen and things like that. So, when Jesus used stories about sorting goats and sheep to make a point, people got it.

In Matthew 25:31–46, Jesus told about the end times. He talked about the judgment day that will occur when all people are held accountable for their lives. Some will live for eternity in heaven. Some will live in eternal separation from God in hell. So, Jesus talked about how the unrighteous people would be condemned to hell. Some of these people thought they belonged in heaven. They basically said to Jesus, "We didn't know we were dishonoring you? We thought we had it all together?" Jesus' response should catch our attention… big time.

Jesus said to these people in verses 45–46, "'I tell you the truth, whatever you did not do for one of the least of these, you did not do for me.' "Then they will go away to eternal punishment, but the righteous to eternal life." We will be held accountable for the things we didn't do. Wow.

God is merciful and seeks to redeem those who suffer. He expects you to join Him in this mission. And, while it's not the best news in the world, there may be consequences for neglecting to help when we see people suffering.

List some opportunities around you in which you might be able to step in and help out someone who is suffering.

justice // **lesson 5 day 1** //38

GOD IS A GOD OF SECOND CHANCES

What if you were told that while God promises to punish the unjust, He also wants to redeem them? How does this create tension in the way you see God?

THE INJUSTICE PROBLEM

This is the point in this study where you might want to stop and shake your head.

This is the point where God being God is almost more than you can take.

It's a glimpse into the heart of the One who is so far apart from us in terms of the way He sees the world. The way He sees His world.

This is one of those moments where the distance between God and us seems to grow by about a million miles. It's a moment where we realize God is Creator, the Master Craftsman not only of the world, but also of the very system that dictates its inner working. It's a moment we honestly might not understand.

Up to this point, we have sort of followed this pathway:
God is just.
God cares about those who suffer.
God judges those who are unjust.
God actively seeks those who suffer.

Got it? Good. Now, look back at those last two phrases up above: God judges those who are unjust. God actively seeks those who suffer. Now prepare to have your mind scrambled. Guess what Jeremiah 12:1–17 says? It says that God also actively seeks those who are unjust. (But don't take my word for it; read it for yourself.) It says God seeks to offer redemption, compassion, and reconciliation to the oppressors.

Huh?

Wait. Isn't this the same God who will raise up and scatter the nations who oppose Him? Well, if you thought that, you were right. God will do that. But here is the crazy thing: The same offer of grace and forgiveness that God extended to you through the death of His Son on the cross is the same offer given to those who perpetrate injustice. God promises forgiveness and salvation to all people. And those who accept it, no matter what their past, receive all the benefits of every other believer.

There are consequences for every evil deed. But God loves all people. And even until the Day of Judgment, there is time for the worst sinners to turn to Him.

Stop and think about that…

25,000 CHILDREN DIE EVERY DAY.

NEARLY A BILLION PEOPLE ENTERED THE 21ST CENTURY UNABLE TO READ A BOOK OR SIGN THEIR NAMES.

600,000 TO 800,000 PEOPLE ARE TRAFFICKED ACROSS INTERNATIONAL BORDERS EACH YEAR AS SEX SLAVES.

6,000,000 JEWS AND 5,000,000 OTHER "UNDESIRABLES" WERE MURDERED IN THE HOLOCAUST.

IN 1994, 800,000 RWANDAN TUTSIS AND POLITICALLY MODERATE HUTUS WERE KILLED, LARGELY WITH MACHETES, IN A MATTER OF A MERE 100 DAYS.

EVERY YEAR 15 MILLION CHILDREN DIE OF HUNGER.

HOW DO YOU ANSWER THIS QUESTION: IF GOD IS JUST, WHY SO MUCH INJUSTICE?

DEVOTION

This is an important moment. You now have the chance to really think about an important concept. It's life changing, actually. Now, it won't take long. And after all, what else do you have to do? Homework? Talk to your boyfriend or girlfriend? Honestly…. That can wait five minutes, can't it? Especially for something as big as this!

Here's your task. Read Revelation 20:11–15. If you remember, Revelation is sort of a crazy book of the Bible. John, one of Jesus' most trusted disciples, was an old man when he wrote Revelation. It is a summary of a vision John was given. Jesus appeared to John and gave him a vision of what the end of the world would look like. John wrote out this amazing vision, making the Book of Revelation available for all people to read.

Now that you know the back-story, read the verses again. Do these verses make you tremble? Well, they should. These verses depict the judgment of all who are going to hell. God sees before Him everyone who has ever died apart from Christ, and He judges each one accordingly. They are sent to hell… forever.

Now here's the part that should get you. There will be people in that group whom you know… whom you eat lunch with… whom you play sports with… You might have even gone on a date with one. There will be someone you know who will spend eternity in hell. And that should really, really grab your attention.

We've learned in this section that God has compassion on even the worst people. God wants all people to have the chance to come to Him. The question you must ask yourself is if you have the same compassion for the lost. Do you see evil people and long for them to come to Christ? Or do you see them and want them to get what they deserve?

Justice is God's. Judgment is God's. But so is compassion. How compassionate are you?

Evaluate your attitude toward people whom you find hard to like— mean people. Do you show compassion toward them?
One reason people might act pretty nasty is that no one has ever shown them the unconditional love of Christ. Ask yourself this: Will you do what it takes today to show someone Christ's love?

justice // lesson 5 day 5 //42

Cause & Effect

Pretend that you are the ultimate judge for ALL wrong that goes on in the world. You decide all the punishments people receive for the wrong they do. You give the last word. Read the following scenarios. For each scenario, write the punishment you think each wrong deserves. Remember, you are the ultimate judge!

Scenario 1
The president of a poor country was found stealing money from the United Nations that was supposed to go toward food for his people. What should his punishment be?

Scenario 2
The quarterback of your football team got a DUI the week before the game with your school's biggest rival. What should his punishment be?

Scenario 3
Two girls at your school have posted a video on YouTube making fun of another girl at your school. What should their punishment be?

Scenario 4
A large tribe in an African country has committed acts of genocide against members of another tribe. Rape, murder, robberies... horrible atrocities have been committed. What should their punishment be?

Scenario 5
A teenager is caught lying to her parents about where she was the night before. What should her punishment be?

Read this passage:
God's Message: "Regarding all the bad neighbors who abused the land I gave to Israel as their inheritance: I'm going to pluck them out of their lands, and then pluck Judah out from among them."

Sounds like justice right? Sounds like they got what they deserve.
Maybe it even sounds like some of the stuff you wrote above. But keep reading...

"Once I've pulled the bad neighbors out, I will relent and take them tenderly to my heart and put them back where they belong, put each of them back in their home country, on their family farms. Then if they will get serious about living my way and pray to me as well as they taught my people to pray to that god Baal, everything will go well for them." —Jeremiah 12:14–17 (MSG)

Hmm... God judges, but then reserves compassion for the enemies of His children?
How compassionate were you in passing judgment?

Aren't you glad God is the ultimate judge and not people?

> **I WILL CLEANSE THEM FROM ALL THE SIN THEY HAVE COMMITTED AGAINST ME & WILL FORGIVE ALL THEIR SINS OF REBELLION AGAINST ME**
>
> ★ JEREMIAH 33:8 ★

We have all been wicked people and enemies of God. That's right. When you sin, you sin against God. He is the standard from which you deviate. The good news? He seeks to redeem and reconcile sinners to Himself. That means you. And that means those who commit injustice. How does it make you feel knowing God desires to redeem even the worst sinners? OK, but, in Gods eyes, how is your sin different from theirs? Thank God for His redemption. No, really. Thank Him now… **right now.**

justice // lesson 6 day 1 // 44

WHAT DOES GOD WANT TO SEE IN YOU?

JUSTICE. MERCY. HUMILITY.

Do you act justly toward those around you?
Do you show mercy to others in all your actions?
Do you walk through this life humbly before others and before God?
Think about it…

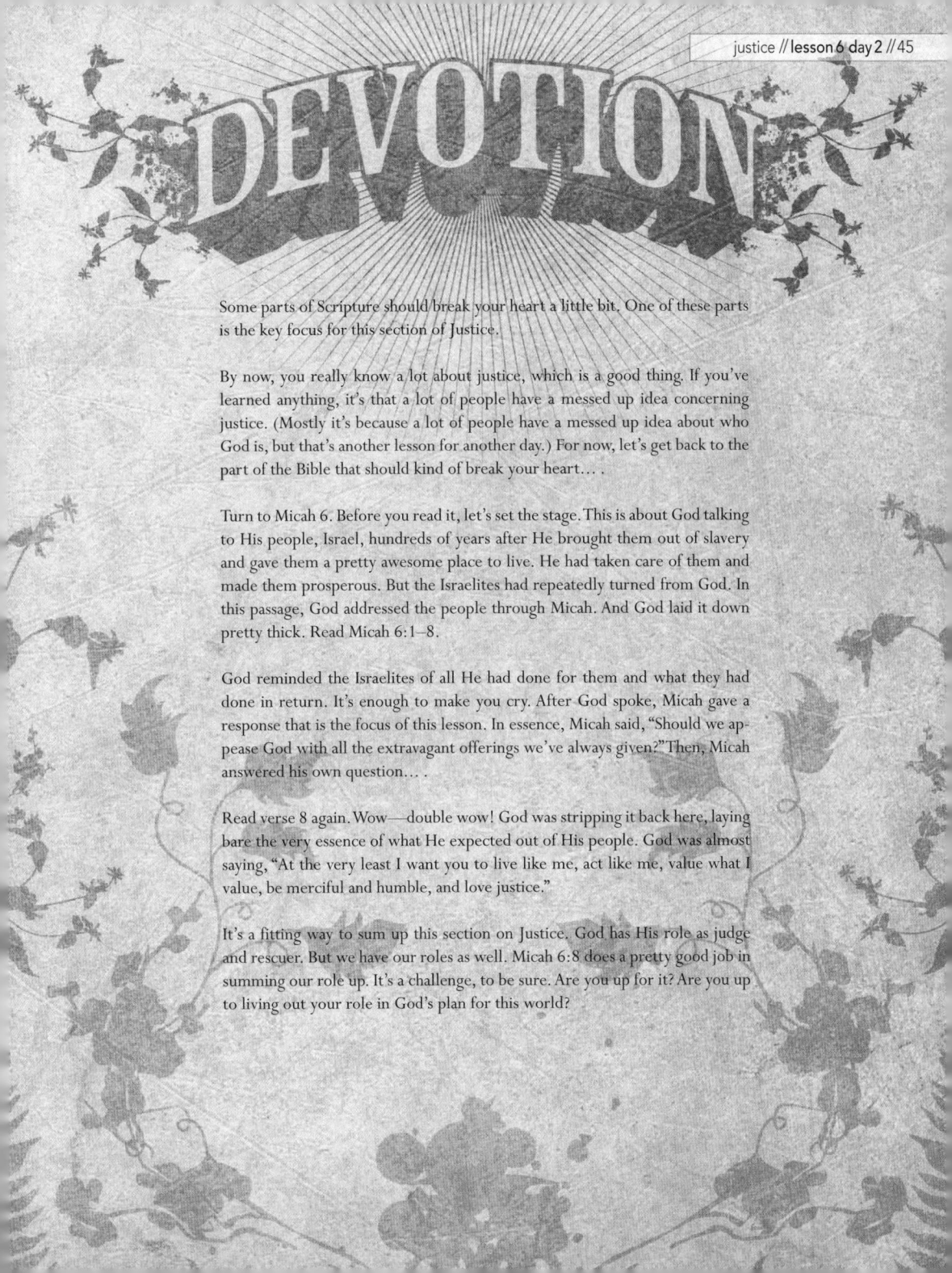

DEVOTION

Some parts of Scripture should break your heart a little bit. One of these parts is the key focus for this section of Justice.

By now, you really know a lot about justice, which is a good thing. If you've learned anything, it's that a lot of people have a messed up idea concerning justice. (Mostly it's because a lot of people have a messed up idea about who God is, but that's another lesson for another day.) For now, let's get back to the part of the Bible that should kind of break your heart… .

Turn to Micah 6. Before you read it, let's set the stage. This is about God talking to His people, Israel, hundreds of years after He brought them out of slavery and gave them a pretty awesome place to live. He had taken care of them and made them prosperous. But the Israelites had repeatedly turned from God. In this passage, God addressed the people through Micah. And God laid it down pretty thick. Read Micah 6:1–8.

God reminded the Israelites of all He had done for them and what they had done in return. It's enough to make you cry. After God spoke, Micah gave a response that is the focus of this lesson. In essence, Micah said, "Should we appease God with all the extravagant offerings we've always given?" Then, Micah answered his own question… .

Read verse 8 again. Wow—double wow! God was stripping it back here, laying bare the very essence of what He expected out of His people. God was almost saying, "At the very least I want you to live like me, act like me, value what I value, be merciful and humble, and love justice."

It's a fitting way to sum up this section on Justice. God has His role as judge and rescuer. But we have our roles as well. Micah 6:8 does a pretty good job in summing our role up. It's a challenge, to be sure. Are you up for it? Are you up to living out your role in God's plan for this world?

justice // lesson 6 day 3 // 46

WHAT IF YOUR ENTIRE BODY, YOUR WHOLE LIFE
WERE AVAILABLE AS AN EXTENSION OF GOD'S JUST WORK IN THIS WORLD?
IN THE BLANKS PROVIDED, WRITE HOW YOU MIGHT USE YOUR LIFE
TO BE A MESSENGER OF JUSTICE.

{HEAD}

{EYES}

{EARS}

{MOUTH}

{HEART}

{HANDS}

{FEET}

JUSTICE, HUMILITY, AND MERCY

Micah 6:8 asks us to do three things: "To act justly and to love mercy, and to walk humbly with your God." If this were the only place in Scripture that asked us to do these things, people might easily dismiss it. Someone might say, "Oh well, that's in the Old Testament. I pay more attention to what Jesus said." Well, that person would be wrong. The Bible is literally full of places that urge us to act in this way.

Don't believe it? See for yourself…

Psalm 37:30 says that a righteous man will speak justice.

Psalm 106:3 says that those who maintain justice and seek to do the right thing will be blessed.

Psalm 112:5 says that "good will come to him" who conducts his affairs in a just way.

Matthew 5:7 says that if you are merciful to others, God will show you mercy.

Romans 12:8 says that showing mercy is actually a spiritual gift from God. Do you have the gift of mercy?

Jude 1:23 says that we are to show mercy to unbelievers. Do you?

Luke 6:36 says that we are to be merciful in the same way Jesus was merciful.

Psalm 18:27 says that God will save the humble, but discipline the proud.

Proverbs 3:34 says that the humble will receive God's grace.

James 4:10 says that if we will humble ourselves before God, He will lift us up.

So, these three words (justice, mercy, humility) capture, in a sense, many of the ways we are meant to conduct ourselves as believers. There really is only one question to ask: Are you willing to shape your life to match the qualities expressed in the Scriptures above?

This is what God desires for your life. But you are not alone. God never calls us to anything without first equipping us for it. The Holy Spirit dwells in you and empowers you to seek these things out. So, you can do it. Commit to showing mercy and humility. Commit to acting in just ways. It is the very call of Scripture for you to do so.

Pray now and ask God to convict you to become more like He desires.

justice // lesson 6 day 5 // 48

DRAW A LINE FROM THE SYMBOL ON THE LEFT TO ITS MATCHING WORD ON THE RIGHT.

COWBOY

BALLET DANCER

SOLDIER

BASEBALL PLAYER

DOCTOR

It was easy for you to match the symbols with their definition. So, in the space below, write or draw three symbols by which **Christians** might be recognized.

NOT SO EASY IS IT? Why is it hard to draw symbols of our beliefs? What if you were known for

HUMILITY? MERCY? JUSTICE?

Describe what your life would look like if you were.

"HE HAS SHOWED YOU, O MAN, WHAT ★ IS ★ GOOD.

WHAT DOES THE LORD REQUIRE OF YOU?

ACT JUSTLY and to LOVE MERCY and to WALK HUMBLY WITH YOUR GOD."

★ MICAH 6:8

LIST AS MANY EXAMPLES AS YOU CAN OF WHAT IT MEANS TO ACT JUSTLY.

NOW, LIST AS MANY EXAMPLES AS YOU CAN OF WHAT IT MEANS TO LOVE MERCY.

FINALLY, LIST AS MANY EXAMPLES AS YOU CAN OF WHAT IT MEANS TO WALK HUMBLY.

STATUS
LONELINESS
PROSPERITY
nature
LOVE
HURT
POWER
INSECURITY
HEALED
FEAR
PRAY
nature
HURT

HAVE YOU EVER TAKEN THE TIME TO THINK ABOUT PEOPLE'S RELATIONSHIP WITH GOD? *NEXUS* IS A SERIES DESIGNED TO HELP YOU UNDERSTAND THE INTRICACIES OF THIS AMAZING RELATIONSHIP. IN *NEXUS* YOU'LL LEARN THAT GOD MADE PEOPLE WITH RELATIONSHIP IN MIND. THIS CONCEPT IS THE FOUNDATION OF HOW GOD RELATES TO US AND HOW WE RELATE TO GOD. AND THIS RELATIONSHIP IS LIKE NO OTHER. IT'S A COVENANTAL RELATIONSHIP, A RELATIONSHIP BUILT ON GOD'S ETERNAL PROMISE TO BE WITH HIS CHILDREN FOREVER.

WHY A COVENANT? AND WHY WITH US? AFTER ALL, WE'RE SINFUL, UNFAITHFUL, AND FALLEN. GOD ESTABLISHED A COVENANT WITH HIS PEOPLE NOT BECAUSE OF ANYTHING WE DID, BUT BECAUSE OF HIS GREAT LOVE. GOD SHOWED THIS LOVE THROUGH SENDING US HIS SON, JESUS. THROUGH JESUS' LIFE, DEATH, AND RESURRECTION, GOD PROVIDED A WAY FOR US TO BE IN PERFECT RELATIONSHIP WITH HIM. AND THIS RELATIONSHIP IS LIKE NO OTHER! WE ARE CHANGED BY IT; OUR CHARACTER BECOMES A REFLECTION OF HIM. AND IN ADDITION TO THAT, GOD'S DESIGN FOR THIS RELATIONSHIP IS THAT WE MIGHT TESTIFY TO THE WORLD ABOUT THE TRUTH OF GOD AND HIS LOVE FOR ALL HUMANKIND. PRETTY COOL, ISN'T IT?

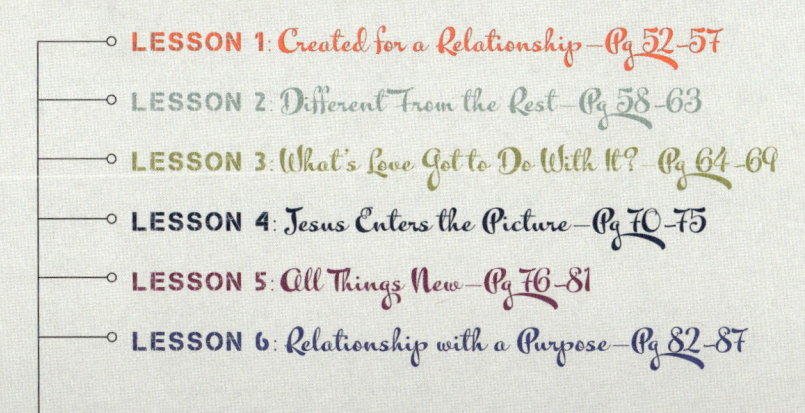

- **LESSON 1**: *Created for a Relationship* — Pg 52-57
- **LESSON 2**: *Different From the Rest* — Pg 58-63
- **LESSON 3**: *What's Love Got to Do With It?* — Pg 64-69
- **LESSON 4**: *Jesus Enters the Picture* — Pg 70-75
- **LESSON 5**: *All Things New* — Pg 76-81
- **LESSON 6**: *Relationship with a Purpose* — Pg 82-87

nexus // lesson 1 day 1 //52

GOD IS NOT SOME DISTANT, FAR OFF, IMPERSONAL [judge] LIVING IN THE [clouds,] SMUGLY GLANCING [down] AT ALL THE POOR LITTLE HUMANS THAT OCCUPY HIS [earth]. GOD IS THE [loving] CREATOR. AND HE CREATED YOU WITH [relationship] IN MIND. YOU WERE LITERALLY MADE IN GOD'S IMAGE. YOU WERE DESIGNED TO LIVE IN [harmony] AND COMMUNION WITH HIM. THIS CONCEPT IS THE FOUNDATION OF HOW GOD [relates] TO YOU, AND HOW YOU [relate] TO GOD.

GOD MADE ALL THINGS. The world around us is a testimony to this truth. We see God's handiwork in the beauty of a sunset, the wonder of a multitude of amazing animals, the majesty of a mountain, etc. But, the most amazing aspect of God's creation is you. That's right. You. Us. People. Humankind is exceptional in the spectrum of God's creation. Don't believe it? Let's go to the Bible and see.

Read Genesis 1:26–31. This passage probably sounds pretty familiar to you. But let's stop for a moment and look at a few specific points that you might have missed before. These points hint at a pretty incredible truth about you and God's purpose for creating you.

Look closely at verse 26. What does God say about how humans will be made? God says they will be made in His image! Think about that. God didn't make the plants in His image, or the birds of the air, or the creatures in the sea, or the animals on the land. People alone are made in God's image. This tells us there is something special about humans in God's eyes. What could that be? The next point in this passage will provide the answer.

Look closely at the beginning of verses 28 and 29. Two phrases appear in both verses that hint at a truly incredible fact about human beings. Did you catch the phrases: "God . . . said to them" and "Then God said . . ."? Whoa! God, the Creator of the universe, spoke to humans! He talked to them. This is incredible. After all, we do not see God having conversations with the trees, or the stars, or the animals. No, only humans find themselves in a personal relationship with God in the garden.

These two truths (the idea that we are made in God's image and the idea that God verbally interacted with humans) point to the fact that God wants to be in a relationship with us. This desire to have a relationship with people is unique in all of creation! God created people so that we could commune with Him. The magnitude of this cannot be understated. It's a truth that should shape every day of your life. God made YOU for relationship with HIM. Let that amazing fact soak in today.

nexus // lesson 1 day 3 // 54

ON DAY 1 GOD MADE THE LIGHT AND THE DARK. IT WAS GOOD.

ON DAY 2 GOD SEPARATED THE WATER FROM THE WATER. IT WAS GOOD.

ON DAY 3 GOD MADE THE LAND, THE SEA, AND THE PLANTS. IT WAS GOOD.

ON DAY 4 GOD MADE THE SUN AND THE MOON. IT WAS GOOD.

ON DAY 5 GOD MADE THE BIRDS AND THE FISH. IT WAS GOOD.

ON DAY 6 GOD MADE THE ANIMALS AND HUMANS. IT WAS VERY GOOD.

ON DAY 7, GOD HAD FINISHED CREATING. HE RESTED.

GOD CREATED YOU FOR A PURPOSE, PUTTING YOU IN THIS WORLD FOR A REASON. REST IN THAT FACT TODAY.

DEVOTION

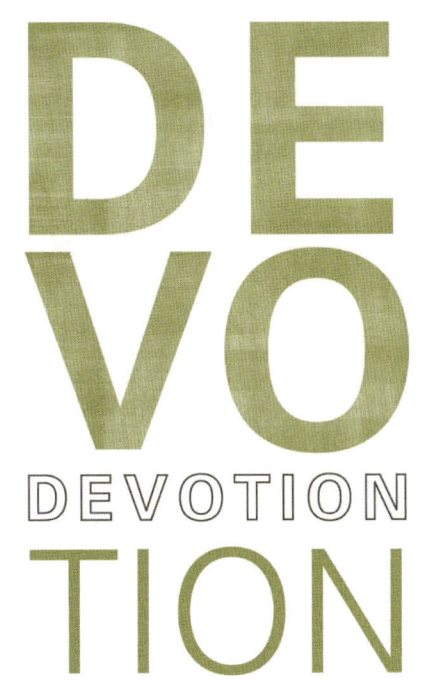

WHEN YOU LOOK IN THE MIRROR, WHAT DO YOU SEE?

Maybe your teeth aren't as straight as you would want. Maybe your hair doesn't quite do what you want it to do. Maybe you are a little overweight. Maybe you're a little underweight. When you look at yourself do you see the imperfections?

When you look in the mirror, do you see your personality flaws? Do you recognize your social awkwardness? Does it bother you that you aren't as confident as you might want to be? Do you recognize your tendency to put others down due to your own insecurities? Do you hate that you can't communicate your thoughts in a group as well as you'd like? When you think of yourself, do you focus most on your flaws?

What would happen if you looked in the mirror and saw yourself as God saw you? According to Scripture, you're a perfect creation.

Stop for a moment and read Psalm 139:13-14. This psalm says that God knew you in your mother's womb. You were no accident. You were no afterthought. God knew before you were born that you would be part of His plan. You. Just as you are. So valuable to God that He wanted you in this world.

What's more, you are wonderfully made! You are no rush-job. You are not a cast-off. The same God who shaped the universe handcrafted you.

Verse 14 contains an assurance you just might need to be reminded of today: "I know that full well." Do you know full well that you are wanted, that you are wonderfully made by God to have a relationship with Him? And if God sees you, His creation, as wonderfully made, who are we to look for imperfections? That'd be sort of like looking at the Mona Lisa and complaining about her eyebrows (or lack thereof). She's a masterpiece! And so are you.

You are a child of God. Do you see that when you look in the mirror? Pray that God would help you see yourself with His eyes.

WHY DO WE BEAT OURSELVES UP OVER OUR FLAWS? WHY IS IT SO HARD TO SEE OURSELVES AS GOD SEES US? NEXT TIME YOU ARE TEMPTED TO FEEL DOWN, WHAT CAN YOU DO TO REMIND YOURSELF OF THIS VERSE AND THE TRUTH IT CONTAINS?

nexus // **lesson 1 day 5** //56

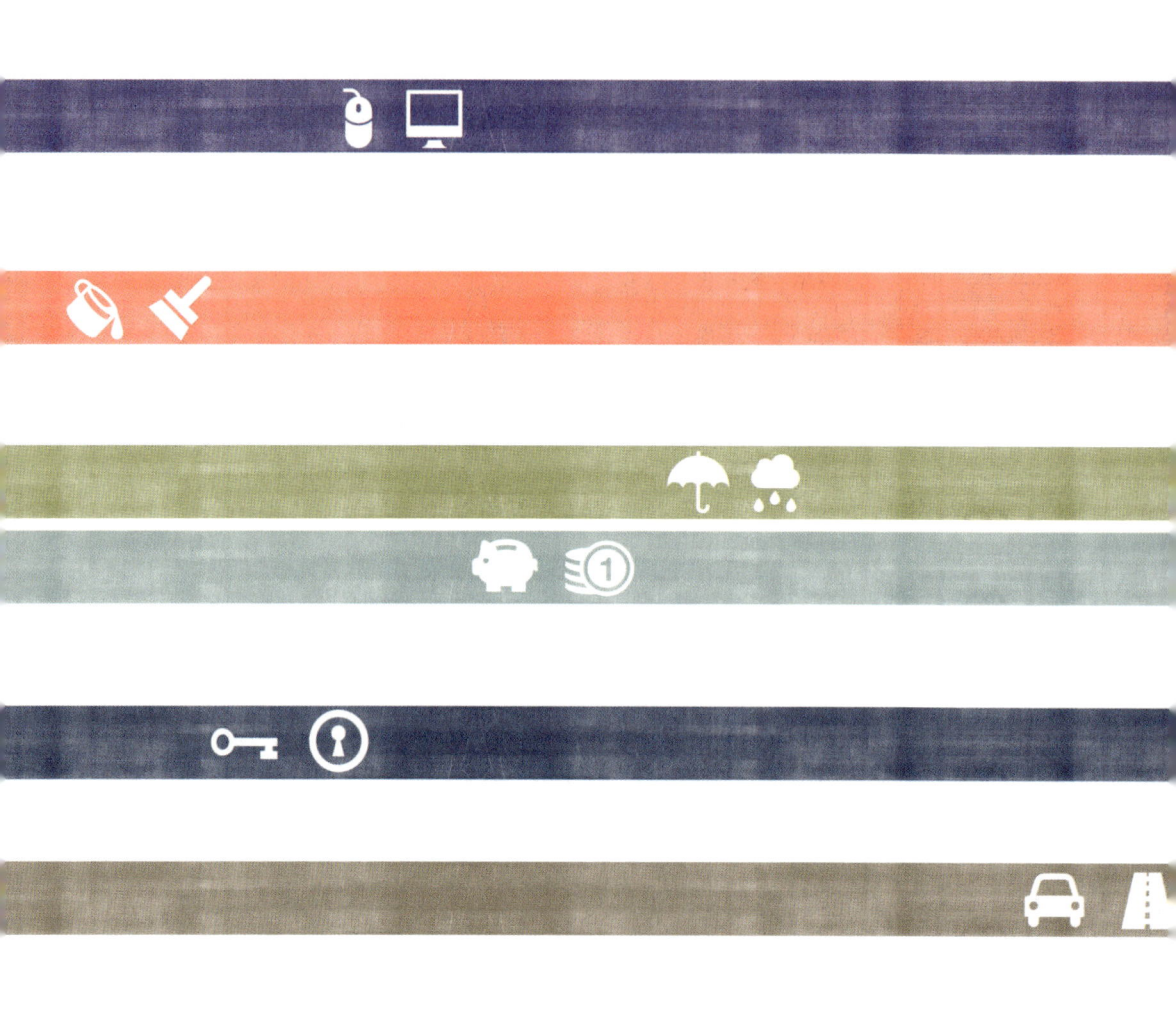

A VIOLIN IS MADE TO MAKE MUSIC.
BASEBALL GLOVES ARE MADE FOR BASEBALLS.
AND PEOPLE ARE MADE TO HAVE RELATIONSHIPS. . . .
NOT JUST WITH EACH OTHER, BUT ALSO WITH GOD. HOW DOES THIS
CHANGE THE WAY YOU LOOK AT YOUR LIFE? YOUR PURPOSE? THE WAY YOU USE
YOUR TIME? SPEND A FEW MINUTES THINKING ABOUT HOW YOUR
RELATIONSHIP WITH GOD CHANGES YOUR OUTLOOK ON LIFE.

GOD IS PRETTY COMPLEX. (NOT SURE WHETHER YOU KNEW THAT . . .) HIS CHARACTER AND NATURE IS NOT DEFINED BY ONE WORD . . . OR BY ONE NAME! BELOW YOU WILL SEE A LIST OF SOME OF THE NAMES GOD IS KNOWN BY IN SCRIPTURE. SPEND A FEW MOMENTS THINKING ABOUT EACH NAME. IN THE SPACE PROVIDED, WRITE HOW YOU MIGHT RELATE TO GOD DIFFERENTLY BASED ON A SPECIFIC NAME.

[The Lord Most High] _____

AΩ [Alpha and Omega] _____

[Comforter] _____

[Deliverer] _____

[Lamb of God] _____

[King of Kings] _____

[Rock] _____

[Savior] _____

[Shepherd] _____

nexus // **lesson 2 day 1** // 58

THE FABRIC OF YOUR LIFE IS HELD TOGETHER BY THE THREADS OF *relationship.* YOUR [*relationships*] WITH YOUR FRIENDS AND FAMILY MAKE UP SOME OF THE MOST VALUABLE AND INFLUENTIAL ELEMENTS IN YOUR LIFE. THINK ABOUT IT: THESE ARE THE PEOPLE WHO BRING **YOU** JOY, HAPPINESS, LAUGHTER, AND SOMETIMES SADNESS. RELATIONSHIPS ARE [*king.*] [*covenant.*]

WHAT MAKES YOUR [*relationship*] WITH YOUR MAKER UNIQUE? HERE'S A HINT: A [*covenant*] IS A BINDING [*relationship.*] GOD IS BOUND TO **YOU** THROUGH AN ETERNAL [*covenant*] HE STARTED AND HAS PROMISED TO ALWAYS KEEP. CAN YOUR FRIENDS SAY THAT?

DEVOTION

HAVE YOU EVER HEARD THE PHRASE, "The only certainties in life are death and taxes"? Ouch. It's certainly not very positive. But, the thought behind it is pretty true, right? Let's be honest: No amount of botox, tummy tucks, facelifts, and wrinkle cream can hold off death. It's inevitable, right? No matter how people try to fight it, we all age and grow old. And eventually—hopefully after a long, fruitful life—we die. Taxes are about as final. Ask your parents what would happen if they were to say, "You know what? I'm not paying any taxes this year." They would find themselves on the wrong end of the IRS. There is simply no choice when it comes to these two things.

But why does such a hopeless statement have a place in the vocabulary of our culture? It comes from a place of skepticism. We've simply been burned too many times. Do jobs last forever? Nope. Do marriages? Sadly, many don't. How about friendships? Unfortunately, too many relationships disappear at the first sign of trouble. All relationships, that is, except one.

Read Genesis 15:1–21. This is an account of God's covenant relationship with Abraham. A covenant is a binding promise – one that should never be broken. This covenant with Abraham is the foundation of your relationship with God. (We'll flesh that out in the next few pages.) And you know what? God will never, ever break His covenant. He will always remain faithful to the relationship He started with His people.

Death and taxes have nothing on God. God is the only eternally faithful thing in this world. He will never leave you. He will never break the terms of His covenant. He can always be counted on, for sure.

HOW DOES GOD'S FAITHFULNESS AFFECT YOUR EVERYDAY LIFE? HOW CAN YOU LIVE IN SUCH A WAY THAT REFLECTS A CONFIDENCE IN GOD'S PROMISE TO NEVER LEAVE YOU?

LOOK AT THE PICTURES ON THIS PAGE. SOME OF THEM ARE MORE SOLID, OUTLASTING OTHERS. CIRCLE THE ICONS THAT REPRESENT THE THINGS THAT ARE FRAGILE, FLEETING, OR EASILY TAKEN AWAY. NOW, UNDERLINE THOSE THINGS THAT LAST MUCH LONGER, THAT ARE MUCH MORE SOLID AND MUCH MORE LIKELY TO STICK AROUND FOR A WHILE. HAVE YOU CONSIDERED THAT YOUR RELATIONSHIP WITH GOD IS EVERLASTING? GOD CANNOT BE MOVED. HE WILL NOT GO AWAY. HE IS SOLID. HOW DOES IT MAKE YOU FEEL TO KNOW THAT GOD IS HERE TO STAY? FOREVER?

IN GENESIS 15:1–21, WE SEE THE ACCOUNT OF GOD MAKING A COVENANT WITH ABRAM. IN VERSE 5 GOD SAID, "LOOK UP AT THE HEAVENS AND COUNT THE STARS—IF INDEED YOU CAN COUNT THEM." THEN HE SAID, "SO SHALL YOUR OFFSPRING BE." PART OF THIS COVENANT WAS TO MAKE A GREAT NATION FROM ABRAM'S OFFSPRING. THE SECOND PART WAS A PROMISE OF LAND. IN VERSE 19, GOD LISTED ALL THE LAND HE WOULD GIVE ABRAM AND HIS DESCENDANTS. THEN, ABRAM AND GOD SEALED THE COVENANT WITH AN ANCIENT CEREMONY.

WANT TO KNOW SOMETHING COOL? THE VERY COVENANT THAT STARTED WITH ABRAM EXTENDS ALL THE WAY TO YOU. HERE'S YOUR CHANCE TO SEE JUST HOW THIS IS SO. SCRIPTURE PLAYS IT OUT PRETTY CLEARLY. WATCH AND LEARN . . .

THROUGH ABRAM GOD CALLED A PEOPLE: THE ISRAELITES.

The LORD had said to Abram, "Leave your country, your people and your father's household and go to the land I will show you. I will make you into a great nation . . ." —**Genesis 12:1–2**

GOD GAVE THEM THE LAW AS THE RULES THAT GOVERNED THIS COVENANT RELATIONSHIP AND SEPARATED THE ISRAELITES FROM OTHER NATIONS.

Now if you obey me fully and keep my covenant, then out of all nations you will be my treasured possession. Although the whole earth is mine, you will be for me a kingdom of priests and a holy nation. —**Exodus 19:5–6**

GOD PROMISED TO KEEP THIS COVENANT FOREVER, EVEN IF HIS PEOPLE DID NOT.

I will not violate my covenant or alter what my lips have uttered. —**Psalm 89:34**

THE OLD COVENANT WAS BUILT ON RULES, WHICH BROUGHT PEOPLE CLOSER TO GOD BUT ALSO BROUGHT GUILT AND CONVICTION OF SIN. THIS COVENANT WOULD ULTIMATELY POINT TO A NEED FOR GOD'S GRACE.

The law is only a shadow of the good things that are coming—not the realities themselves. For this reason it can never, by the same sacrifices repeated endlessly year after year, make perfect those who draw near to worship. If it could, would they not have stopped being offered? For the worshipers would have been cleansed once for all, and would no longer have felt guilty for their sins. But those sacrifices are an annual reminder of sins. —**Hebrews 10:1–3**

ALL ALONG, GOD HAD IN MIND AN EVEN GREATER COVENANT FOR HIS PEOPLE, ONE THAT WOULD TRANSFORM THEIR RELATIONSHIP WITH HIM.

This is the covenant I will make with the house of Israel after that time, declares the Lord. I will put my laws in their minds and write them on their hearts. I will be their God, and they will be my people. —**Jeremiah 31:33**

JESUS IS THE MESSENGER AND THE MEDIATOR OF THE NEW COVENANT.

But the ministry Jesus has received is as superior to theirs as the covenant of which he is mediator is superior to the old one, and it is founded on better promises. —**Hebrews 8:6**

THROUGH JESUS' LIFE, DEATH, AND RESURRECTION, ALL WHO BELIEVE MAY JOIN IN THIS NEW COVENANT OF ETERNAL LIFE.

Yet to all who received him, to those who believed in his name, he gave the right to become children of God. —**John 1:12**

This is my blood of the covenant, which is poured out for many for the forgiveness of sins. —**Matthew 26:28**

SO, THERE IT IS: A FAST LOOK AT THE COVENANT FROM ABRAHAM . . . TO YOU! JUST AS GOD WAS FAITHFUL TO ABRAHAM, HE IS FAITHFUL TO YOU. HE WILL NEVER FORSAKE HIS COVENANT WITH HIS CHILDREN. WHAT AN INCREDIBLE PROMISE!

THERE ARE *different* LEVELS OF COMMITMENT AND KNOWING SOMEONE IN *relationships*...NOBODY KNOWS YOU AND IS COMMITTED TO YOU LIKE *God*.

YOUR RELATIONSHIP WITH A DISTANT RELATIVE

YOUR RELATIONSHIP WITH YOUR NEIGHBOR

YOUR RELATIONSHIP WITH A KID ON YOUR TEAM

YOUR RELATIONSHIP WITH YOUR FRIEND

YOUR RELATIONSHIP WITH YOUR SIBLING

YOUR RELATIONSHIP WITH YOUR MOM OR DAD

YOUR RELATIONSHIP WITH GOD

WHAT MAKES YOUR [covenant] [relationship] WITH [Jesus] *different*?

FOR THE LORD YOUR GOD IS A MERCIFUL GOD; HE WILL NOT ABANDON OR DESTROY YOU OR FORGET THE [covenant] WITH YOUR FOREFATHERS, WHICH HE CONFIRMED TO THEM BY OATH. –**DEUTERONOMY 4:31**

HE REMEMBERS HIS [covenant] FOREVER, THE WORD HE COMMANDED, FOR A THOUSAND GENERATIONS. –**PSALM 105:8**

ALL THE WAYS OF THE LORD ARE LOVING AND FAITHFUL FOR THOSE WHO KEEP THE DEMANDS OF HIS [covenant]. –**PSALM 25:10**

KNOW THEREFORE THAT THE LORD YOUR GOD IS GOD; HE IS THE FAITHFUL GOD, KEEPING HIS [covenant] OF LOVE TO A THOUSAND GENERATIONS OF THOSE WHO LOVE HIM AND KEEP HIS COMMANDS. –**DEUTERONOMY 7:9**

THIS IS THE [covenant] I WILL MAKE WITH THEM AFTER THAT TIME, SAYS THE LORD. I WILL PUT MY LAWS IN THEIR HEARTS, AND I WILL WRITE THEM ON THEIR MINDS. –**HEBREWS 10:16**

I WILL MAINTAIN MY LOVE TO HIM FOREVER, AND MY [covenant] WITH HIM WILL NEVER FAIL. –**PSALM 89:28**

IN THE SAME WAY, AFTER THE SUPPER HE TOOK THE CUP, SAYING, "THIS CUP IS THE NEW [covenant] IN MY BLOOD, WHICH IS POURED OUT FOR YOU." –**LUKE 22:20**

SO, WE'VE ESTABLISHED THAT GOD WANTS A ✻[relationship] WITH **YOU**. AND WE KNOW IT IS A SPECIAL ✻[relationship] ONE RULED BY GOD'S O[eternal] FAITHFULNESS. THE ?[question] WE MUST ASK IS WHY?

WHY DOES GOD WANT A ✻[relationship] WITH **YOU**? NO DISCUSSION OF GOD'S ✻[relationship] WITH HIS PEOPLE IS COMPLETE WITHOUT A DISCUSSION ABOUT WHAT MOTIVATES GOD TO ♾[seek] US.

SIMPLY PUT, GOD CREATED US BECAUSE OF HIS ♥[love].

AND BECAUSE OF THIS GREAT ♥[love], HE SET IN PLACE A PLAN FOR OUR REDEMPTION FROM SIN. IT IS ♥[love] THAT COMPELLED GOD TO DESIRE ✻[relationship] WITH US. DON'T BELIEVE IT? KEEP READING . . . .

DEVOTION

HAVE YOU EVER WONDERED WHY GOD CHOSE TO BE IN RELATIONSHIP WITH US? Why does He want to be our God? After all, we really don't bring much to the table. Think about it. God desires for us to be righteous and sin-free. But, boy do we mess that up! God desires for us to be devoted to Him alone, to give our attention fully to Him. Ouch. We blow that one too, don't we? God desires our total commitment, for us to align all of our decisions with His will and His purposes. Man, how often do we act only out of our own self-interest?

So, why does God want to have a relationship with us? What is the reason for His openness to being in communion with selfish, sinful, rebellious people?

Well, we can find the reason in Deuteronomy 7:6–13. Read this passage, paying close attention to verses 7 and 8. This Scripture passage shows God's commitment to His people. It describes God's desire to call the Israelites to Himself. It reflects God's faithfulness and His steadfastness.

But look back at verses 7 and 8. What did God give as the reason for choosing Israel? Because they were so awesome? Because they were so faithful? Because they were so strong? No! Actually, they were few in number and seemingly insignificant by the world's standards! God felt compassion for them and remained faithful to his promise to Abraham. (Remember, back in Genesis 15?) And He chose the Israelites, according to Deuteronomy 7:8, because He loved them! What an amazing truth.

God chose you because He loves you. He did not choose to have a relationship with you because of what you might have to offer. God chose you because He looked at you through the ages and loved you. And through faith like Abraham, He gave you eternal life and forgiveness for your sins.

IF YOU DO NOT RESPOND IN COMPLETE HUMILITY AND THANKFULNESS... YOU'RE MISSING THE POINT OF THIS LIFE-CHANGING TRUTH. WHAT CAN YOU SAY TO GOD TODAY TO DEMONSTRATE YOUR THANKFULNESS TO HIM? WRITE A PRAYER OF THANKFULNESS IN THE SPACE BELOW.

nexus // lesson 3 day 3 // 66

WILL YOU MARRY ME?

THIS REPRESENTS HOW *the world* SHOWS *love*.

CHOOSE ONE OF THE ICONS.
THINK ABOUT HOW THE EXPRESSION OF LOVE
IS A GLIMPSE INTO GOD'S GREATER LOVE.

nexus // **lesson 3 day 4** //67

DISCIPLINE

THIS REPRESENTS HOW *God* SHOWS HIS *love*.

CHOOSE ONE OF THESE ICONS AND SAY A PRAYER TO GOD THANKING HIM FOR EXPRESSING HIS LOVE THIS WAY.

God's [love] IS AMAZING
...SEE FOR YOURSELF

TURN, O LORD, AND DELIVER ME; SAVE ME BECAUSE OF YOUR UNFAILING [love]. —PSALM 6:4

BUT I TRUST IN YOUR UNFAILING [love]; MY HEART REJOICES IN YOUR SALVATION. —PSALM 13:5

REMEMBER, O LORD, YOUR GREAT MERCY AND [love], FOR THEY ARE FROM OF OLD. —PSALM 25:6

FOR YOUR [love] IS EVER BEFORE ME, AND I WALK CONTINUALLY IN YOUR TRUTH. —PSALM 26:3

ANSWER ME, O LORD, OUT OF THE GOODNESS OF YOUR [love]; IN YOUR GREAT MERCY TURN TO ME. —PSALM 69:16

FOR GOD SO [loved] THE WORLD THAT HE GAVE HIS ONE AND ONLY SON, THAT WHOEVER BELIEVES IN HIM SHALL NOT PERISH BUT HAVE ETERNAL LIFE. —JOHN 3:16

A NEW COMMAND I GIVE YOU: [love] ONE ANOTHER. AS I HAVE [loved] YOU, SO YOU MUST [love] ONE ANOTHER. —JOHN 13:34

AND HOPE DOES NOT DISAPPOINT US, BECAUSE GOD HAS POURED OUT HIS [love] INTO OUR HEARTS BY THE HOLY SPIRIT, WHOM HE HAS GIVEN US. —ROMANS 5:5

BUT GOD DEMONSTRATES HIS OWN [love] FOR US IN THIS: WHILE WE WERE STILL SINNERS, CHRIST DIED FOR US. —ROMANS 5:8

BUT BECAUSE OF HIS GREAT [love] FOR US, GOD, WHO IS RICH IN MERCY, MADE US ALIVE WITH CHRIST EVEN WHEN WE WERE DEAD IN TRANSGRESSIONS—IT IS BY GRACE YOU HAVE BEEN SAVED. —EPHESIANS 2:4–5

MAY THE LORD DIRECT YOUR HEARTS INTO GOD'S [love] AND CHRIST'S PERSEVERANCE. —2 THESSALONIANS 3:5

LET THEM GIVE THANKS TO THE LORD FOR HIS UNFAILING [love] AND HIS WONDERFUL DEEDS FOR MEN. —PSALM 107:21

WE'VE BEEN TALKING ABOUT RELATIONSHIPS. SO, LET'S TAKE OUR DISCUSSION A STEP FURTHER. THINK ABOUT THE RELATIONSHIPS IN YOUR LIFE. THINK ABOUT ALL OF THEM—THE GOOD ONES AND THE BAD ONES.

NOW, AS YOU THINK ABOUT SPECIFIC RELATIONSHIPS WRITE SOME OF THE REASONS YOU ARE IN THESE RELATIONSHIPS IN THE SPACE BELOW. THINK ABOUT WHAT MOTIVATES YOU TO STAY IN RELATIONSHIPS THAT MAY NOT BE SO GREAT. THINK ABOUT WHAT KEEPS SOME OF YOUR FRIENDS IN A RELATIONSHIP WITH YOU. THEN, RECORD YOUR THOUGHTS.

_____

_____

_____

OK, IF YOU WERE HONEST WITH YOURSELF, YOU LISTED BOTH POSITIVE AND NEGATIVE REASONS. AS YOU THOUGHT ABOUT WHY OTHERS ENGAGED IN RELATIONSHIPS, DID YOU MENTION ANY OF THESE REASONS?

Blessing — FEAR — convenience — STATUS — *comfort* — POWER — LONELINESS — PROSPERITY — *manipulation* — INSECURITY

THERE ARE MANY REASONS TO HAVE A RELATIONSHIP WITH SOMEONE. LOOK BACK AT THE WORDS ABOVE AND REFLECT ON YOUR RELATIONSHIPS. ARE ANY RELATIONSHIPS IN YOUR LIFE MOTIVATED BY SOME OF THE NEGATIVE QUALITIES?

HERE'S A THOUGHT THAT WILL LEAVE YOU FEELING MORE POSITIVE: GOD'S SOLE MOTIVATION FOR HAVING A RELATIONSHIP WITH YOU IS HIS LOVE. THAT'S IT. GOD DOES NOT WANT TO MANIPULATE YOU. HE DOES NOT WANT TO CONTROL YOU. HE IS NOT LONELY WITHOUT YOU. IN FACT, HE DOES NOT EVEN NEED YOU TO EXIST. YET, YOU NEED HIM FOR YOUR EVERY WAKING BREATH. KIND OF COOL, ISN'T IT?

AS YOU GO THROUGHOUT YOUR DAY, THINK ABOUT THAT VERY SIMPLE FACT. THEN THANK GOD THAT HE LOVES YOU ENOUGH TO WANT A RELATIONSHIP WITH YOU.

nexus // lesson 4 day 1 //70

WE HAVE DISCUSSED ✞[relationships] FOR THE LAST THREE WEEKS. SORRY TO BRING THIS UP, BUT WE CANNOT TALK ABOUT OUR ✞[relationship] WITH GOD WITHOUT FIRST DEALING WITH A DISCOMFORTING FACT:

WHEN LEFT TO OUR OWN MEANS, OUR SINFUL *nature* MAKES HAVING A ✞[relationship] WITH GOD IMPOSSIBLE.

THE GOOD NEWS IS THAT GOD ALREADY KNEW THIS AND PUT A PLAN IN PLACE TO STRAIGHTEN IT OUT. THOUSANDS OF YEARS AGO, GOD CALLED A PEOPLE, THE ISRAELITES, TO HIMSELF.

HE LED THEM OUT OF SLAVERY AND INTO THE PROMISED LAND. YET, THEY STILL TURNED AWAY FROM HIM. WE'RE NO DIFFERENT TODAY.

GOD KNEW FROM THE BEGINNING HE WOULD HAVE TO BE THE ONE TO PROVIDE THE MEANS FOR US TO HAVE A ✞[relationship] WITH HIM…… ENTER THE †[Christ.]

JESUS WAS GOD'S PLAN FOR PERFECTING THE ✞[relationship] WITH GOD BECAUSE OF ⊙[Jesus.]

WE CAN ONLY HAVE A ✞[relationship] WITH GOD BECAUSE OF ⊙[Jesus.]

DEVOTION

SO, WE'VE SPENT A LOT OF TIME TALKING ABOUT OUR RELATIONSHIP WITH GOD. We've learned that God created us for relationship, that He will always be in relationship with us, and that this desire flows out of His love for His children. But, there's a question we have not asked.

How can we, being sinful and selfish, ever expect to come to God for a relationship?

God is perfect. We are imperfect.
God hates sin. We seem to embrace it.
God is true. We often lie.
God is graceful. We can be pretty stubborn or just plain mean.
God is eternal. We shift and change with the wind.
How can we ever hope to have a relationship that we are so obviously incapable of sustaining?

Enter Jesus.

Take a moment and read Jeremiah 31:31–34 and Hebrews 9:15. Here's the deal: Before the beginning of time, God knew the plan He would set forth. He knew He would call a people. He knew His people would be set apart. He knew His people would also forsake Him. God knew that if He did not make a provision for His people, they would never be able to come to Him. We are simply too broken, too imperfect. So from the beginning of time, God planned to send His Son as a once-and-for-all sacrifice for the sins of all humankind. By doing so, Jesus became the mediator of the new covenant. Jesus is the means by which we gain access to God.

Jesus' death on the cross was not an afterthought. It was the essential moment in God's plan: a plan to redeem all humankind—a plan to redeem you.

TAKE A MOMENT AND RESPOND WITH A PRAYER OF THANKS TO GOD FOR HIS AMAZING PLAN THAT PAVED A WAY FOR YOU TO COME TO HIM.

nexus // **lesson 4 day 3** //72

THIS IS YOUR PAGE. TAKE A MOMENT AND WRITE HOW YOUR LIFE HAS CHANGED AS A RESULT OF YOUR RELATIONSHIP WITH GOD. IF YOU DON'T WANT TO WRITE, THEN DRAW. IF YOU DON'T WANT TO DRAW, THEN TEAR OUT A PICTURE OR TWO FROM A MAGAZINE AND PASTE IT. DO WHATEVER YOU WANT TO REPRESENT GOD'S CHANGING FORCE IN YOUR LIFE.

lesson 4 day 4

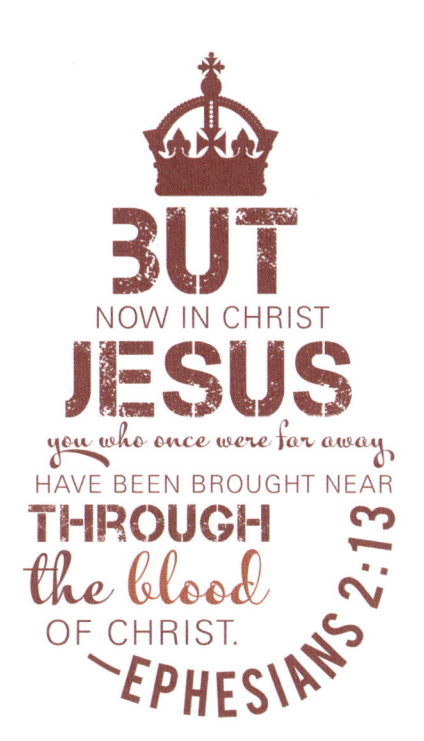

BUT NOW IN CHRIST JESUS *you who once were far away* HAVE BEEN BROUGHT NEAR THROUGH *the blood* OF CHRIST. —EPHESIANS 2:13

CHRIST *forgiveness* MERCY GRACE

BOTH THE OLD AND NEW TESTAMENT ("TESTAMENT" IS ANOTHER WORD FOR "COVENANT") REVEAL GOD'S WRATH TOWARD SIN AND LOVE AND MERCY FOR HIS PEOPLE. BUT THERE IS A DIFFERENCE IN THE WAY WE RELATE TO GOD NOW. NO MORE SACRIFICES EVERY TIME YOU BLOW IT, SELFISHLY REBELLING AGAINST GOD. CHRIST WAS THE ULTIMATE SACRIFICE, ONCE-AND-FOR-ALL. NOW, A NEW WAY TO RELATE TO GOD IS POSSIBLE THROUGH FAITH IN JESUS AND HIS SACRIFICE ON OUR BEHALF.

AREN'T YOU GLAD YOU LIVE ON THIS SIDE OF THE CROSS?

lesson 4 day 6

OLD TESTAMENT PROPHECY: But you, Bethlehem Ephrathah, though you are small among the clans of Judah, out of you will come for me one who will be ruler over Israel, whose origins are from of old, from ancient times. —Micah 5:2

NEW TESTAMENT FULFILLMENT: After Jesus was born in Bethlehem in Judea, during the time of King Herod, Magi from the east came to Jerusalem. —Matthew 2:1

OLD TESTAMENT PROPHECY: Therefore the Lord himself will give you a sign: The virgin will be with child and will give birth to a son, and will call him Immanuel. —Isaiah 7:14
NEW TESTAMENT FULFILLMENT: "How will this be," Mary asked the angel, "since I am a virgin?" The angel answered, "The Holy Spirit will come upon you, and the power of the Most High will overshadow you. So the holy one to be born will be called the Son of God." —Luke 1:34–35

OLD TESTAMENT PROPHECY: He was oppressed and afflicted, yet he did not open his mouth; he was led like a lamb to the slaughter, and as a sheep before her shearers is silent, so he did not open his mouth. —Isaiah 53:7

NEW TESTAMENT FULFILLMENT: Then the high priest stood up and said to Jesus, "Are you not going to answer? What is this testimony that these men are bringing against you?" But Jesus remained silent. The high priest said to him, "I charge you under oath by the living God: Tell us if you are the Christ, the Son of God." —Matthew 26:62–63

OLD TESTAMENT PROPHECY: I offered my back to those who beat me, my cheeks to those who pulled out my beard; I did not hide my face from mocking and spitting. —Isaiah 50:6
NEW TESTAMENT FULFILLMENT: Then they spit in his face and struck him with their fists. Others slapped him. —Matthew 26:67

OLD TESTAMENT PROPHECY: "The time is coming," declares the LORD, "when I will make a new covenant with the house of Israel and with the house of Judah." —Jeremiah 31:31

NEW TESTAMENT FULFILLMENT: This is my blood of the covenant, which is poured out for many for the forgiveness of sins. —Matthew 26:28

OLD TESTAMENT PROPHECY: Then will the eyes of the blind be opened and the ears of the deaf unstopped. Then will the lame leap like a deer, and the mute tongue shout for joy. Water will gush forth in the wilderness and streams in the desert. —Isaiah 35:5–6

NEW TESTAMENT FULFILLMENT: Then the chief priests and the Pharisees called a meeting of the Sanhedrin. "What are we accomplishing?" they asked. "Here is this man performing many miraculous signs." —John 11:47

OLD TESTAMENT PROPHECY: Rejoice greatly, O Daughter of Zion! Shout, Daughter of Jerusalem! See, your king comes to you, righteous and having salvation, gentle and riding on a donkey, on a colt, the foal of a donkey. —Zechariah 9:9

NEW TESTAMENT FULFILLMENT: Saying to them, "Go to the village ahead of you, and at once you will find a donkey tied there, with her colt by her. Untie them and bring them to me. If anyone says anything to you, tell him that the Lord needs them, and he will send them right away." —Matthew 21:2–3

nexus // **lesson 5 day 1** //76

GOD LOVES [relationship.] **YOU** SHOULD HAVE A FIRM GRASP ON THIS BY NOW. BUT WHAT ABOUT THAT [relationship] [changes] **YOU**? THROUGH CHRIST, YOUR [relationship] WITH GOD IS DRAMATICALLY [changed.]

BUT **YOU** KNOW SOMETHING ELSE? YOUR [relationship] WITH THE [world] [changes.] TOO. YOUR CHARACTER REFLECTS CHRIST'S CHARACTER.

BY LIVING OUT YOUR FAITH, YOU SHOW THE [world] THE DIFFERENCE [Jesus] HAS MADE.

PAUL KNEW THIS AS WELL AS ANYONE. PAUL ONCE LIVED AS AN ENEMY TO CHRISTIANS. BUT THEN PAUL ENCOUNTERED CHRIST AND WAS FOREVER [changed]. THIS LESSON FOCUSES ON THE NEW LIFE THAT IS AVAILABLE TO THOSE WHO WALK IN COMMUNION WITH GOD THROUGH CHRIST. (THAT MEANS **YOU, YOU** KNOW . . .)

DEVOTION

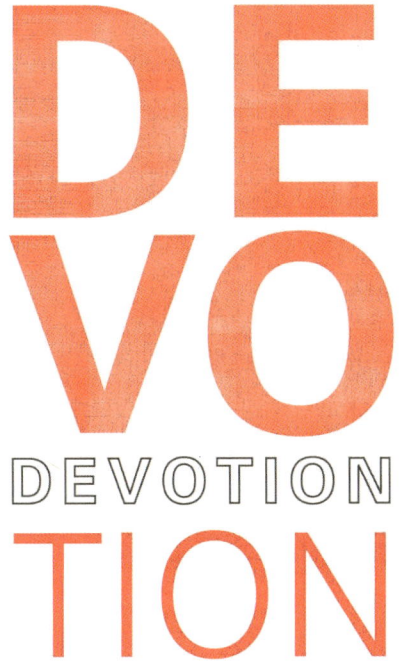

CAUSE AND EFFECT. You're familiar with this principle. Something happens (cause), and there is a result (effect). The funny thing is that one cause and one effect can lead to a long list of causes and effects. Take the weather for instance: Pressure changes in the atmosphere (cause), and the temperature changes accordingly (effect). The weather gets warmer (cause), and you put on shorts (effect). The problem is that you've been wearing jeans lately (cause), so your legs are really pale (effect). Your friends see your pasty legs (cause) and burst out in laughter (effect). So, a change in atmospheric pressure results in your friends laughing at your pale legs! See how that works?

Now, take a break from visions of your pale legs and read Colossians 3:1–14. This is a great passage of Scripture. In it, Paul talked about how the people of God's Kingdom should live and act. It is a wonderful call to live as a Christ-follower.

Pay close attention to verses 1 and 2. They are the first of a few cause and effect statements. Verse one says, "Since, then, you have been raised with Christ (cause), set your hearts on things above" (effect). See how that works? When you professed faith in Christ as God's Son and accepted His sacrifice on the cross for your sins, you became a new person. That's the cause. The effect? You are to set your heart on heavenly things, not earthly things.

Look now at verses 5–14. Here is where we see multiple causes and effects coming into play. Because you believed in Christ (cause) you set your heart on godly things (effect). Because you have set your mind on godly things (cause) you live a life embracing "compassion, kindness, humility, gentleness and patience" (effect). And because you embraced such Christlike character (cause) you will be a light to others, forgiving them and bearing with their struggles (effect).

CHRIST IN YOU RESULTS IN AMAZING CHANGE. HE IS THE CAUSE. THE CHANGE IN YOUR LIFE IS THE EFFECT. HOW WILL THE WORLD SEE JESUS (THE CAUSE OF YOUR TRANSFORMATION) THROUGH YOU TODAY?

WHICH LIFE IS BETTER: PAUL'S LIFE WITH OR WITHOUT A RIGHT RELATIONSHIP WITH CHRIST?

ENEMY OF †[Christ]

☑[Approved] OF STEPHEN'S MURDER

ATTACKED CHRISTIANS

RADICAL ENCOUNTER WITH †[Christ]

VISITED ANTIOCH [Church]

WENT ON FIRST [missionary] TRIP

[Healed] AND TAUGHT IN ICONIUM

STONED IN LYSTRA

WENT ON SECOND [missionary] TRIP

🔒[Imprisoned] AT PHILIPPI

[Taught] IN ATHENS

ESTABLISHED THE CORINTHIAN [Church]

WENT ON THIRD [missionary] TRIP

RIOT IN EPHESUS

[Arrested] IN JERUSALEM

WENT BEFORE FELIX, FESTUS, AND AGRIPPA

HOUSE [arrest] IN ROME

BEHEADED IN ROME

nexus // lesson 5 day 4 //79

The acts of the sinful nature are obvious: sexual immorality, impurity and debauchery; idolatry and witchcraft; hatred, discord, jealousy, fits of rage, selfish ambition, dissensions, factions and envy; drunkenness, orgies, and the like. I warn you, as I did before, that those who live like this will not inherit the kingdom of God. BUT THE FRUIT OF THE SPIRIT IS ♥ [love,] ☺ [joy,] ☮ [peace,] ⌛ [patience,] 🤝 [kindness,] ✝ [goodness,] 🙏 [faithfulness,] 🐑 [gentleness] AND ⊘ [self-control.] AGAINST SUCH THINGS THERE IS NO LAW. THOSE WHO BELONG TO CHRIST JESUS HAVE CRUCIFIED THE SINFUL NATURE WITH ITS PASSIONS AND DESIRES. SINCE WE LIVE BY THE SPIRIT, LET US KEEP IN STEP WITH THE SPIRIT.

-GALATIANS 5:19-25

DID YOU EVER PLAY WITH PAPER DOLLS AS A CHILD? HERE'S THE DEAL ABOUT A PAPER DOLL: YOU CAN PUT NEW CLOTHES ON A DOLL, BUT THE DOLL DOESN'T CHANGE. THE SAME IS TRUE WITH YOU IF YOU HAVE COMMITTED YOUR LIFE TO FOLLOWING JESUS. YOU CAN DRESS HOWEVER YOU WANT, HANG OUT WITH WHOMEVER YOU WANT, LIVE WHEREVER YOU WANT, DO WHATEVER YOU WANT . . . BUT YOU'RE STILL GOD'S CHILD. YOU HAVE STILL BEEN TRANSFORMED INTO A NEW CREATION.

YOU ARE NO LONGER YOU. YOU ARE SOMETHING NEW. THINK FOR A SECOND. HOW IS THIS BOTH A FREEING TRUTH AND ONE THAT CARRIES GREAT RESPONSIBILITY?

THIS IS GUT-CHECK TIME. You will have the chance to compare yourself to God's Word and see how you match up. Now, the point of this isn't to make you feel guilty. Hopefully, as you compare your life to what you're about to read, you'll find some things you already do pretty well, things that are already taking root in your life. And you might discover some areas that could use a little more of your attention. The point is to take inventory of the way you express your Christian life each day.

You will look at a passage of Scripture you read a few pages back. It's from Paul's letter to the Colossians. The cool thing Paul does here is list behaviors and characteristics from a life without Christ and also from a life with Christ. Evaluating our lives in comparison with these two lists can help us review our lives. Let's get started.

In Colossians 3:5–14, Paul says the following things have no place in the life of a Christ follower:

Sexual Immorality	Impurity	Lust	Evil Desires
Greed	Anger	Rage	Malice
Slander	Filthy Language	Lies	

What from this list do you still struggle with? Be honest! Don't run from the conviction of the Holy Spirit. Pray specifically about each sin listed above. After you pray about something, cross it off the list, symbolizing that it no longer has any place in your life as a Christ-follower. Then, once you've identified your struggles, remember Paul said that these have no place in the life of a Christ-follower. What if you could begin to weed these behaviors out of your life? It takes prayer and self-discipline. But with the Lord's help, you can do it. (Technically, He can do it in you. You just cooperate by surrendering it all to Him.)

Now, look at this list. Paul said these behaviors and characteristics should fill the lives of Christ-followers:

Compassion	Kindness	Humility	Gentleness
Patience	Forgiveness	Love	Unity

Put stars next to the things that are already evident in your life. Take a moment and thank God for changing you and for empowering you to live in this way. Now, circle areas that you would like to see become more prominent in your life. Prayerfully ask God to help you in this way. Consider doing some Scripture searches to find passages that address this area. And keep in mind that growing as a Christian is what God expects from us! He will equip you to grow and will honor your desire to be more like Him.

YOUR ✞ [relationship] WITH GOD IS UNLIKE ANY OTHER ✞ [relationship] IN YOUR LIFE.

GOD DOESN'T JUST WANT TO HANG OUT WITH YOU. HE DIDN'T 📞 [call] YOU TO HIM SO HE'D HAVE A BIG ENTOURAGE.

HE CERTAINLY DOESN'T NEED YOU (OR ANYONE, FOR THAT MATTER).

HOWEVER, GOD CHOSE US—HIS CREATION, HIS CHILDREN—TO BE HIS MOUTHPIECE IN THIS 🌍 [world.]

FROM THE OLD TESTAMENT TO THE NEW, SCRIPTURE TESTIFIES TO THIS FACT. GOD WANTS THE RESULTS OF OUR COLLECTIVE ✞ [relationship] WITH HIM

TO BE A BODY OF PEOPLE READY TO DEMONSTRATE TO THE 🌍 [world] THE WONDERFUL REALITY OF COMMUNION WITH THE ONE TRUE GOD.

WE ARE TO BE LIKE THE PRIESTS OF OLD, LEADING OTHERS IN THE KNOWLEDGE AND UNDERSTANDING OF GOD. HOW DO YOU 📧 [communicate] TO THE 🌍 [world]

THE AMAZING DIFFERENCE ✝ [Christ] HAS MADE IN YOUR LIFE?

DEVOTION

THINK ABOUT THE LAST TIME YOU SOMEONE ASKED YOU TO DO A JOB. Maybe your dad or mom asked you to cut the grass. To complete the task you had to create a plan. You had to consider the right tool for the job (lawnmower) and account for the proper usage of it (fill up the gas, make sure to not run over any rocks, etc.).

Want to know something cool? God works the same way. Check it out...

Read Exodus 19:1–6. Do you see what God said about the purpose of the nation of Israel? God actually outlined His plan and how He would go about it.

What did God say the Israelites would be?

Did you answer "a kingdom of priests and a holy nation"? In the Old Testament, a priest was someone ordained by God to lead the people in worshiping God. The priest would facilitate sacrifices and lead worship. In other words, the priest helped connect the people to God.

By calling Israel a nation of priests, God was saying that Israel would serve to show people God. Sounds awesome, right? Here's another question: What nationality was Jesus and to whom did He first come to preach? The answer to both is the same: Jesus was born into the Jewish nation and aimed His message initially at the Jews. See how God's plan is starting to take shape?

But where do you fit in? Jump to Matthew 28:16–20. This is the Great Commission, Christ's last words of instruction to His disciples. God's plan was to let the whole world know about Him. And when He laid out the groundwork for the plan, it included Jewish disciples . . . and you. God has given you the same call He gave the disciples. When God set His plan in place for the entire world to know about Him, you were on His mind. You are a vital part of God's plan.

HOW DOES THIS MAKE YOU FEEL? DO YOU FAITHFULLY USE YOUR LIFE TO FULFILL GOD'S DESIRE FOR YOU? WHAT CHANGES DO YOU NEED TO MAKE TO BECOME A MORE VITAL PART OF GOD'S PLAN? WRITE OUT A PRAYER HERE, RESPONDING TO THIS AWESOME TRUTH.

nexus // lesson 6 day 3 //84

YOU HAVE A PURPOSE. WE ALL HAVE A PURPOSE.

ARE YOU BEING **[faithful]** TO God's **[call]** IN YOUR LIFE TO BE A WITNESS FOR HIM?

SEE WHAT SCRIPTURE HAS TO SAY ABOUT LIVING A LIFE WHERE YOU TESTIFY TO THE WORLD ABOUT GOD'S WORK IN YOUR LIFE AND IN THE WORLD.

It is written: "I believed; therefore I have spoken." With that same spirit of faith we also believe and therefore speak. —**2 Corinthians 4:13**

That is why I am suffering as I am. Yet I am not ashamed, because I know whom I have believed, and am convinced that he is able to guard what I have entrusted to him for that day. —**2 Timothy 1:12**

We are therefore Christ's ambassadors, as though God were making his appeal through us. We implore you on Christ's behalf: Be reconciled to God. —**2 Corinthians 5:20**

"Come, follow me," Jesus said, "and I will make you fishers of men." — **Matthew 4:19**

Ask the Lord of the harvest, therefore, to send out workers into his harvest field. —**Matthew 9:38**

I proclaim righteousness in the great assembly; I do not seal my lips, as you know, O LORD. I do not hide your righteousness in my heart; I speak of your faithfulness and salvation. I do not conceal your love and your truth from the great assembly. —**Psalm 40:9-10**

MEASURE YOUR LIFE AGAINST THE CALL IN SCRIPTURE. ARE THERE THINGS YOU ARE DOING TO LIVE AS A GOOD "AMBASSADOR" OR "FISHER OF MEN"? IDENTIFY SOME AREAS WHERE YOU ARE DOING WELL AND OTHER AREAS WHERE YOU COULD DO BETTER. WRITE YOUR ANSWER BELOW:

_____
_____
_____

IDENTIFY A FEW EASY WAYS YOU CAN START SHOWING FAITHFULNESS TO GOD'S CALL TO MAKE HIS NAME KNOWN.

_____
_____

HOW, THEN, CAN THEY CALL ON THE ONE THEY HAVE NOT BELIEVED IN? AND HOW CAN THEY BELIEVE IN THE ONE OF WHOM THEY HAVE NOT HEARD? AND HOW CAN THEY HEAR WITHOUT SOMEONE PREACHING TO THEM? AND HOW CAN THEY PREACH UNLESS THEY ARE SENT? AS IT IS WRITTEN, "HOW BEAUTIFUL ARE THE FEET OF THOSE WHO BRING GOOD NEWS!" —ROMANS 10:14–15

> IN THE SAME WAY, LET YOUR [light] SHINE before men, THAT THEY MAY see YOUR GOOD DEEDS AND PRAISE YOUR FATHER IN HEAVEN.
> —MATTHEW 5:16

YOU ARE CALLED TO BE A WITNESS TO GOD'S WORK IN YOUR LIFE, TO TESTIFY TO GOD'S GRACE, LOVE, AND POWER, TO SHARE THE DIFFERENCE GOD HAS MADE IN YOUR LIFE.

SO OFTEN WE THINK OF THIS IN TERMS OF WORDS. WE MEMORIZE LITTLE WAYS TO PRESENT THE GOSPEL. WE MIGHT EVEN DISTRIBUTE PAMPHLETS OR TRACTS. BUT THERE ARE OTHER WAYS TO SHARE YOUR FAITH.

LOOK AT THE VERSE ABOVE. HOW DO WE SHOW GOD TO PEOPLE? RIGHT: GOOD DEEDS. DOING GOOD DEEDS, OR IN OTHER WORDS, LIVING THE WAY GOD CALLS YOU TO LIVE, CAN HAVE A DRAMATIC EFFECT ON SOMEONE. THEY SEE YOUR WAY OF LIVING, NOTICE SOMETHING IS DIFFERENT, AND SEARCH FOR THE DIFFERENCE. WHEN THEY FIND THAT THE DIFFERENCE IS GOD, THEY WANT TO KNOW HIM AND THE DIFFERENCE HE MAKES.

SO, YOU CAN TURN PEOPLE TO GOD WITH MUCH MORE THAN SIMPLY YOUR WORDS. WORDS ARE IMPORTANT. YOU NEED TO BE ABLE TO ACCURATELY AND CLEARLY TELL SOMEONE ABOUT THE LORD BY USING SCRIPTURE. BUT IF YOUR ACTIONS DO NOT MATCH YOUR WORDS, YOU WILL NEVER BE ABLE TO SHOW PEOPLE THE LOVE OF CHRIST.

Bridging the Gap

God

Isaiah, to be honest, can be a confusing book of the Bible. It starts off with God telling His people that He's sick and tired of their hypocritical worship, followed by a vision of an angel putting a hot coal on a dude's tongue, and gets more intense from there. Prophecy uses language and imagery that may seem harsh or just plain weird. But Isaiah is also full of amazing promises and a story of God's redemptive work with His people. For example, the hot coal incident, that was an act of grace not punishment, purifying God's prophet. The book also contains some of the most famous prophecies about the birth, life, and death of the Messiah, stuff you may have heard at Christmas and Easter.

Ultimately, the message of Isaiah is one of hope. At the beginning, people are hopelessly lost in their sinfulness, separated from a holy God. This is how not only the Book of Isaiah starts, but how all of our lives start. Something had to be done to reunite God and His people. But man could never get back to Him. The distance was too great. He had to come to them. Rescue them. Cross over and bridge the gap.

- **LESSON 1:** Reason Together—pg 90-95
- **LESSON 2:** Righteous Wrath—pg 96-101
- **LESSON 3:** Quick Grace—pg 102-107
- **LESSON 4:** Safe And Secure—pg 108-113
- **LESSON 5:** Suffering Servant—pg 114-119
- **LESSON 6:** Free Future—pg 120-125

bridging // lesson 1 day 1 // 90

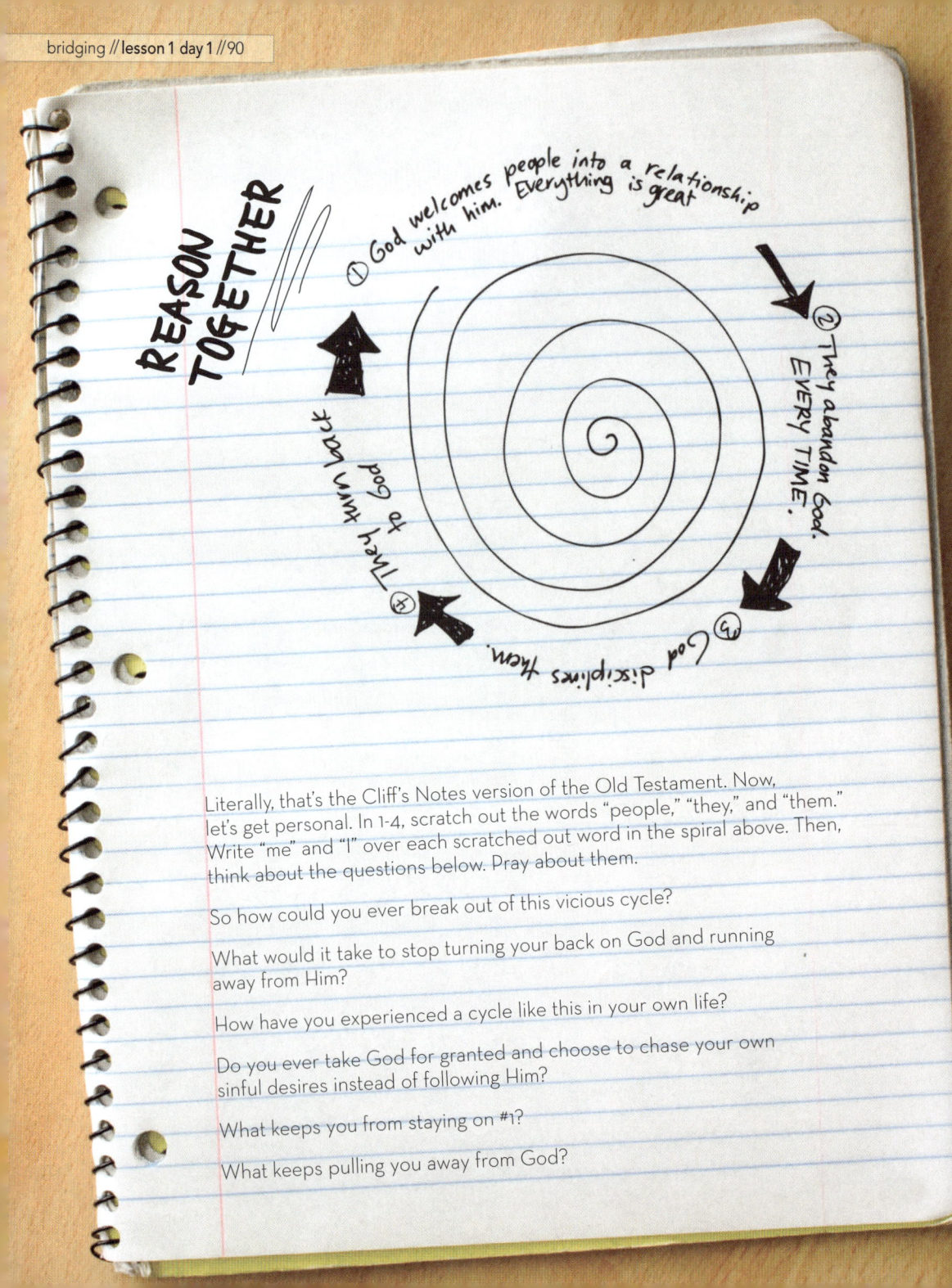

REASON TOGETHER

1. God welcomes people into a relationship with him. Everything is great.
2. They abandon God. EVERY TIME.
3. God disciplines them.
4. They turn back to God.

Literally, that's the Cliff's Notes version of the Old Testament. Now, let's get personal. In 1-4, scratch out the words "people," "they," and "them." Write "me" and "I" over each scratched out word in the spiral above. Then, think about the questions below. Pray about them.

So how could you ever break out of this vicious cycle?

What would it take to stop turning your back on God and running away from Him?

How have you experienced a cycle like this in your own life?

Do you ever take God for granted and choose to chase your own sinful desires instead of following Him?

What keeps you from staying on #1?

What keeps pulling you away from God?

PURIFIED

Isaiah was an Old Testament prophet who lived over 700 years before Jesus. Isaiah showed how far the Israelites had strayed from God but foretold how God would not give up on them. Although Isaiah's message seemed bleak at times, it was a message of hope to the Hebrew nation. God would not forget them; He would restore them.

In Isaiah 1:21-22 he gave vivid images of what Judah and Jerusalem had become:

1. The faithful city had become a harlot:

In the original language of Hebrew, this image is of a man and his bride. The literal translation could be, "My once faithful bride suitable for marriage has now become a prostitute." That was the heartache God felt toward His people in Jerusalem and Judah. Although God chose them and rescued them, they disobeyed Him and chased after other gods.

2. Their silver had become worthless:

Silver was a very precious metal during that day, as it is today. It was something to be desired and very valuable. Dross was the worthless part of a metal that forms at the top during the purification process. It was basically a mass of impurities to be thrown away. Isaiah used this metaphor to describe the condition of their hearts. Their hearts and actions were one big mass of impurities. They'd traded the pure for the impure.

3. Their choice wine was diluted with water:

Isaiah said that the Israelites had taken what was valuable and turned it into something cheap. He gave the image of someone pouring water into their most valuable wine, which essentially meant that they had cheapened something of worth.

But what does God say in Isaiah 1:25-26? He said that he would purge, or get rid of, the dross and remove the impurities. He said that the city would be called the City of Righteousness; God was going to restore the city to its original state of purity and godliness. But how?

What Israel could not do for itself, Jesus did. What Israel did to itself, Jesus undid. God's way of accomplishing Isaiah 1:25-26 was sending His Son, Jesus. Jesus had to be for Israel what Israel could not be for itself.

Home Remedies

Toenail Fungus? Paint your toenails with Listerine and a Q-Tip!

Got Zits? Soak your face in a bowl of hot spinach!

Cold Sores Got You Down? Just dip into your ear canal and wipe some of that wax on it!

Oversweating? Rub a potato on your armpits!

Asthma? Get a pet chihauhua!

Runny nose? Wear garlic on a string around your neck!

Someone, at some point in time, had a really terrible cold. And they tried everything to make it go away. And nothing worked. And so they got really desperate and said, "I guess I'll just rub this cow dung on my chest." And lo and behold, it worked. A home remedy was born.

People believe (and do) all kinds of weird things... especially when they are desperate for a solution to a personal problem.

There's more than one way to skin a cat, but there's one and only one way that you can be forgiven of your sins. We can be thankful that we live in a time when sweating can be stopped with something other than a potato, and also that there is ONE REAL way to be free of the cycle of sin. Give God a word of thanks for making a way where there was no way, and for freeing us with Jesus Christ!

bridging // lesson 1 day 4 //93

No Way Out Maze

Our sin keeps us in a massive maze that it is impossible to be free from. The hedges that form the maze are too thick and too high. We don't have any way to climb over them. Every time we think we've found a hole or a pathway that leads us out, we run into a dead end. This will inevitably go on for our whole lives.

There is a way out of the maze. One way. And we have nothing to do with it. Every once in awhile, a helicopter starts buzzing over our heads. A rope ladder gets tossed down. A man shimmies down the ladder and reaches for our hand. He yells over the blades, "Hey! I know you're lost in this maze. And to be real honest, the maze is of your own doing. But come with me. Grab my hand. Climb up this ladder and get in the helicopter with me. The only thing I require of you is your life. Come on!"

Is life in the maze or the helicopter better? What do you think?

DEVOTION

John was called the "beloved disciple," or "the one whom Jesus loved." He was one of Jesus' closest disciples and was present at Jesus' death. John focused much of his writing on the love of Christ that he experienced through his time with Jesus. The Scripture for today talks about that very love. John chose to use a word like "lavish" to describe just how much God loves us. Lavish means "to give exceedingly or in excess." God loves us so much that we are called children of God. He has adopted us into His family despite our sins. The sin that was once a barrier separating us from God has been bridged with Jesus' life, death, and resurrection.

When a child is adopted, barriers exist between the child and the parents: There are laws separating them. Sometimes there are far distances between them. However, the parents overcome all of these obstacles to get to their new, chosen child. When that process is complete, the child is in the family forever. Nothing separates them any longer.

Nothing separates us from our Father. Because God has adopted us into His family, just as John says in 1 John 1:3, we are to live as part of His family. Sin will strain our relationship with Him, but God cares for and loves us so much that He wants to see us grow into His image. He is patient to lead us back into fellowship with Him. Sin is real, and God doesn't tolerate it. However, we can be confident that He will not reject us from His family but will always offer His forgiveness. We are His and belong to Him for eternity.

How does it affect your relationship to God to think of yourself as one of His own children?

What sin is in your life now that you need to address?

Thank God for His love and for being patient with you, even when you have sin in your life.

Barriers

Sin is a barrier to our relationship with God. And we have a lot of barriers. What are some of the barriers that you have in your relationship with Him? Write them below. Then spend some time in prayer asking God to help you overcome that sin.

_____
_____
_____
_____
_____
_____
_____
_____

Righteous Wrath

We tend to focus on the side of God that's loving and merciful and wise. And, make no mistake. He is all of those things. But God is also wrathful. And rightly so. We have turned away from his holiness, from his good gifts. The Bible talks about God coming in fire to consume the earth. It talks about the moon turning into blood. It talks about God killing you with a sword. God's wrath is not to be taken lightly or not considered. God's wrath is terrifying and deadly and quick.

As believers we can be thankful that Christ took the entirety of God's wrath upon himself when He died on the cross. But in order to fully understand the sacrifice, we must fully comprehend the wrath.

Grab your Bible and head to the concordance, looking for the word "wrath". Read some of these verses and meditate on His wrath and Christ's sacrifice that shields you from it.

God Doesn't Take Sin Lightly

Like Mordor, *War and Peace*, and Abraham Lincoln, sin is serious stuff. Because we live on this side of the cross, sometimes we don't give it the weight it deserves. Our sin grieves God. You know when people use the word "grieve," they are typically referring to a funeral. He does not take our sin lightly.

What are some sins in your life that you don't take seriously that grieve the heart of God?

SAVED

Paul wrote the Book of Romans for the church in Rome. Although Paul had not started the church in Rome, he felt a close bond to the believers there. In chapter five, Paul used some really "big" words like: justification, perseverance, and reconciliation. In verses 6-9, there are a few things we need to notice.

Verse 6
- Paul called us powerless. This shows that we cannot complete "salvation" on our own. It requires God's intervention. If we were powerful enough to save ourselves then we wouldn't need God's help.

- Paul said, "Christ died for the ungodly." That means you and me. Everyone on earth is ungodly. So, at this point Paul described us as powerless and ungodly. It makes sense, right? Why would Christ die for godly people? If we were capable of being godly in the first place, then Christ wouldn't have had to die at all.

Verse 8
- Paul called us "sinners." Now we are powerless and ungodly sinners. Do you feel the love? God doesn't see us as little children who can do no wrong. He sees us for what we are. We are flawed and messed up human beings that cannot save ourselves.

- Paul said, "While we were still sinners, God died for us." Dying for us is how God showed His love to us. That means it is no surprise to God that we are sinful. We can't hide our sins from Him. That means that we don't have to come to God and put on a fake front by acting like we are good enough to deserve salvation.

We are weak, ungodly sinners. Christ died so that, in Him, our weakness would turn into strength and we would be made righteous before God.

But what's next? What happens after salvation?

Verse 9
- Paul said that we are "saved from God's wrath"! Woo hoo! Bring out the banners and let's party! Right? Sure that is cause for a celebration, but at whose cost? You see, God's wrath had to be poured out onto somebody. But instead of pouring it out on us, He chose to pour out His wrath on His Son. So while we celebrate the wrath of God being turned away from us, God's wrath turned toward Jesus.

- Whenever you think about God's wrath not coming down on you, remember that God's wrath did come down on Jesus. You and I didn't get away with our sins; Jesus just took the punishment for our sins in order that we might have peace. The penalty had to be paid, and Jesus signed the check with His blood.

Cause & Effect

Cause and effect. You learned about it in school, and it is active in your life. Take a look at the situations above. What do you think the effects are for each of these pictures? Write what you think they might be. Get as creative as you can.

Now, here's a question: what is the effect of your sin? Think about it for a minute. When you sin, who is affected? Just you? Just God? Really take a moment to think about the potentially far-reaching consequences of your sin.

DEVOTION

Have you ever wanted to belong to an exclusive group? I'm not talking about an exclusive group in which you can pay a certain amount of money and join like a country club. I'm referring to a group of like-minded individuals who choose to get together and not let others join—kind of like clubs from your childhood or cliques in high school? Think about if for a second.

John wrote this letter near the middle to end of the first century to a group of people being led astray by false teachers, called the Gnostics. I hope you can see John's heart in this passage. John did not condemn their foolishness or mistakes with a "holier than thou" attitude. He wanted to show them their mistakes through love. Why? Because he'd seen this love and experienced it through following Jesus.

Now, think about the church or ministry to which you belong. Is the mindset of your church or youth group intentional about including people in your fellowship so that we can show them the love of Christ?

Why do you think people come to your youth group? Is it the riveting communicator behind the pulpit? Is it the food? Is it the cutting edge music? Those things may help people come the first time, but they will stay because people want to find something different—something the world cannot offer them. They come in hope of finding unconditional love and acceptance. Most people know the mistakes in their own lives. They are just looking for someone to look past those mistakes and love them unconditionally as they show them the way to Christ.

If your youth group is not known for loving God and loving people, make a change. (Not make a change by changing churches.) Be the change you want to see in your youth group. Start loving people as Christ commanded. Be the change!

It's Ok. I love you!

We tend to think of ultimate love as ultimate freedom. When our parents deny us the opportunity to go to that death metal concert with our new serial killer friends, we claim that they "don't love us." But what would you think of the parent that allowed their child that "freedom"? We'd call them neglectful, selfish, and, above all, unloving.

So this applies to your relationship with God too.

The next time you feel that God is unfair or ruining your fun, remember that it is because He loves you that He doesn't let you do everything you want.

If you love me, you'll let me stick my finger in this electric socket.

It's ok! I love you!

Buddy proceeds to electrocute himself.

If you love me, you'll let me dive into this tank of boiling hot water, infested with flesh-eating piranhas.

It's ok! I love you!

Buddy proceeds to be eaten by piranhas.

If you love me, you'll let this car drag me from its bumper while I balance on a surfboard.

It's ok! I love you!

Buddy proceeds to be tossed from a moving vehicle at 70 mph.

bridging // lesson 3 day 1 // 102

Quick Grace

We hear a lot about fast things in our world. Internet companies promise the fastest speeds. You can literally cook a meal in 90 seconds. If we wait in a drive-thru longer than 3 minutes we get highly irritated. We want it now, we want it fast, whatever it is.

There is one thing we can always count on for speed: God's grace. It's there, waiting in the gates to be sent immediately to you. All you have to do is ask for it.

Think of a recent moment when you have been a recipient of this gift and write about it here.

bridging // lesson 3 day 2 // 103

Grace is fast. It comes right on time; it comes the second you ask for forgiveness in Jesus' name. No pizza delivery service can compare to its swiftness.

Take a moment to write some words describing God's grace.

grace
HOT, FAST, & READY!

God's grace is like a massive eraser that is capable of removing otherwise-permanent marks from the Sharpie sin on your life.

How do you imagine God's grace? A laser beam on a spaceship that destroys the Death Star of sin? A huge fly swatter with perfect aim, killing the annoying flies of sin? Be creative. Tell how you view God's grace and sin.

THE FAMILY

In Isaiah 30, the Israelites can't seem to understand how to follow God. God made it simple for them: just follow Him and do what He says. But the Israelites had to make things more difficult on themselves. When threatened, they decided to seek help from Egypt instead of relying on God. How quickly they forgot that Egypt had enslaved them for over 400 years! It was God who delivered them then, but now they sought their captors for help instead of their Deliverer.

God called the Israelites "obstinate children," which meant that they were disobeying and doing things without seeking their Father. He said that they heap sin upon sin. That was the history of Israel: the nation commits idolatry and then lies about it and then murders and so on. Israel was renowned for heaping sin upon sin. God warned the Israelites that they would only receive shame and disgrace when they sought Egypt and Pharaoh.

Jumping forward to verses 4-17, Isaiah showed us just how disobedient the Israelites were. God revealed His displeasure and judgment against them. However, in verse 18 we see a very important phrase: "Yet the LORD." This short phrase shows up all throughout Scripture. Some people refer to it as the "Big 'but' in the Bible." The word "yet" in Hebrew means, "in spite of." We see it many times interchanged with the word "but," as in "but God. . . ." Many times when we see this phrase, we see God's grace revealed. For example, in verse 18, the phrase "yet the LORD" means, "even though you are rebellious, disobedient, sinful, deceitful, and stubborn; despite all of that which I just mentioned, the Lord longs to be gracious to you."

That kind of grace is huge. That is the heart of a loving Father to his disobedient children. God loves us and longs to restore us and show us grace. He wants us to depend on Him, not on some temporary power as Egypt was to the Israelites. God loves protecting His children. The Israelites' problem was that they failed to remember what a loving God they had. "Yet the LORD" never grew weary in trying to remind them. "Yet the LORD" will never give up on you as well.

Fast v. Slow

Baseball pitch: 107 mph

Peregrine Falcon: 200 mph

Usain Bolt: 100m in 9.58 seconds

SSC Ultimate Aero: 0-60mph in 2.7 seconds

Light: travels 186,282 miles per second

Baseball pitch: .5mph (thrown by your brother's PeeWee team's girl pitcher)

Three-Toed Sloth: reaching speeds of 0.07mph

Your Grandmother using a walker: 100m in 9.58 hours

The beat-up 1994 sedan that you "inherited": taps out at 49mph

Time it takes you to turn on the light in the morning: 3 snooze hits

It's pretty easy to see which column contains the fastest things and the slowest things (unless, that is, you have a very fast grandmother). Some things are made to be fast. Usain Bolt, the fastest man that has ever lived, was made to be fast. The three-toed sloth was made to hang from a tree by its claws and eat mangoes... slow. God's grace was meant to be fast. Faster than Usain, faster than the speed of light, even.

How fast are you to ask for His forgiveness?

DEVOTION

Samuel was a prophet, priest, and judge who led Israel. God sent Samuel to find the future King of Israel in a very unlikely place--Bethlehem. There was a man there named Jesse who had many sons. God told Samuel that he would find the next King of Israel in that group of Jesse's sons. Jesse brought out seven of his sons and presented them to Samuel. Undoubtedly, some of them looked like they could be king. But God said something in 1 Samuel 16:7 that we never need to forget: "Man looks at the outward appearance, but the LORD looks at the heart." After all but one of the sons passed by Samuel, he asked if Jesse had more sons. Jesse sent for his youngest son, David, who was tending sheep in the fields. God told Samuel to anoint David as the next King of Israel. King David ruled for many years because he had the heart of a king that followed God, not because he had the appearance of a king.

Some of the most interesting home renovation shows demonstrate how to buy a run-down house and flip it for more money than you paid for it. The people on these shows take a fairly rough looking house, gut it from the inside out, and then renovate everything in it to make it attractive. But, sometimes builders try to cut corners and just apply a fresh coat of paint to make the walls look new. This approach may be less expensive, but unless they go inside the walls, they'll never know if something such as termites, mold, or rot might have destroyed the invisible parts of house. It doesn't matter how many coats of paint the builder applies to a house like this, eventually the house will crumble from within. The best way to approach these run-down homes is to leave the infrastructure and then build from there.

God knows if we've applied a fresh coat of paint to try and cover our sins. He knows when we try to cut corners on fixing our heart. If we do not address the sin in our lives, we will eventually crumble from within just like a termite-infested house. God knew there were others who may have looked more like a king, but He was more concerned with finding the one who had the heart of a king who followed God. David wanted to follow God completely. How is your heart? Have you done a full-scale renovation of your soul or have you simply applied Sunday clothes to cover your sin?

What sins do you try to cover up?

If other people could see your heart would they see the same person you present on the outside?

How does God see your heart?

Safe & Secure

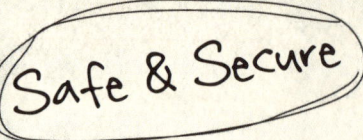

Close your eyes. Wait. Don't. You can't read the rest of this if you do that. Now, I want you to think of the safest place you can imagine. Is it your house? The vault in the bank? Sitting with a friendly law enforcement officer enjoying a delightful treat? It can be anything.

Did you know that when you have God's grace you have absolutely nothing to fear? You are in the safest place possible. Maybe not safe to the outside world. You will still have hard times and hardships. But you walk the road with God. He's always there for you, He will never forsake you, He is a rock to cling to. The safe place in the storm.

Draw or describe the safest place you could imagine. Go crazy with it. Think over-the-top, ridiculously secure.

THE STANDARD

The Apostle John wrote 1 John as a pastoral letter with the purpose of encouraging churches to have confidence that God is the source of salvation. At this time there were many false teachers claiming that salvation came through realizing an inherent "light" within each person and coming to an enlightened knowledge of this personal power; this claim indicated that people did not have a problem with sin that only Christ could overcome. John wanted to challenge Christ-followers to not fall victim to this teaching. He wanted them to stick to the truth of Christ that they had been taught. In 1 John 1:8-10 we see John addressing the issue of sin and forgiveness.

In verse 8, John called believers to examine their lives. He told them that every one of them had a sin problem and that to deny it would be lying. We often lie about our sin problem by comparing ourselves to others. If you compare yourself to others, you'll always find a way to become complacent. It's really easy for us to use the excuse, "I'm not as bad as them," or "At least I haven't done that." There will always be people to whom we can compare our lives, but we fall short every time when we compare our lives to Jesus.

What areas in your life do not measure up to Jesus' standards?

In verse 9, John said that God would forgive sins when His people acknowledge them and seek forgiveness from Him. But John didn't stop there. He said that God would purify His people from all unrighteousness. When God purifies our lives, He takes away what doesn't belong; He removes the part of us that don't measure up to His standards. There will always be an area in your life that God needs to purify for you. We can be encouraged that God is patient to help us become more like Him and is ready to forgive us when we repent.

What is God trying to remove from your life that you don't want to let go?

John emphasized in verse 10 that each person has sinned and that problem is why Jesus died. If we claim to be sinless, then we are saying that Jesus didn't have to die. If we are sinless then we are strong enough to earn salvation on our own. Therefore, there is no need for Christ, God, or God's Word. But that is not the case. Only Christ was sinless, and His sacrificial death and work in our lives is the only way that we can be made righteous before God.

bridging // lesson 4 day 3 //110

The USSS, United States Secret Service, is the government agency in charge of preventing and investigating acts of counterfeit money. But you probably also know them for their other main responsibility: protecting the president.

The legislation to create the Secret Service was, ironically, rumored to be on Abraham Lincoln's desk the night he was assassinated, and the agency was put fully in charge of presidential security in 1902. They run every tiny detail of presidential security. From code names to armored cars to standing in front of bullets, these men and women make it their business to protect the president of the United States.

As highly trained as these special agents are, our security in God's grace is something even they can't touch. Paul said it best when he informed us that neither life nor death, nor the future or the present, nor anything this side of heaven or the other will ever separate us from God through Christ. It's as secure as you will ever be.

Do you feel secure in God's love and grace? Why or why not?

DEVOTION

Paul wrote his letter to the Philippians from his prison cell, but he used the word "joy" or "rejoice" 14 times in this letter. Paul understood joy to be a state of mind. He knew that there was a difference between happiness and joy: happiness is related to your circumstances, but joy is what you have when Christ lives in your heart. In Philippians 1:3-6, Paul told the Philippians how much joy he felt because of their partnership for the gospel and their involvement in his life. He encouraged them in their work for the gospel because God would never leave them but would continue His work in and through their lives until the return of Christ.

Have you ever tried to go to a Website only to find the homepage displaying the message, "Website Under Construction"? Frustrating isn't it? Often this means that the site is undergoing improvements to make it more user-friendly. What about when you're driving and you see traffic backed up in a construction zone? Very frustrating isn't it? You know the roads will drive well once they're finished, but it's inconvenient at the moment. These signs are somewhat of a nuisance, but they are actually signs of progress. If Websites aren't updated they would not be able to keep up with the latest software or designs. If roads weren't repaired we'd be driving on dangerous highways. Construction and repairs are good things. They are for our benefit.

Sometimes people feel that they should have everything figured out once they become Christ-followers. That is far from the truth. Paul understood that God is continually at work in the lives of His people, and He will finish His perfect work in them. If you are not where you think God wants you to be, then be encouraged that God is not finished with you yet. You and I are still works in progress. God is always working to make us into who He wants us to be.

How is God working on your life?

What part of your heart and actions are under construction?

How can we appreciate God's work in our lives, even when it may be painful?

How Would You Respond? (Part 1)

The way we respond to situations and the way God responds are...well, as different as you can get, for the most part. Today and tomorrow, we're going to look at the differences in the two. Take a look at these situations. Put yourself in them. How do you respond? Don't just write down what you think you should say. Be brutally honest with yourself. It's ok. No one but you will see it. Write down your answers and tomorrow, we'll look at God's response.

Your younger sister just told the family that she is pregnant.

You find out that a friend has been spreading rumors about you being gay.

Your father takes away your car keys for not making straight A's this semester.

Your basketball coach decides to start a freshman guard, while you sit on the bench.

Your boyfriend is cheating on you with another girl in your class.

A police officer writes you an extremely expensive ticket for going 4 miles over the speed limit.

Your mother loses her job and you're asked by your family to help with expenses by handing over the money from your summer job.

The college you've been hoping to attend your entire life rejects you.

How Would God Respond? (Part 2)

Yesterday we took a hard look at our responses to difficult situations in our lives. And if we're honest with ourselves, we know that even when we try, we don't have the most grace-filled attitudes.

Today, let's have a look at the same scenarios through God's lens. How might He respond? Take what you know about God through His Word and Christ and fill in God's responses. Back it up with scripture. Use that concordance, baby!

How do these responses differ from the ones you wrote yesterday? How are they the same?

Your younger sister just told the family that she is pregnant.

You find out that a friend has been spreading rumors about you being gay.

Your father takes away your car keys for not making straight A's this semester.

Your basketball coach decides to start a freshman guard, while you sit on the bench.

Your boyfriend is cheating on you with another girl in your class.

A police officer writes you an extremely expensive ticket for going 4 miles over the speed limit.

Your mother loses her job and you're asked by your family to help with expenses by handing over the money from your summer job.

The college you've been hoping to attend your entire life rejects you.

bridging // lesson 5 day 1 // 114

Suffering Servant

It's amazing to think that part of God's ultimate plan of salvation includes a very important part where His Son must suffer. To suffer means to bear pain. To live with it. To have it deep in your bones. Suffering is long-term. Suffering happens over weeks, months, years.

Maybe you have suffered. Maybe you have a friend with cancer. Maybe you lost a parent at an early age. Maybe you are ridiculed every day at school.

Christ was the bearer of our sin, and he suffered for it. Don't forget: Jesus sweat drops of blood the night he was arrested. He is the Suffering Servant, taking our sin on himself and fulfilling God's ancient plan of salvation.

How may I serve you?

The Difference between Prisoners and Servants

Prisoners
Prisoners are captured and held against their will.
Prisoners have no choice in doing what their Master orders.
Prisoners are kept in chains.
Prisoners are mentally, emotionally, and sometimes physically abused.

Servants
Servants come to work because they want to.
Servants have free will.
Servants are kept informed.
Servants are here because they want to be, and they take on responsibility because they love their Master.

Christ was the perfect example of a servant. He submitted Himself to God, and gave Himself up for our sake. The ultimate in humility, the ultimate in sacrifice.

How will you surrender your will and your life to Christ? (This doesn't make you a prisoner; you can choose to be a servant of Christ.)

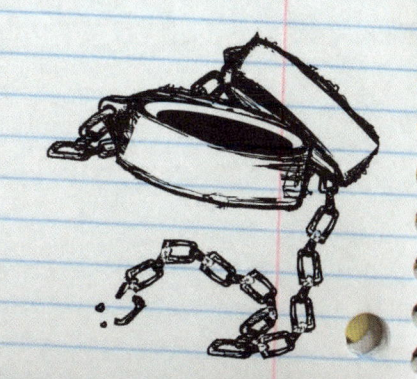

RECONCILED

Paul spent about a year and a half living with the Corinthians and working as a tent maker during his second missionary journey. He knew these people well and loved them despite the many problems they had within the church. In 2 Corinthians 5:17-21, Paul is explaining the ministry of reconciliation to the church. In verses 17-21, Paul used the word "reconciliation" or its variation five times. Sounds like an important word to understand. It means to make things right by settling a debt.

The word "reconciled" is used for the first time in verse 18. Here it means that God traded in His wrath toward us for a right relationship with us through Jesus. Christ paid the price for our sin. God did the reconciling. We were the ones who were reconciled to Him. We cannot reconcile ourselves to God, but God can reconcile us to Himself.

The second time the word appears is later in verse 18. Here Paul told us that since God reconciled us, we now have the example of ministry to follow. Since we have been reconciled, we have a responsibility to carry out the ministry of reconciliation. The ministry of reconciliation is something that we could not understand unless God showed it to us. And He did just that. He showed us the ministry of reconciliation when He fixed the broken relationship between God and humanity. How did He fix that relationship? Through sending His Son, Jesus, to pay for our sins with His death on a cross.

In verse 19, Paul further explained an aspect of reconciliation. Since God does not count our sins against us, we too must show that same amount of grace to our brothers and sisters. If we are to carry out the ministry of fixing broken relationships between each other and helping them see a right relationship with God, we have to show each other the same grace God showed us.

Later in verse 19, Paul told us that God has committed to us the message of reconciliation so that we have now become messengers. God has entrusted to us this message so that the world will receive it, understand it, and pass it on. If we are to serve as Christ's ambassadors but are not reconciled to each other whether in a family relationship, a friend relationship, a racial relationship, or a broken relationship, we are not carrying out God's message of reconciliation. We have to share the gospel. Both in deed and word. Sometimes we think it is enough to just act godly or to just tell people about Jesus, but we need to do both.

Finally in verse 20, Paul said that this is the message we should spread to others, "Be reconciled to God." We are Christ's mouthpieces and reconciliation is the message. Paul urges us to go and spread the word of reconciliation to the world so that they too can be reconciled to God. The world's relationship with God needs to be fixed so that they will see how He turned His wrath into love. The world needs to hear what God did for them through Jesus and how He did it. Verse 21 tells exactly what Jesus did. He took upon Himself the sins of the world and became a sin offering for us so that we didn't have to receive that punishment. Jesus took our punishment, and God gave us His righteousness. Without Jesus, our relationship with God would still be broken.

What person in your life is someone to whom you need to be reconciled?

Based on these verses, what does reconciliation mean to you?

Grace Match

Stealing a $20 from your mom's purse _____

Stealing 8 million dollars in a international Ponzi scheme _____

Gossiping about a friend on Facebook _____

Gossiping about all your friends on Facebook _____

Underage drinking _____

Thinking lustful thoughts about someone _____

Jealousy towards a friend that has better grades, a cuter prom date, and an overall better life than you _____

Anger towards your parents for getting a divorce _____

Write the word "grace" next to each scenario.

For the believer in Christ, the answer is always grace. But we don't just need grace when something big happens, when we mess up royally. We need it every second of every minute of every hour of every day. We are in a constant need of grace. And although we are always offered grace, it doesn't mean we should keep on sinning. The goal is to become more like Christ.

Taking One for the Team

While the business of Christ taking on our sin and dying for us is a great deal more serious than Buddy taking a cartoon bullet, you get the idea. Christ selflessly threw himself in the path of sin and death, and absorbed the consequence for us.

Take a moment and thank God for sending Christ to do what you could have never done.

DEVOTION

The writer of Hebrews is unknown. Some people speculate that they know or have an idea who wrote it, but the truth is that we just don't know. What we do know is that the writer was very smart. He was educated in Jewish history and laws. We know that it was written to Jews to show that Christ was the way to salvation. In chapter 9, the writer tried to show the Jews that Jesus made the ultimate sacrifice for all sins. He gave the readers a history lesson about how Moses used the blood of calves to purify the tabernacle and the items used in ceremonies. Our key verse for today is Hebrews 9:22. The writer made the connection between Moses and Jesus by explaining that Moses knew there would be no forgiveness of sins without the shedding of blood. Then, in verses 27-28 he showed that Jesus made the ultimate sacrifice with His own blood for the sins of the world. Jesus' perfect sacrifice was greater than anything Moses on the Jewish Law could accomplish; true and lasting forgiveness of sin was now a reality.

Have you ever heard the phrase, "That's just water under the bridge"? What that phrase means is that all has been forgiven and is now in the past. For instance, if two people had an argument and then resolved things before one person moved away and years later they saw each other again and one of them brought back up the argument, the other one could say, "That's just water under the bridge." What he or she would mean is that all was forgiven, and it is not important because it is in the past;
it is time to move on.

Read John 19:33-34

Jesus is our bridge to God. Without Him, we cannot be made right before God. Jesus' death and resurrection bridged the gap between God and humanity so that we could be restored to the right relationship with God. When blood and water flowed beneath the cross of Jesus, God was washing away our sins forever. They would never be held against us again. Let's move on.

Next time you hear that phrase, "Water under the bridge," think about the sacrifice God made for you so that there could be forgiveness. Think about the time when blood, water, and tears flowed beneath the bridge shaped like a cross.

Pray that you will never forget the pain and suffering that Jesus went through to give you forgiveness.

Free Future

God's got a plan in mind. He's always had it, since before the beginning of time. The plan is this: one day, this world will be completely and totally free from sin. And it's not just that I will send my Son to remedy the sin problem. There will be a world in which sin does not exist. Where sin doesn't ruin everything.

Spend a minute thinking about the top three things you can't wait to see gone from this world when that future plan becomes reality. Write these in the thought bubbles. Then thank God for the hope you can have knowing that some day those things will be so far gone, that they will not even be distant memories anymore! They'll never cross your mind again. Give those troubles and worries to Him today.

WISDOM

Solomon, King of Israel and son of King David, was considered the wisest man in the world. He wrote most of the Book of Proverbs. There are different sections in Proverbs, and this passage falls in the section that your Bible may label: Sayings of the Wise. Each of the verses in this section is considered to be a rule of thumb on how to live wisely. Wise sayings from a wise man on wise living. Got it? Let's break down these two verses: Proverbs 23:17-18

"Do not let your heart envy sinners"
Have you ever wondered why it seems like "bad people" get all the breaks? Just turn on the TV and you'll be bombarded with stories of the rich and famous. Why is an adulterer the best golfer in the world? Why are thieves the CEOs of large companies? Sometimes it is easy to envy these people due to their success on earth. But we know ultimately there are more important things – eternal things – to live for and that everyone will be judged in the end for their actions. Proverbs tells us not to envy these people, but instead to have a fire for the Lord.

"But always be zealous for the fear of the LORD."
To be zealous means to be enthusiastic without restrictions. Proverbs says to be that enthusiastic about fearing the Lord. That doesn't mean to shake in your shoes when you think about God. To fear the Lord means to have a reverence or to be in awe about God when you think of him. This is the kind of fear you should have toward your parents and other people in leadership roles. You are reverent to them, look up to them, and respect their power and authority, but you are not scared of them either. The fear you should have for God is a healthy fear that draws us to worship Him. This proverb tells us that we should be enthusiastic about our reverence toward God. Usually we associate reverence with being solemn. Have you ever seen enthusiastic reverence? That is how we are to act instead of being jealous of sinners. Be zealous, not jealous.

"There is surely a future hope for you"
One reason this wise saying tells us to not envy sinners is because our reward is not necessarily here on earth. Our hope is in heaven. If sinners have everything on earth they want and all the toys they could ever buy, that is their treasure. It's OK if Christ-followers never have a dime to spare here on earth. Our treasure is in heaven. Christ-followers have a future hope that one day we will live with God in heaven. Heaven is described as having streets of gold. Ironic isn't it? It will be such a great place that the most valuable things here on earth are what people trample on in heaven. Why should we envy people who collect trash for treasures?

"And your hope will not be cut off."
Not only does our hope rest in the fact that one day we will be in such a great place as heaven, but also we will be in God's presence for eternity. We will not be cut off from Him. Being in God's presence is the best part of living in heaven. Hell is being separated from God for eternity. If we trust in God in this life, He will not cut us off in the life to come. That is why we should not envy sinners. Sinners should envy us because we have the eternal treasure and an everlasting hope.

Protect your heart. Make God the one for whom you heart aches. The things of this earth will pass away but your soul lives forever. A soul that longs for God is one that will be with God throughout eternity.

Your Own Perfect World

Everyone has their perfect world. What they would dream up if they were in control. Maybe that guy you have a crush on would have one on you in return. Your fingernails would be made of chocolate. Water would taste like Diet Coke. The list goes on. In the box below, draw or describe your perfect world. Be creative and have fun with it.

knowing the future

Does knowing the future change the present? If someone time-traveled and told you that something was going to happen in the future, how would it change the way you lived right now? What if you knew you were going to be rich? What if you knew when you would die? What if you knew who you would marry? What if you knew who won the World Series? You get the idea.

Now. Think about this. You DO know something about the future. Grab your Bible. Look up Revelation 21. Read the whole chapter if you want, it is AWESOME! But pay close attention to verses 1-8. Notice that it says in verse 5 that these things are true. What future does God promise to all who love Him? What future awaits those who do not believe in God? So, how does this glimpse into the future change the way you live starting right now?

Write about or draw the things described in Revelation 21 and think about how this future changes your life today.

DEVOTION

The Apostle John wrote Revelation based on a vision God gave him. In Revelation 21:1-7 God showed John what the end of time would look like. John saw a lot of destruction poured out on the earth, but that is not the end. In this passage, John saw the very end, and it is good. Focus on verse 5 when God said, "I am making everything new!" How exciting is that! In this world as we know it everything is dying. From the time you take your first breath you are dying. When flowers bloom they are on their way out. Everything in this world is dying. For God to say He is making all things new is awesome. Regardless of what destruction the end will bring, God will make everything new in the end.

How many doomsday or end-of-the-world movies have you seen?

All these movies picture the end of time as a bleak event in which all hope is seemingly lost. However, that is not what God promised. God promised to restore the earth. The end time is a time of renewal for Christ-followers. It is a time of hope for those who've remained faithful. Followers of Christ should not fear the end times. We should look forward to what God is going to do. It should excite us to know that pain, suffering, and persecution will be no more. God will make all things new! The earth will not be without hope like the movies depict. God created this earth as good and plans to restore it in the end.

Sin is the reason this earth is in its current state of confusion. God knows that. That is why He sent Jesus to die for us, so that we might be restored to God. God not only restores us here in this life, but He will restore us for eternity as well. God will restore the earth by doing away with the sin that plagues the earth now. We will not recognize an earth without sin. We have no idea what that will be like since sin infects everything we know. When God said He will make all things new, that means that He will make things new in His eyes—not ours. We know what our "new" might look like, but we cannot fathom what God's "new" will look like. Get excited! God is about to do something new during the end times.

The End

There is a plan for the future. It is free of sin and suffering. And just like after everything is set right in the movies, the heroes walk off into the sunset, we, along with Christ will do the same thing. A future of love. A future of happiness, of joy. There will be no sorrow. There will be no tears of sadness. We will walk into the sunset and experience Christ and his kingdom forever.

The Means

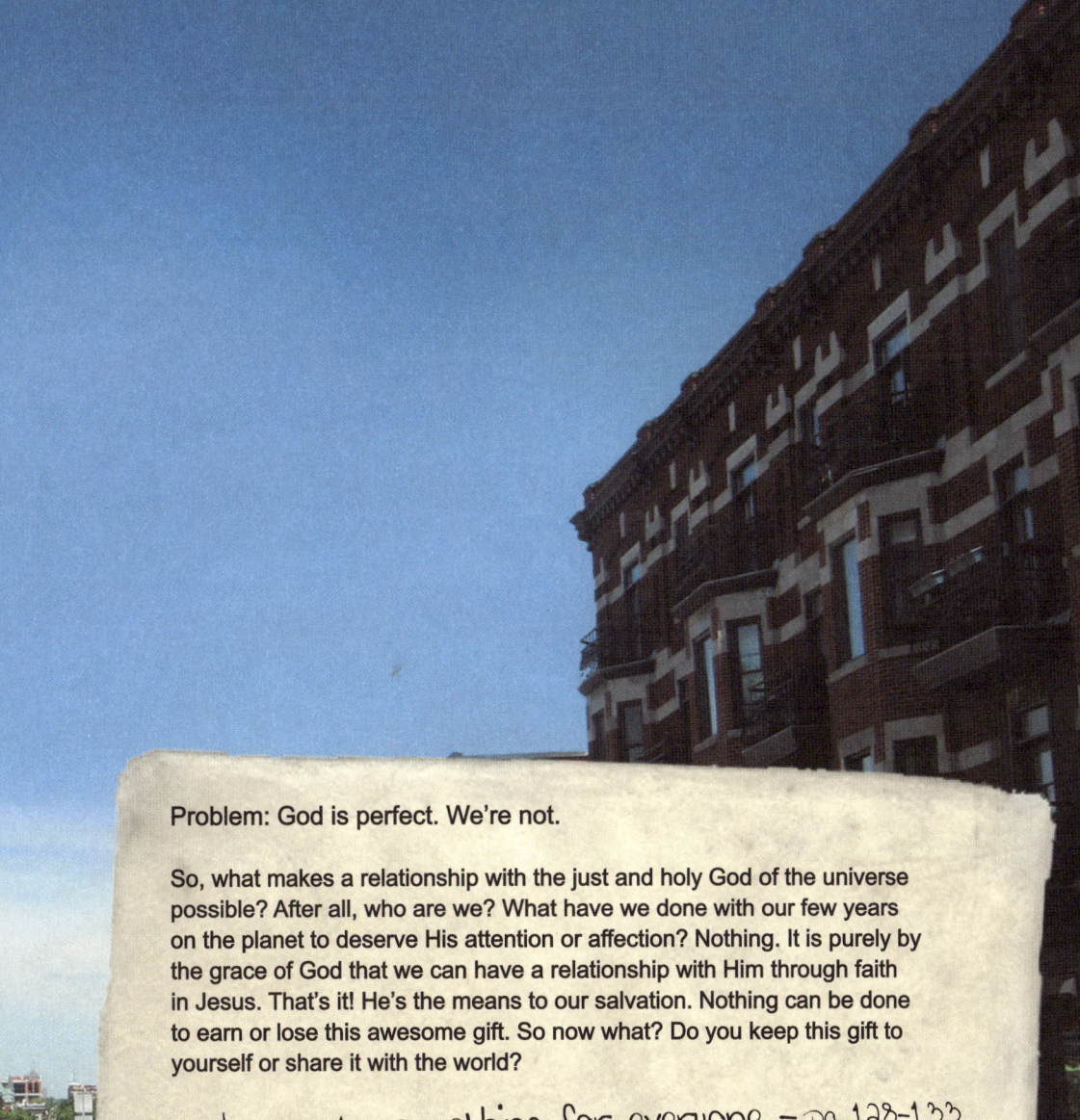

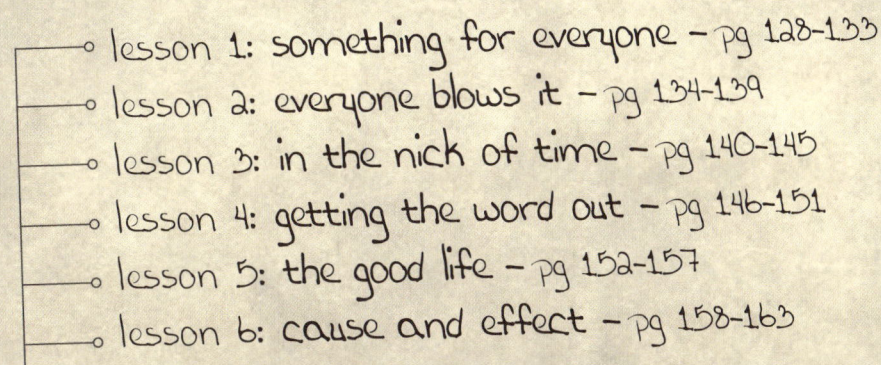

Problem: God is perfect. We're not.

So, what makes a relationship with the just and holy God of the universe possible? After all, who are we? What have we done with our few years on the planet to deserve His attention or affection? Nothing. It is purely by the grace of God that we can have a relationship with Him through faith in Jesus. That's it! He's the means to our salvation. Nothing can be done to earn or lose this awesome gift. So now what? Do you keep this gift to yourself or share it with the world?

- lesson 1: something for everyone – pg 128-133
- lesson 2: everyone blows it – pg 134-139
- lesson 3: in the nick of time – pg 140-145
- lesson 4: getting the word out – pg 146-151
- lesson 5: the good life – pg 152-157
- lesson 6: cause and effect – pg 158-163

the means // lesson 1 day 1 // 128

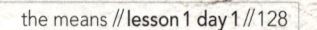

WHAT SINS FROM YOUR PAST HAVE LEFT A MARK ON YOUR LIFE?

Thank God for covering over your sins, FORGIVING YOU.

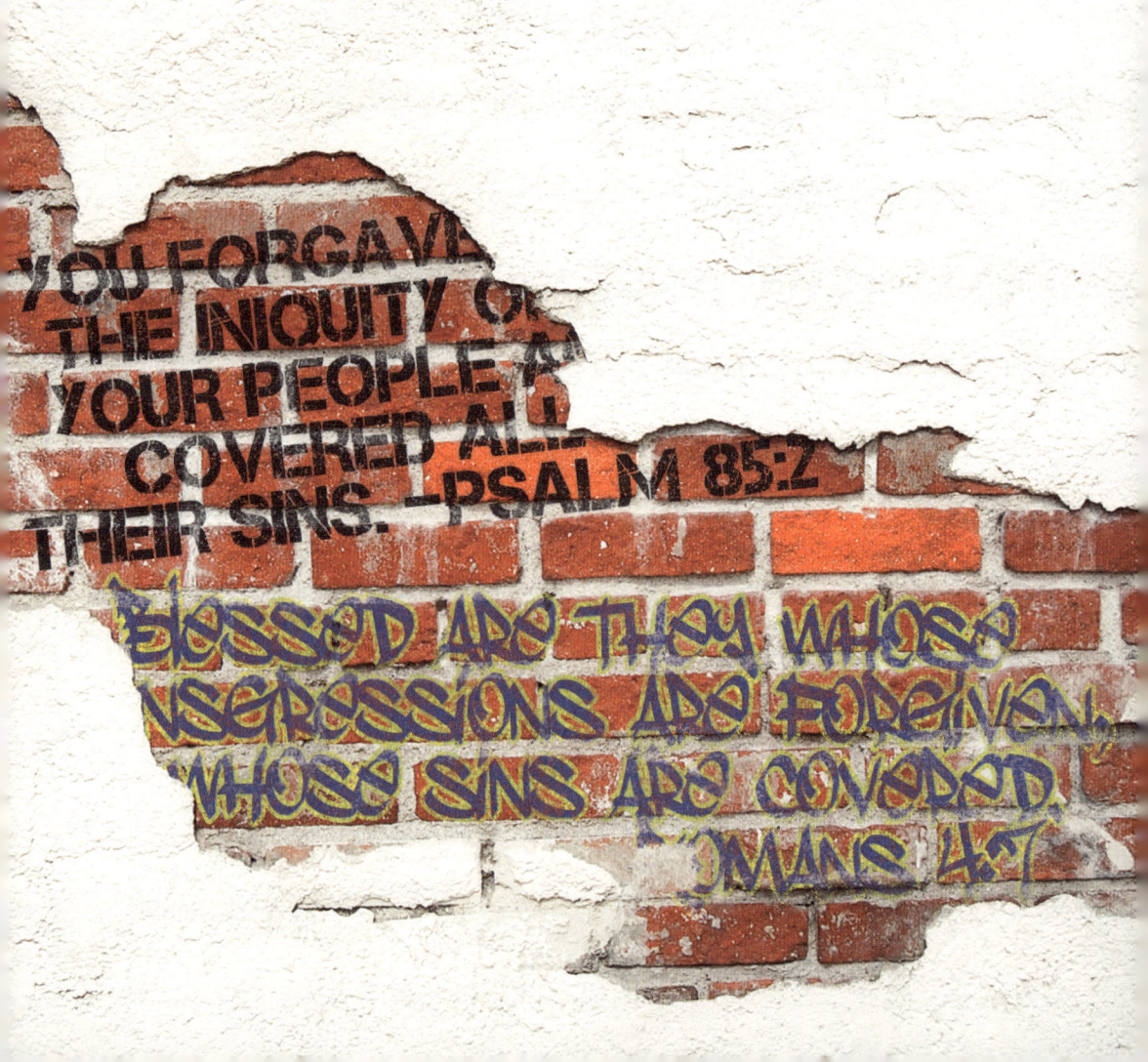

YOU FORGAVE THE INIQUITY OF YOUR PEOPLE & COVERED ALL THEIR SINS. —PSALM 85:2

Blessed are they whose transgressions are forgiven, whose sins are covered. —Romans 4:7

the means // lesson 1 day 2 // 129

GOD

YOU

Think about your own life. How do any of these things get in the way of your relationship with God? Fill in a few specific things that are currently coming between YOU and GOD.

DEVOTION

Nobody is perfect. Right?

We've all experienced this fact. And we've all said something like this before. The Bible even agrees with this fact. However, the Bible says this is not an excuse. It's sin. (Do you think that sounds a little severe? After all, "nobody's perfect." Right?)

Well, what is sin? Maybe you've heard before that the word "sin" is an archery term. It means to miss the mark. In other words, anything other than perfection, right in the middle of the bull's eye, is a sin. So for your life, if you aim to please God and remain in the center of His good and perfect will, but you stray even the slightest from perfection . . . it's a sin.

God is perfect. By definition, perfection has no part of imperfection. The two simply can't coexist. However, this understanding of sin is incomplete and softens the idea of sin to merely "not being perfect." But honestly, it's not like we've always tried to honor God perfectly but just can't live up to His unrealistic expectation; we don't even try. We don't even want to try. We are aiming at different targets all together. We justify selfish desires in all kinds of ways: "It's no big deal." "Everybody else does it." "I'm not hurting anyone." "It's just for fun." "I can't help it." "Nobody's perfect . . ."

Open your Bible to Romans 3 and read verse 23. You're probably quite familiar with that verse by now. Let's explore what Paul means by "nobody's perfect."

Back up and read verses 9–20. Paul uses Old Testament Scriptures to show that not only is everybody imperfect, but nobody is even trying to honor God. And in all the years that have passed since the Psalms were written, nothing has gotten any better. These verses cover three major categories of sin: heart and mind (11–12), speech (13–14), and action (15–18).

So if everyone has sinned in his or her heart, mind, speech, and actions then we're all completely sinful. What's left? That pretty much covers it!

In verse 19–20, Paul clarifies that Scripture reveals God's holiness and our sinfulness. God's Word shows the world that it needs God. Not only are people imperfect, they are completely sinful and unable to even get close to a holy God.

The good news is that He has provided the means for our salvation. That's what this section of the book is all about. But for now, as unusual as this may sound, don't try to skip past your sin to your salvation. Don't make excuses. Don't even say: "I'm forgiven." Allow the reality of your sinfulness apart from God to sink in. Let the weight of sin feel heavy so that you'll have a truer appreciation for that from which He has saved you.

Pray now that God would make you aware of your total need for Him.

the means // lesson 1 day 4 // 131

Sin took you hostage. It was crouching right outside your door ready to pounce. Once it had a foothold capturing your mind and corrupting your heart, it was your master. Sin owned you. You were slave to sin. And the wages of sin are death. There was no escape. No way out. Nothing could be done in your own strength. You were trapped. Captive. Dead.

So who could rescue you? Who could save you, set you free and give you life? Only Jesus could pay the ultimate price for your freedom. Only your Heavenly Father could deliver you from sin. It is by grace you have been saved. It is through Christ you have been redeemed. You were ransomed with the blood of God's son. He has set you free!

Share the good news of life and freedom today. Tell someone that Christ has paid their ransom.

IDENTIFYING SINS

OK. The idea here is not to beat yourself up or to obsess over sin. Yet before you fully experience the freedom of Christ's redemption, you need to have a realistic view of sin.

You looked at the big picture a few days ago. Write down the effects of sin in general, using what you know and what you've learned.

So, you know that people are completely sinful apart from the grace of God. And you know that sinful people cannot be in relationship with a holy God. Once you acknowledge those realities about sin in general, you need to begin dealing with specific sins. That's what you'll do here.

Look up each of the following Scripture passages, and write down the sins mentioned in these verses. (It'll take a little time, but it'll be valuable.)

Exodus 20:1–20

1 Corinthians 6:9–10

2 Corinthians 12:20

Galatians 5:19–21

2 Timothy 3:2–5

Matthew 25:41–46

Obviously, this is not a complete list of every possible sin. Some seem worse than others. And you will not struggle with all of these. It's hard to believe disobeying your parents is on the same list as murder or witchcraft, huh? Or how did coveting (wanting what somebody else has) make the "Top 10" list? Had you ever thought about the things Jesus mentioned in Matthew as sins? (Kind of a shocker that He wasn't running through the list of "big bad sins" that we saw, but rather things like not helping the poor . . . wow.)

Now, go through and mark (circle, box, underline, star) any of these sins to which you need to pay extra attention (but don't cross any out). Which of these do you struggle with the most? Any new revelations? Feel free to add anything specific that you know is a struggle for you.

Finally, pray that God's grace would free you from these sins. This must be an ongoing process—a daily prayer habit of going through these steps.

THE BASIC STEPS IN DEALING WITH SINS ARE:
1. Identify (You've gotta know what they are in the first place, right?)
2. Confess (You've gotta admit that they are wrong.)
3. Repent (You've gotta want to stop doing them.)
4. Surrender (You've gotta let go of those desires and let Christ change your heart.)
5. Resist (You've gotta move on and avoid doing them again.)

the means // lesson 1 day 6 // 133

we have a real problem.
But there is a solution.

Consider these factors:

People = Sinful
God = Gracious
SIN = DEATH

GRACE = LIFE
God > People
Grace > Sin

So, which equation best defines your life?

People - God = SIN = DEATH

People + God = GRACE = LIFE

the means // lesson 2 day 1 // 134

THINK ABOUT IT: How have you seen God's grace displayed in your life? How are you displaying His grace to the world around you?

> I delight greatly in the LORD;
> my soul rejoices in my God. For
> he has clothed me with garments
> of salvation and arrayed me in
> a robe of righteousness.
> Isaiah 61:10

the means // lesson 2 day 2 // 135

BREAK IN CASE OF EMERGENCY

If you were literally rescued from a near-death experience, how would your life change forever? Would you refuse to keep doing whatever had almost killed you? Would you be more thoughtful about decisions and behavior? Would you have a new appreciation for the small things in life? Would your priorities change? Would you be forever grateful to the person who saved you?

Why is it so easy to forget that Christ literally saved your life? ("Yeah, spiritually." You might think. But why is that less real? It is MORE real. It has eternal consequences AND changes our lives today too!) Reread these questions, thinking about the eternal death and earthly experiences from which Jesus has saved you. If you want, write down, in the space above, some of things from which Christ has saved you and/or how your life will be different because He saved your life.

DEVOTION

Dead. You're dead. Those are the only words that keep running through your mind as you look at the bill. How in the world did you rack up thousands of dollars on your new cell phone?!?! There must be some mistake. You've seen the Youtube videos of people with outrageous cell phone mix-ups. Like the guy with the $62,777 Sprint bill! It was a decimal point problem. The bill should've read $627.77, which is better, but still a killer.

But no. Your bill is legit, they say. You opted out of the data plan. You had no idea those "few" times you checked Facebook "real quick" could add up so quickly. Downloading apps, streaming music and videos, texting. . . . Oh, and going over your minutes. You'll have to sell your own body to science. That's after you cash in your college fund, say goodbye to your car, and pawn your guitar. But that still wouldn't cover it.

As that scenario hangs over you, check out Colossians 2:13-14. Those two little verses are HUGE!

Now, back to the phone bill. Imagine the relief you would feel as breath refilled your lungs and fresh blood pumped through your veins after you received another bill, this time marked PAID IN FULL. You quickly follow up with customer service and discover through notes on your account that the company's president caught wind of the largest bill in history and had mercy on you. No, he didn't just wave the charges. But having children of his own, he knew what you were going through. So he had your debt transferred, putting it on his son's account instead.

The bill was fair. It was your fault. You could never pay it, but the amount had to be paid. So this son that you had never met took on your debt, and his father settled your account so that all charges against you would be forever dropped.

Now reread that paragraph. Read it in light of what Colossians says about our spiritual debt that literally deserves our physical and eternal spiritual death.

You were dead. No way of saving yourself. You could never repay your debt against a perfectly holy God. You justified a sin here and there, never realizing how great the consequence. You were eternally separated from God. Now if you can imagine the joy and freedom you would feel after getting a cell phone bill paid and relieving you of those consequences, how much greater is the reality of the grace of your Heavenly Father and the price Jesus paid on your behalf? He forever canceled your debt, nailing it to the cross.

PAID IN FULL.

Two other men, both criminals, were also led out with him to be executed. When they came to the place called the Skull, there they crucified him, along with the criminals—one on his right, the other on his left. Jesus said, "Father, forgive them, for they do not know what they are doing." And they divided up his clothes by casting lots. The people stood watching, and the rulers even sneered at him. They said, "He saved others; let him save himself if he is the Christ of God, the Chosen One." The soldiers also came up and mocked him. They offered him wine vinegar and said, "If you are the king of the Jews, save yourself." There was a written notice above him, which read: THIS IS THE KING OF THE JEWS. One of the criminals who hung there hurled insults at him: "Aren't you the Christ? Save yourself and us!" But the other criminal rebuked him. "Don't you fear God," he said, "since you are under the same sentence? We are punished justly, for we are getting what our deeds deserve. But this man has done nothing wrong." Then he said, "Jesus, remember me when you come into your kingdom." Jesus answered him, "I tell you the truth, today you will be with me in paradise." It was now about the sixth hour, and darkness came over the whole land until the ninth hour, for the sun stopped shining. And the curtain of the temple was torn in two. Jesus called out with a loud voice, "Father, into your hands I commit my spirit." When he had said this, he breathed his last. The centurion, seeing what had happened, praised God and said, "Surely this was a righteous man."

(Luke 23:32-47)

He suffered death, so that by the grace of God he might taste death for everyone. Hebrews 2:9

WHY THE CROSS?

Crosses. You see them everywhere. You may even be wearing one right now. But the cross was not always an ornate piece of art or jewelry. It was once used for public humiliation and painful execution. So why is the cross now beautiful? Because, it is God's grace on display.

But why did Jesus die? Why did you need the cross?

Look up 1 Peter 2:22–23. Jesus was perfectly innocent. Besides the overwhelming love and grace He displayed in His self-control as people mocked and beat Him, the spiritual significance is in verse 22 (which quotes Isaiah 53:9). Complete this sentence by filling in the blank:

HE COMMITTED _____ _____.

Now read verse 24. This is a great summary of what Jesus did on the cross (or the NIV says "tree" since it is made of wood). This is also a great summary of what it means to you, personally. Fill in the blanks.

He himself bore _____ _____ in his body on the tree, so that we might _____

_____ _____ and _____ for righteousness; by his wounds you have

been _____.

Christ was the perfect sacrifice, taking away your sins. Remember in the Old Testament when you read about sacrifices? Take a look at a couple important things about why a sacrifice is needed in the first place.

Look up the following verses:

Genesis 3:3 From the very beginning of history, God warned that the consequence for sin is _____.

Leviticus 4:23 The sacrifice for sin must be without _____.

Leviticus 16:15 The _____ of the sacrifice will be brought into the holy presence of God to make atonement for your sin by sprinkling it on the _____ cover.

Finally, read how Christ became both your priest and your sacrifice in **Hebrews 9:11–15.** When you read, watch for these words: greater, perfect, once for all, eternal, much more, unblemished, and new.

Pretty amazing. Did you notice in verses 14–15, that Christ even cleanses our _____ from acts

that lead to death, so we can serve the Living God. He set us _____, giving us an _____ inheritance. (This means we're part of His family now and forever!)

Thank God for displaying His grace through the cross of Christ. Thank Him that His mercy is poured out on you because Christ's perfect blood was shed for you. Thank Christ for taking your sin and putting it to death. Thank Him that even your conscience is free from guilt. Pray for His Spirit to empower you to live free as you serve Him today and every day!

the means // lesson 2 day 6 // 139

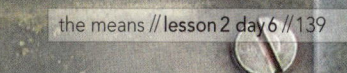

GRACE

If a picture is worth a thousand words and actions speak louder than words, then God's grace is loud and clear in the life, death, and resurrection of Jesus Christ. How will you show and tell the world about this perfect picture of grace?

the means // lesson 3 day 1 // 140

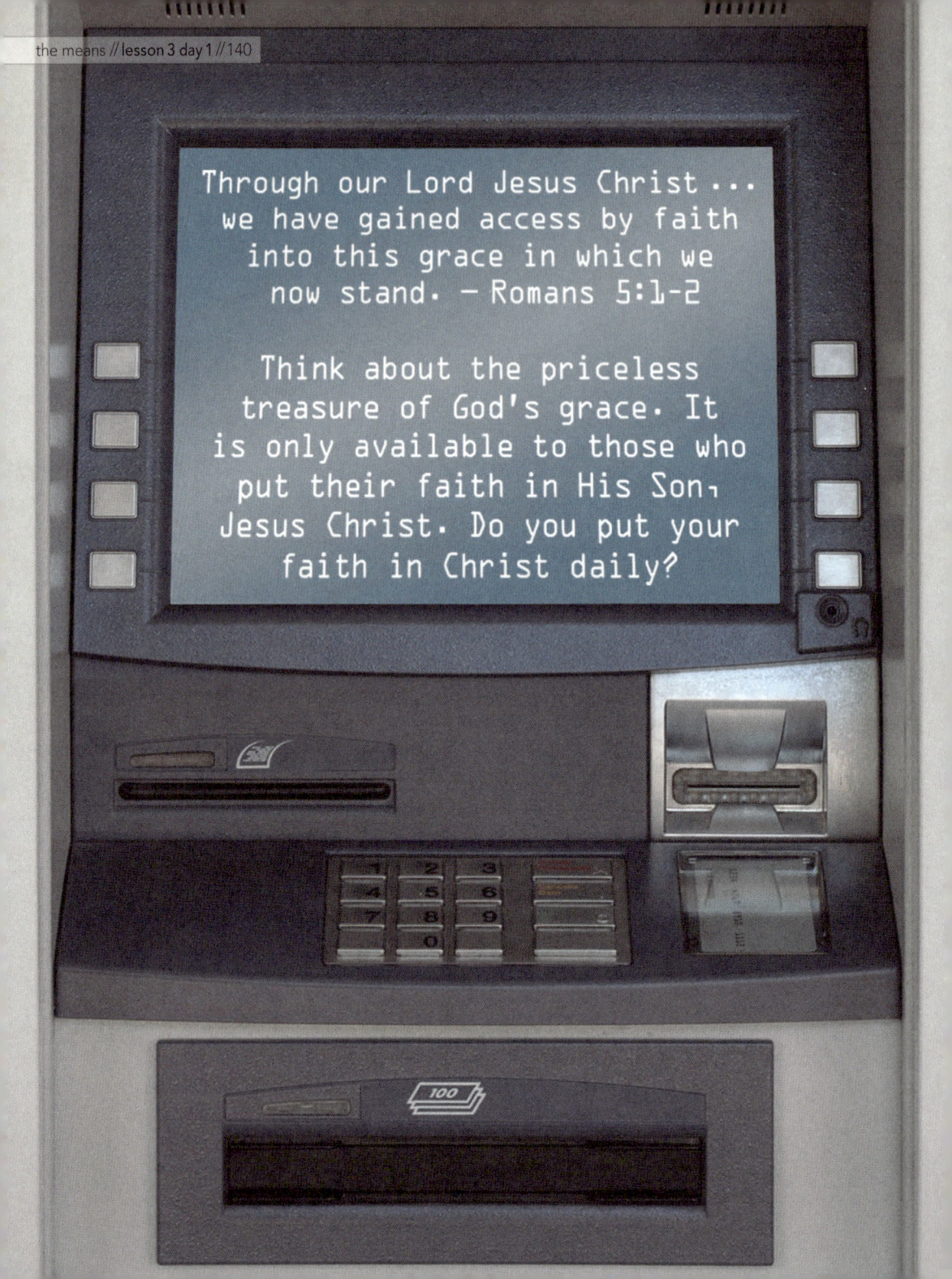

> Through our Lord Jesus Christ... we have gained access by faith into this grace in which we now stand. — Romans 5:1-2

Think about the priceless treasure of God's grace. It is only available to those who put their faith in His Son, Jesus Christ. Do you put your faith in Christ daily?

the means // lesson 3 day 2 // 141

WHAT IF SOMETHING YOU NEEDED WAS INSIDE YOUR LOCKER? YOU'D SPIN THE DIAL: RIGHT, LEFT, RIGHT, AND GIVE THE METAL DOOR THE BUMP NEEDED TO POP RIGHT OPEN ...

WHAT IF A FRIEND GAVE YOU A NEW IPHONE? YOU'D SLIDE YOUR FINGER ACROSS THE BOTTOM OF THE SCREEN TO UNLOCK THE SEEMINGLY INFINITE NUMBER OF APPS ...

WHAT IF THE RADIO DJ SAID YOU WERE THE WINNING CALLER AND TOLD YOU TO GO ONLINE TO PICK UP YOUR TICKETS AND BACKSTAGE PASSES FOR YOUR FAVORITE BAND'S CONCERT? YOU'D ENTER THE PASSWORD HE PROVIDED AND REARRANGE YOUR SCHEDULE ...

WHAT IF YOUR PARENTS LET YOU HAVE THE CAR FRIDAY NIGHT? YOU'D BE SURE TO KNOW EXACTLY WHERE THE KEYS WERE AT ALL TIMES ...

WHAT IF A DISTANT RELATIVE HAPPENED TO BE ROYALTY AND GAVE YOU A DEBIT CARD WITH AN UNLIMITED BALANCE? YOU'D COMMIT THE PIN NUMBER TO MEMORY ...

What if God made the eternal richness of His grace available to you? To unlock this incomparable treasure, you simply had to believe in Christ? Would you accept it in faith? Would you access His grace?

DEVOTION

There he is. The crazy fan with the rainbow clown wig. As always, he's waving the sign with the world's most famous Bible verse. Everybody recognizes that name and two numbers, whether they believe the truth of the verse or not. You could probably look it up in your Bible right now without even seeing it in this book . . .

Say John 3:16 out loud, right now from memory if you can (and if you're willing). Go ahead. Do it. Now look it up.

Jesus is talking to a super-religious guy named Nicodemus. Nic knew all the rules and obeyed them. He knew Scripture and wanted to please God. He even thought Jesus was a great man of God. But Jesus told him that eternal life in God's Kingdom was only possible for people who were "born again" spiritually. We're familiar with what that means, but Nic wasn't. So Jesus explained to Nic what is required to gain access into God's eternal Kingdom.

Read John 3:16–18.

It doesn't matter how good or religious you act, or if you know all the right "Sunday School" answers. If you're not born again, if you have never chosen to believe in Christ as your Lord and Savior, then you do not have eternal life. You cannot have a relationship with God the Father without having a relationship with His only begotten Son.

That is why God sent Christ into the world. He came not to judge you, but to save you. Sin will be judged. Anyone who chooses to ignore the free gift of God's grace through Christ is condemned . . . guilty. Only believing in Him can save you! But in God's perfect love, He's left the choice up to you.

Will you choose to believe, be saved, and experience eternal life with Christ? Tell God whether you believe in His Son. If you do, thank God for His grace through Christ.

Belief is...

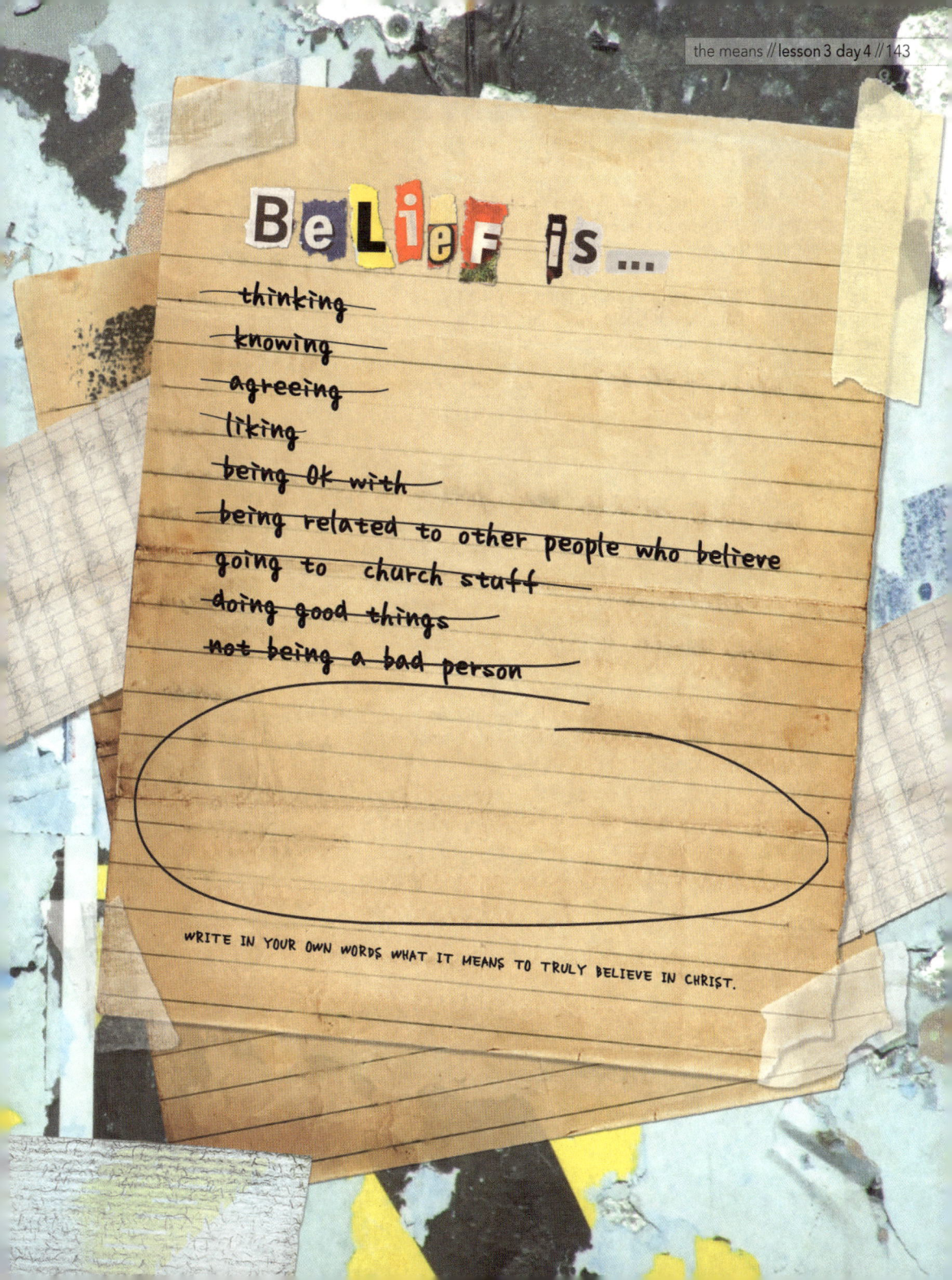

~~thinking~~
~~knowing~~
~~agreeing~~
~~liking~~
~~being OK with~~
~~being related to other people who believe~~
~~going to church stuff~~
~~doing good things~~
~~not being a bad person~~

WRITE IN YOUR OWN WORDS WHAT IT MEANS TO TRULY BELIEVE IN CHRIST.

A BIG, BIG HOUSE

Do you ever worry about life? What about "the afterlife"? (Maybe you do, maybe you don't. But if not, you have friends who worry.) How can we really know there is a heaven? And how can people know they will go to heaven when they die?

Read John 14:1–3. The disciples are hanging out after the Last Supper. Judas has left to betray Christ. Everyone else is probably still lounging around the table. Jesus is telling them that He will be "leaving" soon, meaning that He will die on the cross. But they don't know He is going to die, so Peter and then Thomas ask Jesus, "Where are you going?" You can imagine they are freaking out a little bit. (Wouldn't you?) They've left everything in their lives in order to follow Christ, which caused the religious leaders to get more and more hostile toward them, and now He's talking about leaving and saying that they can't come with Him for now. What?!?!

In verse 1, Jesus says not to worry, but instead, to _____ in God, and _____ also in me (Christ). Depending on the translation of your Bible, this verse may read either "trust" or "believe." As you read about on the last page, "trust" is a good, short definition of true belief. So, Jesus says to trust Him—if we believe in Him then we don't have to worry about this life or the next.

In verse 2, Jesus promises that His followers will live eternally with Him. He even says "if it weren't true, I wouldn't tell you it was true." (Sounds obvious, but how many things does the Bible say that we don't take seriously?) Jesus talks about adding rooms to His Father's house. This is what was done in that culture when someone was getting married (and it's still done in many cultures around the world today). The man would build a new room for he and his bride to live. They would join his family, and everyone would live together. (You can see why Thomas asks Jesus in verse 5 what on earth He is talking about!) Christ says that if a person has a relationship with Him, then He will become part of His family and live forever with Him in a new life and new home beyond death.

Now read verse 6. Jesus says "I am _____ _____ and the truth and the life. _____ comes to the Father except through me." You can know for sure if you are going to heaven or not. There is only one way.

In your own words, as obvious as this may sound, explain verse 6.

Pray about how you could put all of your trust in Christ. Thank God for making you a part of His family. Thank Him that you can believe everything His Word says. Thank God that you know "the way." Ask for help in trusting "the truth." Pray that you would live "the life" that He has made known to you through a relationship with Jesus Christ.

belief → result

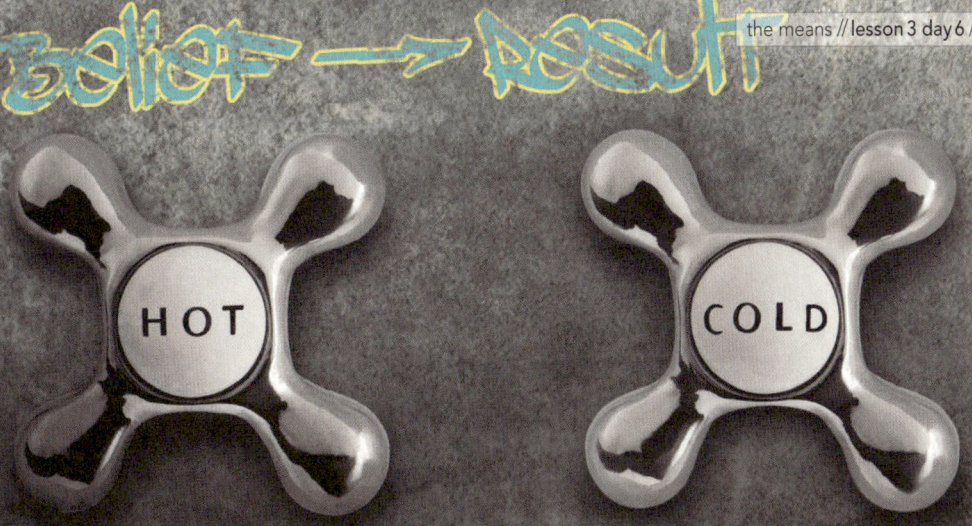

the means // lesson 3 day 6 // 145

HOT   **COLD**

Think about how strongly you believe something impacts your life. For example: If you strongly believe that a leprechaun has left a pot of gold at the end of a rainbow, you're going to be sprinting like a crazy person toward the horizon every time it stops raining.

Using the spectrums, indicate how "hot" (strong) or "cold" (weak) your beliefs are about each thing. Then, think about how each belief affects your attitude and actions.

THE WAY I LIVE MATTERS AS A FOLLOWER OF CHRIST.

SIN HAS NO POWER OVER ME AS A CHRIST-FOLLOWER.

GOD'S GRACE IS ENOUGH TO CHANGE MY LIFE.

GOD LOVES ME REGARDLESS OF MY PAST.

I HAVE BEEN MADE HOLY BY GOD'S GRACE.

How would your life be different if you warmed up to each of these truths?

the means // lesson 4 day 1 // 146

CLEANING & LAUNDRY

"COME NOW, LET US REASON TOGETHER," SAYS THE LORD. "THOUGH YOUR SINS ARE LIKE SCARLET, THEY SHALL BE AS WHITE AS SNOW; THOUGH THEY ARE RED AS CRIMSON, THEY SHALL BE LIKE WOOL." —ISAIAH 1:18

HAVE YOU BEEN HONEST WITH GOD CONCERNING THE SIN STAINS IN YOUR LIFE?

the means // lesson 4 day 2 // 147

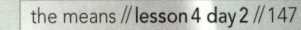

NEW! FRESH!

FREE GIFT

HAVE A STUBBORN STAIN YOU JUST CAN'T SEEM TO GET RID OF? YOU'VE TRIED AND TRIED, BUT NOTHING SEEMS TO WORK IN REMOVING IT?

Don't let dirt stick around. Get clean once and for all.

Try it for yourself and see. It's Amazing!

USE DAILY.

Pray that God would make you better than new. He is willing and able to wash away every sin.

DEVOTION

The "Dog Star," Sirius, is the brightest star in the sky. It is part of a constellation that resembles a big dog (Canis Major). Now that star-eyed puppy in outer space makes sense as the Sirius satellite radio logo doesn't it?

It appears so bright, not because it puts off the most light but because of its closeness to earth. A star called Betelgeuse, like "Beetle-juice" in The Hitchhikers Guide to the Galaxy, is actually one of the most luminescent stars. This means it exerts a lot of energy. Betelgeuse radiates 105,000 times more energy than our sun. Even though this star is huge, it doesn't seem as bright as Sirius (which is only about 26 times brighter than our sun). Both the amount of energy put forth and the distance from us affect how bright a star "shines." Thanks for the science class right?

With those factors in mind, read Philippians 2:12–16. Paul, the writer of this book, is telling Christ-followers to live in a way that shows respect for the God who saved them. God is the one working in and through His people to do the right thing. When people follow Christ and are filled with the light of His Word, they are going to stick out from the dark world. Paul says that Christ-followers should stand firm in the life of Christ while surrounded by a corrupt culture.

You don't have to be the most talented or most popular person in your group. You don't have to do the biggest, most noticeable acts. You just have to use whatever energy you have to shine God's light on those close to you. You are surrounded by friends and other people close to you.

Now read one more verse from Paul. Look up Ephesians 5:8 and write it in the space below, then pray.

Thank God for changing your dark heart, turning you into a child of light. Pray that your life would shed light on the truth of God's grace, so that others may see the glory of the One who saved you and who works through you.

Think about this old hymn today...

Amazing Grace
John Newton (1725–1807)

Amazing Grace, how sweet the sound,
That saved a wretch like me.
I once was lost but now am found,
Was blind, but now I see.

T'was Grace that taught my heart to fear.
And Grace, my fears relieved.
How precious did that Grace appear
The hour I first believed.

Through many dangers, toils and snares
I have already come;
'Tis Grace that brought me safe thus far
and Grace will lead me home.

WHO'S THE BOSS?

As a child of God, you have been given a new life. Not a better life. Not an improved life. A brand new life. You didn't earn or deserve it. God gave you this incredible gift of new life purely by His grace.

So what should this new life in God's grace look like? **Open your Bible to Romans 6.**

Read verses 1–4.
Is it OK to keep sinning since God will forgive all of my sins? ❏ yes ❏ no
What action testifies to your old life being buried with Christ and raised with Him to newness of life?

Read verses 5–11.
According to verse 7, does any sin have power over you? ❏ yes ❏ no
So is it a reasonable excuse to say "I can't help it. I just keep doing it."? ❏ yes ❏ no

In light of verse 11, ask yourself honestly, "Do I live like I'm _____ to sin and

_____ to God though Christ?" ❏ yes ❏ no

Read verses 12–15.
There are no cravings or desires that are too strong to resist. Sin is no longer your master. You don't have to obey it. Can you live in both your new life and your old life?

"MY BODY WILL ONLY BE USED TO DO UNRIGHTEOUS THINGS."
If this is no longer a true statement for you as a Christ-follower. Cross out the letters "un," leaving the word "righteous." Now reread the sentence as a prayer.

Read verses 16–18.
By dying to sin, you're free from it. A dead employee can't do the work his old boss tells him to do, right? But you're not free to do whatever you want. You have a choice now. You're not the boss, but you are free to decide for whom you will work.

Serving sin leads to _____ but wholehearted obedience to God's instructions leads to

_____.
Shade in the heart to represent your level of devotion. Are you currently wholehearted? Halfhearted? Somewhere in between? Or less?

Read verses 19–20.
Paul clarifies that he's using human terms to explain a spiritual truth. Basically, he says: "Just like you used to do whatever your sinful desire told you to do, now do whatever righteousness tells you to do."

Read verses 21–23.

When sin was your boss, what payment did you deserve? _____
Now that you have been set free from sin and work for God instead, what free gift do you receive?

_____

the means // lesson 4 day 6 // 151

Arrogance

Doubt

SELF-RELIANCE

Lost

dark
crooked
apart

Guilty

WAGE

Match each word to it's opposite.

Saved
Obedience
faith
Righteousness
Gift
Trust
Grace
Light
FREE
Truth
Upright
Life
with
Respect
Blameless
Dependence

Judgment

Lie
Sin

rejection

Earned

Death

LUST

the means // lesson 5 day 1 // 152

BAKERY

JESUS ANSWERED, "IT IS WRITTEN: 'MAN DOES NOT LIVE ON BREAD ALONE, BUT ON EVERY WORD THAT COMES FROM THE MOUTH OF GOD.'" — MATTHEW 4:4

Do you believe Jesus when He said that you need God's Word as much as you need food? Do the habits of your life reveal that you hold one more important than the other?

the means // lesson 5 day 2 // 153

Use this page as a reference for your well-balanced diet. Look up the different verses to see what you need daily in order to be spiritually healthy.

"Daily" Nutrition Guide

Trust God's provision...	Matt. 6:11
Take up cross...	Luke 9:23
Read scripture...	Acts 17:7
Pray...	Ps. 88:1
Rejoice...	Ps. 118:24
Be satisfied in God's love...	Ps. 90:14
Encourage each other...	Heb. 3:13
Meet needs...	Jas. 2:15
Fellowship...	Acts 2:46-47
Share gospel...	Acts 19:9
Persevere hardship...	2 Cor. 4:16

DEVOTION

Your baby is so... ummm... GINORMOUS. What do you say to the new parents? "Congratulations," or just "whoa!" This must've been the dilemma for Ani's friends and family in September 2009 when the Indonesian woman delivered her "little" baby boy weighing over 19 pounds and measuring over 2 feet long! Akbar (which means "the great") was easily the largest newborn in the country's history but still several pounds shy of the world record for healthy babies (A baby born in 1879 was a whopping 23 pounds!). Akbar's father joked that he hoped he could afford to keep feeding the new addition to the family. The doctor told reporters, "He's got a strong appetite, every minute, it's almost nonstop feeding." You think?

With big, hungry babies in mind, read 1 Peter 2:2–3. This passage of God's Word reminds us that part of living is eating and growing. It's natural. Babies crave milk. Nobody has to tell them to discipline themselves and make regular time for eating. They don't have little baby calendars with reminders scribbled in crayon and drool to try their best to eat today if they're not too tired or busy. If you've ever been around a baby that is even the slightest bit hungry, you know that nothing satisfies that longing except the milk he or she so desperately wants. They just know it's good, nobody has to convince them of this obvious fact.

By this point, you have at least "tasted" the Lord's goodness. And if nothing else, you have been getting a healthy sampling by going through this book, devouring a variety of Scriptures. God is SO good. But once you've really tasted that for yourself, nobody has to convince you of this fact. You know that only He can satisfy your natural cravings and soothe your deep achings for whatever you're missing. His Word gives you strength. His Word helps you grow spiritually. Babies aren't just born and then glad to be in the world. They eat and grow. They can't help it. It's natural. You have been given a new nature. Like Akbar "the Great," are you constantly hungry for God's Word? Do you have a healthy appetite for spiritual things? The great news is that your Heavenly Father always has plenty of good things to satisfy your every need.

Grow up. It only sounds harsh if you're stuck in stunted growth. Healthy, living things are hungry on a regular basis, and they eat and grow. So grow up. Big and strong and healthy. Pray for God's daily grace. Pray for a constant hunger for His Word. Pray for a craving that draws you desperately closer to Him. Pray that He would mature you daily.

the means // lesson 5 day 4 // 155

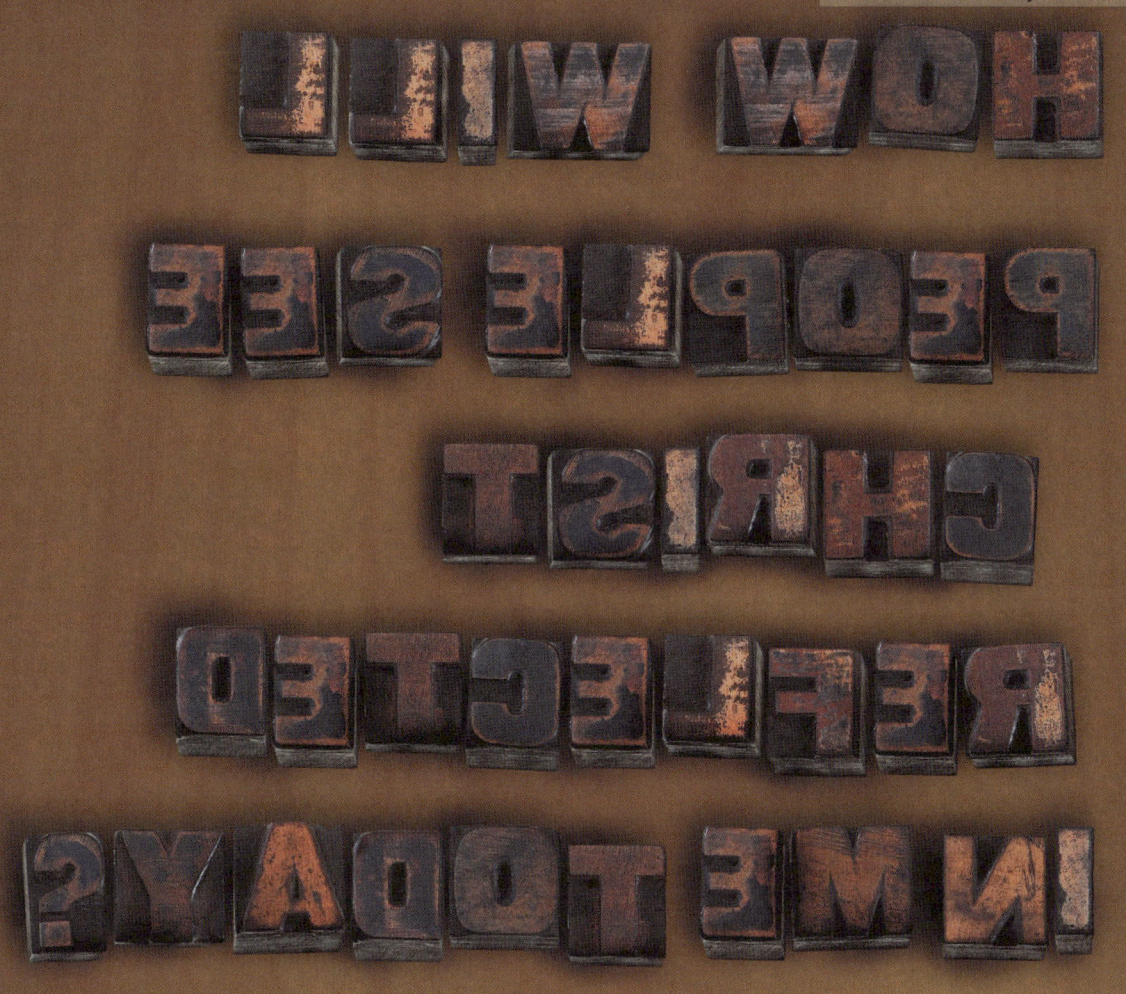

HOW WILL PEOPLE SEE CHRIST REFLECTED IN ME TODAY?

✦ HOLD THIS PAGE UP TO A MIRROR. PRAY ABOUT IT.

GET DRESSED

Another major part of growing up, other than eating, is dressing yourself, right? You don't have your "mommy" come in, pick out your clothes, and dress you each day, do you? Can you imagine walking down the halls of your school every day wearing whatever crazy outfit someone else chose for you to wear? In a similar way, the New Testament teaches that by God's grace, Christ-followers have taken off their old lives and tossed them aside like dirty laundry on the floor.

Sin doesn't decide what you look like anymore. Instead of continuing to wear the old habits from the lifestyle you used to feel so comfortable in, you put on a "new self," clothed in the righteousness of God. So it would be a good idea to look at a few of the things God says in your Bible about getting dressed.

Go to Colossians 3.

Read verses 1–4. This kind of summarizes what you have read about over the past few weeks. It's a good reminder of God's grace.

How do verses 1–2 say you start living this new life in Christ? Set your heart and mind on

_____ _____ not on _____ _____ .

Simple enough. What you think and dream about, what you desire and focus on, is what your life will naturally be drawn toward. What you think about impacts your decisions and attitudes. So your heart and mind relates to your speech and actions (remember?). So if you're going to grow more into the likeness of Christ, you need to focus on Him, not on the world. Makes sense.

Next Colossians goes into a few lists. Don't think of them as "do's" and "don'ts" necessarily, but rather as descriptions of who you used to be and what you used to do instead of who you are now and what you live for now.

Read verses 5–10. Write down all the things named under each "category." (Each category is introduced with a "put" phrase, but your translation may say something slightly different, such as "consider," "rid yourself," or "take off.")

PUT TO DEATH (VV. 5–7)   PUT AWAY (VV. 8–9)   PUT OFF (9)

Read verses 10–17. Now write down all of the characteristics of the NEW SELF that you are to put on or clothe yourself with.

PUT ON (VV. 10–17)

Look back over everything you have written in each space. How will you set your mind on things above?

What in your earthly nature needs put to death immediately? (Notice that these are all heart/mind issues.)

How is your speech revealing a sinful attitude? What habits and actions are inconsistent with a heart and mind set on things above?

All of those things (desires and expressions) add up to the Old Self.

Which traits of the New Self are you already comfortable in? Which do you need to be extra mindful to put on? Read through the "New Self" list again. Consider specific ways you can grow in each of these things.

Finally, rewrite verse 17 as a prayer, replacing the word "you" with "I."

linked // lesson 1 day 1 // 157

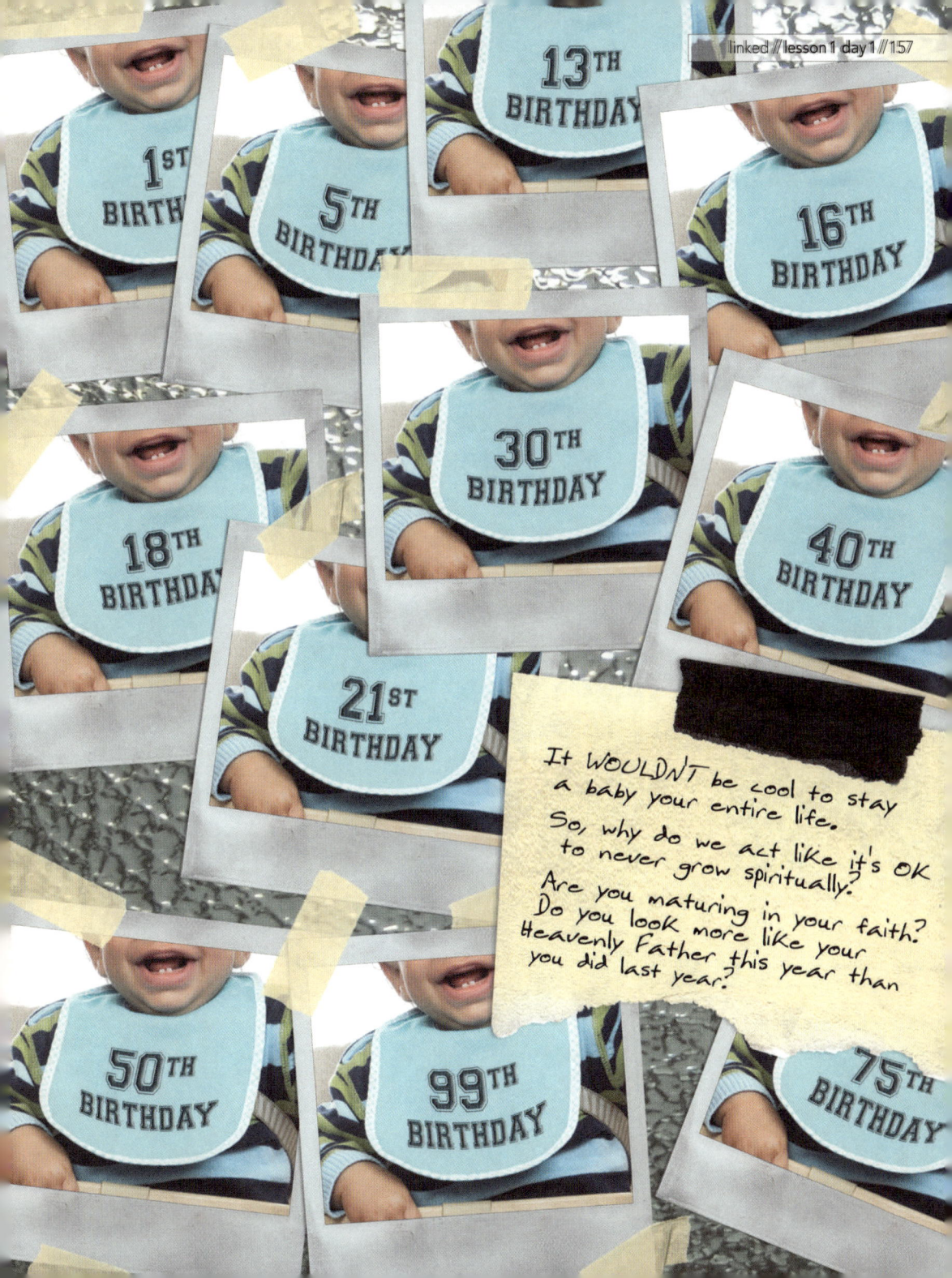

1ST BIRTHDAY
5TH BIRTHDAY
13TH BIRTHDAY
16TH BIRTHDAY
18TH BIRTHDAY
21ST BIRTHDAY
30TH BIRTHDAY
40TH BIRTHDAY
50TH BIRTHDAY
75TH BIRTHDAY
99TH BIRTHDAY

It WOULDN'T be cool to stay a baby your entire life. So, why do we act like it's OK to never grow spiritually?

Are you maturing in your faith? Do you look more like your Heavenly Father this year than you did last year?

the means // lesson 6 day 1 // 158

NEWS

Daily News

FOR WE CANNOT HELP SPEAKING ABOUT WHAT WE HAVE SEEN AND HEARD. —ACTS 4:20

That which was from the beginning, which we have heard, which we have seen with our eyes, which we have looked at and our hands have touched—this we proclaim concerning the Word of life. The life appeared; we have seen it and testify to it, and we proclaim to you the eternal life, which was with the Father and has appeared to us. We proclaim to you what we have seen and heard, so that you also may have fellowship with us. And our fellowship is with the Father and with his Son, Jesus Christ. We write this to make our joy complete. —1 John 1:1–4

PULL

free

ARE YOU SPREADING THE WORD?

the means // lesson 6 day 2 //159

LOOK, HE IS COMING WITH THE CLOUDS, AND EVERY EYE WILL SEE HIM. —REVELATION 1:7

DEVOTION

Funnel or balloon?

It sounds random now, but it's an important question. . . . You'll see. Go ahead and pick one.

Have you ever poured oil into a motor of some kind or filled a glass bottle with colored sand for a craft as a kid? Here's where the first question comes into play. In order to pour the oil or sand through a small opening into the desired destination, would you be better served by a funnel or a balloon? What would happen if you were able to pour your greasy or grainy substance into each? The brightly colored latex would stretch until it held as much possible. The ordinary plastic or metal would redirect everything, keeping as little as possible.

Read Psalm 67:1. In this first verse, God's people cry out for His gracious blessing. We're familiar with that attitude. God bless us; fill us up abundantly.

Read verses 2–7. The reason God's people are asking for His blessing is so that other people will experience God's salvation and God will get the glory. They are not singing about their own happiness, but rather other people's joy. And in the end, God will bless His people and get great glory from all nations.

So do you want to be puffed up, serving no real purpose other than to look good? Do you believe God desires for you to be swollen up with His blessings and for grace and goodness to end with you?

Or would you rather be continually used by God so that others can experience the same grace that He has poured out on you? Do you realize that He has blessed you so that you can bless others? Should salvation and praise end with you, or should everyone everywhere give God glory?

So which will you be: funnel or balloon?

the means // **lesson 6 day 4** // 161

WHAT LABELS DO YOU PUT ON PEOPLE? WHAT LABEL HAS BEEN PUT ON YOU? PRAY TO SEE PEOPLE WITH "GOD'S" EYES.

So from now on we regard no one from a worldly point of view. – 2 Corinthians 5:16

Stop judging by mere appearances, and make a right judgment – John 7:24

The Lord does not look at the things man looks at. Man looks at the outward appearance, but the Lord looks at the heart – 1 Samuel 16:7

There is neither Jew nor Greek, slave nor free, male nor female, for you are all one in Christ Jesus. – Galatians 3:28

hot **LOSER** **band member** slacker emo **poor** goth **SNOB** athlete **drama queen** **LONER** gamer church kid **POSER** RICH skater "that girl" CHEERLEADER **PLAYER** art kid "that guy" computer nerd **REDNECK** punk hippie

CALLED OUT

Your life is significant. God created you, saved you, and is now using you to accomplish His will. But you're not the only one. You're not the only one He is using, nor are you the only one He has created and desires to save. His grace does not stop with you, remember? He has a mission, so you have a mission.

Read 1 Peter 2:9. This is your identity and purpose. Look at each phrase below to get a good grip on what this verse means in your life. First, fill in all the blanks. Then, read about each phrase.

But you are a _____ people,
How does it make you feel to know that God "chose" you? He sought you out personally and saved you. You're not trying to earn His approval. God, the Creator of the universe, has already chosen you!

a _____ _____ ,
This "royal" status is no reason to boast. Just like royalty today, there is nothing you can do to earn this position. It is a benefit enjoyed by those of royal blood. Through the blood of Christ, you have been adopted into the family of the King of kings.

The "priesthood" was entrusted with special responsibilities. They offered sacrifices on behalf of other people. They represented a connection to God and experienced His presence firsthand. The life of a priest was dedicated to serving God and other people. They did not spend theirs lives pursuing comforts and possessions. Are you devoted to serving God and people, helping them know His grace? Or are you pursuing worldly pleasures instead?

a _____ nation,
What do you think of when you hear or see the word "holy"? Usually the first thing to come to mind has to do with being pure, perfect, and sinless. Absolutely. God is each of those things. He is perfectly good. But holy also means "other" or "set apart." So for Christ-followers to be "a holy nation" means that they are set apart from the sins of the world and purified to be used for God's perfect plan.

a people _____ to God,
You "belong" to God. He made you. He has total rights over your life, like an artist over His creation. There is great comfort, security, and humility in this truth. This means you can trust Him completely, but it should also remind you that you're not in control and have no right to say you would rather do things your own way. He owns you. But you're not just His property; it literally says you are his "own possession." Emphasizing the personal nature to this ownership. You are His prized possession! He takes great joy in you!

that you may _____ the _____
Everything up until now has explained your identity. Now here is your purpose:

"Declare" means that you are not making up stories, you are relaying the truth. This word comes from another word meaning "messenger." That means you God has entrusted you with passing on His message to the world. You have tasted and seen that the Lord is good, and you can't help but tell everyone about it! Who do you know that needs to hear the praiseworthy truth of grace and salvation?

of him who called you out of _____ into his wonderful _____ .
Finally, He transformed your life. He took you out of "darkness" (representing sin, death, and ignorance) and brought you into His wonderful light (God's great glory, abundant life, and holy truth). What life change has occurred as a result of knowing Christ?

the means // lesson 6 day 6 // 163

Being an ambassador of Christ and a minister of reconciliation is a pretty awesome identity and purpose in life. But how do you start?

First, identify the different places you go. For example: If you go to school, write "school" in one of the spaces. Do this for all of the main places you spend time.

Next, name some specific things about Christ that people need to know. For example: If people need to know that He is the only way to live eternally with God or that they don't have to earn His love or forgiveness, write those things down, too.

Finally, how will you make sure that the people in the places you wrote down know the things you wrote down? Showing God's grace, living in His power, and trusting in His authority in your life is what being an ambassador is all about. It's a 24-7, 365-days-a-year-plus, leap year kind of deal. So if you haven't already, get started! Be His ambassador.

TOGETHER

You're not alone. There are 6.7 billion people on this planet. Yes, billion with a "B." But more significant than the fact that you're not literally alone in this world, is the fact that God created you for relationships. They didn't just happen as a result of bumping into other people. From the very beginning of human history, God has designed life in such a way that people need relationships. Good or bad, we are in relationship with God and with other people. Hopefully, you want those relationships to be "good." So what does God have to say about how to live this life together? Glad you asked. Turn the page . . .

- LESSON 1: MADE FOR EACH OTHER—PG 166-171
- LESSON 2: LOVE ONE ANOTHER—PG 172-177
- LESSON 3: ESTABLISHED RELATIONSHIPS—PG 178-183
- LESSON 4: LASTING RELATIONSHIPS—PG 184-189
- LESSON 5: UNIFIED TOGETHER—PG 190-195
- LESSON 6: MUTUAL RESPECT—PG 196-201

together // **lesson 1 day 1** // 166

THE PERSON WHO TRIES TO LIVE alone WILL **NOT** SUCCEED AS A HUMAN BEING,

his heart withers

if it does not answer another heart. HIS MIND SHRINKS AWAY IF HE **HEARS ONLY** *the echoes of his own thoughts* and finds no other INSPIRATION.

—Pearl S. Buck

God said it, and God meant it. It is not good for us to be alone. Even after He looked around and saw that all of these things He had created were good, it was not good for man to be alone. Pray that God would open up your heart and mind to what it means to live in a community of believers.

together // lesson 1.day 2 // 167

GOOD

GOOD

Pay attention today to the relationships all around you, even in nature. What do your relationships look like?

GOOD

GOOD

GOOD

NOT GOOD

DEVOTION

Peanut Butter and Jelly. Bacon and Eggs. Spaghetti and Meatballs. Mac and Cheese. Burger and Fries. Chips and Salsa. Popcorn and M&M's. (If you haven't tried dumping a bag of M&M's into your popcorn, try it—neither snack will ever be the same!)

So, you get the idea. Some things are just meant to be together. It's like they were made for each other. One perfectly complements the other.

Read Genesis 2:18. You're super familiar with this story. And if you weren't before, you are by now! God has created everything on and above the earth, speaking it into existence. How's that for power? God just speaks and things appear. Even "nothing" obeys Him and becomes "something." Finally, the Lord creates man and assigns him the job (and honor) of overseeing His creation. But notice that God didn't just speak Adam and Eve into existence; He personally formed them "by hand." People have a special relationship with God. And as that which is uniquely created in God's image, man has authority over everything else on earth—not to abuse it, but to care for it (tending the garden) and to maintain order (naming animals). Everything is good except for man to be alone. Remember?

Ironically, the Hebrew word meaning "alone" in this verse is pronounced "bad." In other words, it is not good for man to be "bad." So, notice what God does. He made Adam a helper. Not just a companion. Not just a friend or someone to keep him company. Not a servant or someone inferior. God took a rib from his side and made someone to walk beside him, someone to live with him as an equal partner.

This is a big deal, because the Bible isn't saying that people should never be alone or that God simply wants people to find just anyone to spend time with. God created someone for Adam to be a helper in the work that God had given him to do. Every other time that word "help" or "helper" is used in Scripture it is in relation to God. He is the source of man's help. He is ultimately our helper. So when God created Eve as Adam's helper, this means they were created to work together (literally side by side) doing God's work.

So, with whom do you spend most of your time? Are the closest relationships in your life with people who will help you honor God? It is not good for you to be alone . . . or in "bad" company. Some things are just better together . . . made for each other. You're one of those things. You were created for relationships. Seek out relationships that naturally bring out the best in you (and that you help bring out the best in them). Together, do whatever God has given you to do!

together // lesson 1 day 4 // 169

Not every relationship we have is lovey-dovey, sappy marriage. But Adam and Eve walked with God. TOGETHER, HELPING, and SHARING. Wow. Think about that. So, what work has God given you? Pray that God's Word will help you see how to live in relationship: loving God and loving people.

together // lesson 1 day 5 // 170

Dear Diary: (Is it girly to keep a diary? I wondered about that today, but then I wondered what "girly" even meant... since I've never met a "girl." Oh well...)

Today was another day in paradise. I ate some delicious fruit; I called it: TANGERINE. Isn't that a great name? After this naming every plant and animal thing is over, I'm gonna try my hand at coming up with names for all the colors. Not that I need to describe what anything looks like. There's nobody to talk to. But these colors are incredible! I wonder if I could find a way to melt these awesome colors into little sticks... I think I'd call those crayons. But there are so many colors, where would I put them all? Maybe a little box with a flip top lid? Anyway, I also named that big grey animal, finally. Elephant. Nice, huh?

Oh, who am I kidding? Why didn't I take God up on that offer to create a suitable helper? There are no suitable helpers to be found in this garden. I ask the monkey for help naming YET ANOTHER ANIMAL (HOW MANY CAN THERE POSSIBLY BE?) and he just scratches his head, scratches his rear, shows me his teeth... Did you know that monkeys throw poo? It's gross. I venture to see if the giraffes would care for a delicious TANGERINE, but they just STARE AT ME.

I'm going crazy. I mean, I love hanging out with God and everything, but I wish I had someone to TALK to about how awesome it is to be with God every day. The tangerines don't care. They just sit there, waiting to be eaten. I try to talk to the tigers, but those claws are sharp. I try to talk to the rhinos, but they're so big and clumsy, and that horn is a little dangerous. The other day, I invented this sweet new game called Rock, Paper, Scissors. Except I can't play it with a meerkat. So I play it on my own. Left hand vs. right hand. (Which, by the way, is incredibly hard.) I keep losing! Or do I keep winning? It's extremely confusing...

I need someone else here. Another me, except different. Maybe with long hair, and big eyelashes. Someone that talks. Someone to share everything with and do everything with. No claws. No horns. No Trunks. No tail. Just, another person. Yeah, that would be nice...

Anyway, I better run. TTYL. (You like that? I was getting creative with my letters the other day while naming the opossum. Yeah, I put an "o" up front just to entertain myself. I think using letters instead of words could really catch on someday if there were someone else to talk to... but... you're the only one I can TTYL.)

Well, more NAMING OF THE ANIMALS to do. Hurrah.

Peace out, diary.

Your Bro, Adam

AREN'T YOU GLAD YOU'RE NOT ALONE? THANK GOD FOR THE PEOPLE HE HAS PUT IN YOUR LIFE.

RELATIONSHIPS

If you are made for relationships, and those relationships should be God-honoring, who are the people in your life that help you honor God? Who do you help to honor God?

Check out the different relationships that the Bible specifically teaches you about. Read each passage of Scripture. To the right of each, write the name of the relationship that passage describes. (Leave the big space underneath each one empty for now. . . . you'll come back to it.)

Matthew 22:37–38

Matthew 22:39–40

Ephesians 6:1–4

1 John 3:16

Luke 19:17

Leviticus 19:34

Deuteronomy 15:11

Acts 9:31

Luke 6:27

Romans 13:1

Now, look at your list of biblical relationships. This doesn't spell out every single type of relationship you may have. Obviously. This isn't even a complete list of relationships the Bible mentions. But it's a starting point for thinking biblically about how and why you interact with other people.

All the way back in the garden, the very first couple, God brought people together in order to help each other. Remember? They were to fill the earth with His image. So, how might each of the relationships you've identified help you honor God with your life, filling the world with a true picture of His character?

Using the larger space under each relationship above, write ideas for how these people may help you know God and serve Him. It may help to write the names of specific people that fit each category. You may also write ways you can help these people honor God with their lives. After all, relationships work both ways, right?

Take a minute to pray for each of these relationships specifically. Ask for help in honoring God, regardless of whom you happen to spend time with during the day.

CHRISTIANITY IS NOT ABOUT BUILDING AN ABSOLUTELY *secure* little niche IN THE WORLD WHERE YOU CAN LIVE WITH YOUR PERFECT little wife AND YOUR PERFECT little children *in your beautiful* little house WHERE YOU HAVE **NO GAYS OR MINORITY GROUPS ANYWHERE NEAR YOU.** CHRISTIANITY IS ABOUT LEARNING TO LOVE *like Jesus loved* AND JESUS LOVED **THE POOR** AND JESUS LOVED **THE BROKEN**

— Rich Mullins

Christ was not interested in not loving people. It didn't matter if they were rich or poor, able-bodied or disabled, children or elderly. He also called His disciples to love others (everyone) with the same love. Amazingly and impossibly, this is what Jesus has called us to do. What does it look like? And how do we do it? Pray that God would help you love everyone, remembering that He loves you even when you're "unlovable."

DEVOTION

Team jerseys. Popped collars. Skinny jeans. Trendy haircuts. Band tees. Boots and belt buckles. Black hair and fingernails. All kinds of traits are dead giveaways as to what "group" someone belongs. This doesn't mean an athlete and a scenester or a prep and a redneck can't be friends. And obviously, it doesn't mean that people are all the same or that you know everything about a person by what he or she is wearing or what music he or she likes. But if you're honest, some things tell you a lot and are easy to spot. Think about it this way: if you were at a new school and needed to find a seat for lunch, who would you see as potential friends and at which lunch table would you probably not have much to talk about? People express themselves in ways that reveal what matters to them.

Read John 13:34–35. Jesus told His disciples (His closest group of friends) that His time on earth was almost over. He would soon leave this world, and they would enter a brand new period of their lives (and of human history!). So sitting around the table, Jesus told them that everyone should be able to recognize them as belonging to this group. What was the dead giveaway as His disciples? Love.

Now when Jesus said this was a new commandment, He meant that a fresh and deeper understanding was being provided. God's people have always been commanded to "love God and love people." But, Jesus told His group of followers to love each other like He loved them. So how do you love people just like Christ loves you? All of your relationships should be characterized by Christlike love. Humble, sacrificial, God-honoring love. Notice He didn't say people would know you are His followers because you go to youth group or have a Christian fish on your car. He said they would know by the incredibly unique way you love each other. It's unlike anything this world has ever seen.

If you truly care about the love God has shown you, it should be obvious in the way you treat others. You can't keep that a secret. Imagine your surprise to find out that the school's star quarterback has a passion for knitting kitten mittens. Yeah. That's right. Little booties for cat paws. Wow. Nobody would ever figure that one out. Would people be surprised to find out you are a Christ-follower? Is your so-called passion for Christ such a little-known fact that someone would have to be pretty close friends with you before they discovered that part of your life? Following Christ isn't some ridiculous hobby to hide or reserve for your spare time and private life. His love should be easy to spot. Is it?

Like the generic brand of peanut butter that sits next to Jif in the grocery store, we come into contact with the world's version of love everyday. And like that peanut butter, it looks the same, but there's something off about it. Below are some characteristics of "love" the world has to offer. Have you ever experienced this type of so-called love before? Fill in a few examples of your own in the space provided. Ask God to help you discern between His love and the fake love that the world holds up.

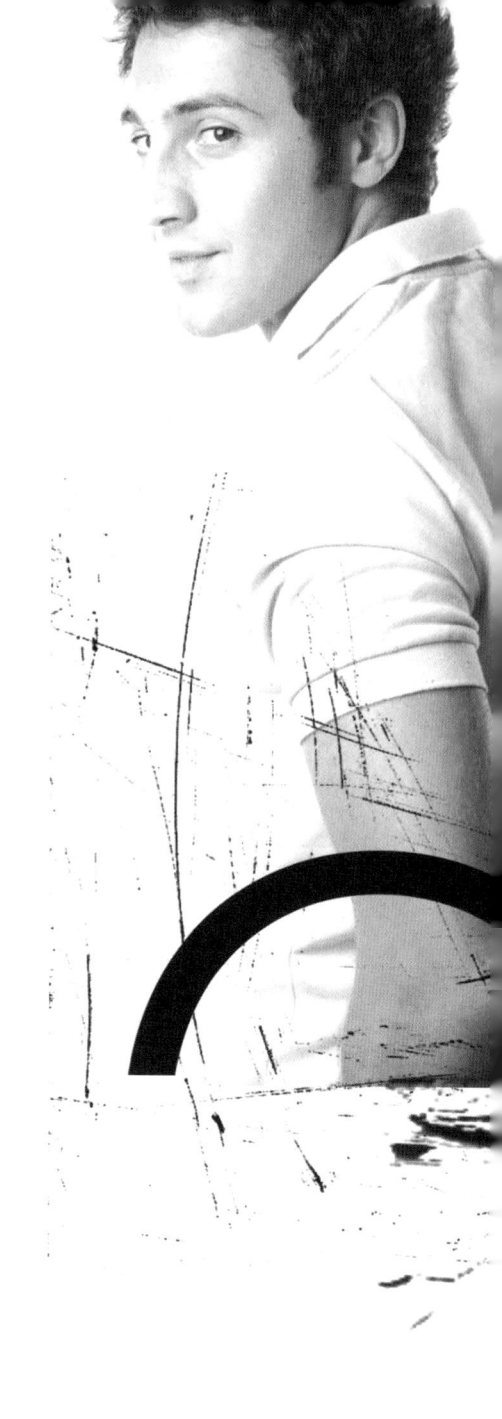

WORLDY love is . . .

- SELFISH
- SELF-ABSORBED
- VENGEFUL
- INCOMPETENT
- NAÏVE
- STUBBORN
- GUNNING TO BE FIRST
- IRRITABLE
- SELF-IMPORTANT
- DRAMATIC
- BOSSY
- SMOTHERING
- SPITEFUL
- OBSESSIVE

together // lesson 2 day 4 // 175

GODLY
love is . . .
SIMPLE
CHRIST-FOCUSED
HUMBLE
SINCERE
HONEST
TRUSTWORTHY
KIND
PATIENT
FORGIVING
FILLING
SATISFYING
LOOKING OUT FOR OTHERS
NEVER FORCED OR MANIPULATED

God's love is Jesus' love. It never changes. It never fails. It's hard to accept that because every kind of love we have ever known is fallible. Even your mother's love. Sometimes, especially your mother's love. Yesterday, we looked at love that the world says is real. Today, let's see what God says about it. How have you seen God's love at work in your life.

together // **lesson 2 day 5** //176

We hear all the time about how we should love as Jesus loved. But, HOW exactly did Jesus love? Look up these examples. Read these stories. And read them out loud, if you can. Listen to the different characters. Try to put yourself in the scene. Look for tangible ways that Jesus exhibits His love in these instances. How can you do the same?

HOW DID **HE** LOVE?

Mathew 8:5–13
Mark 6:30–44
Mark 10:13–16
Mark 15:21–41
Luke 5:27–32
Luke 11:1–4
Luke 15:11–32
Luke 24:1–12
John 11:1-38
John 2:12–22
Matthew 4:23–25

HOW CAN **WE** LOVE

You may be wondering how in the world you're supposed to love others just like Christ loved you. You understand that He loved others, but let's be honest . . . you're not Jesus. It's believable that the Son of God perfectly loved people, even His enemies, but what about "normal people"? Remember, in some great mysterious way, Jesus was not only God with us, but He was also 100 percent human. He was unique but also normal. So it wasn't "easy" for Him either. He had some seriously messed up relationships (misunderstood by his family, hated by the in-crowd, betrayed by a so-called friend, falsely arrested, beaten up, made fun of, and publicly humiliated before being murdered). He was tempted. He wrestled with emotions. But He never sinned. He chose to love God and love people, laying down His life sacrificially on our behalf. He told us to love like He loved us, so how is that possible?

Read John 15:9–17. This is the Scripture you discussed in your group this week. What word comes up over and over and over again? (Nine times!)

First let's clarify what is meant by "love." We're not talking ooey-gooey mushy love. No baby talk, cuddling, or annoying nicknames. We're also not talking about really liking something such as pizza rolls and ranch dressing. If that was what Jesus had intended, loving our enemies would mean we really enjoy snuggling with those meanie-weenies. See? That would be absurd!

The Greek word Jesus uses for "love" is *agape*. This is a special kind of love in the Bible. In simple terms, it means "unconditional love" or "godly love." It is the kind of love God has for us, and therefore, that Jesus showed us. In the Bible, only God *agapes* people. So we can only agape each other if God is in us and loving people through us.

Now back up and read John 15:1–8.

To "abide" means to *remain* in. And when the Bible talks about "bearing fruit," it means evidence of God's truth having deep roots in your life. Fruit is something that shows up on the outside revealing the true nature of what's on the inside. For example, could you tell the difference between a watermelon vine and a pumpkin vine? Probably not until the fruit appeared. So with that in mind, look back at verses 1–8 and answer the following questions.

In verse 1, what does Jesus mean when He says that He is the true vine?

In verses 2 and 6, what does Jesus say will happen to branches not abiding in Him and producing fruit?

In verse 5, what does Jesus promise will happen if you do abide in Him and He in you?

Also according to verse 5, what can you do apart from Christ and without Him being in you?

Catch that? This is the whole point: In your own ability, you can't love others just like Christ loved you. You also can't be everywhere at once. But God can. While He doesn't give you the power of omnipresence (a big word meaning "being everywhere") He does give you the power to love with His unique love. This is possible only because He is loving people through you.

That kind of takes some of the pressure off too, if you think about it. You may or may not like someone. But no matter who they are or what they've done, God can love them. It's not something you have to muster up in your own personality, and it has nothing to do with your feelings. It's literally the love of Christ. So, back to where we started. . . . Can we love perfectly? NO. But can God perfectly love people through us when He is in us? YES.

Are you abiding in Him, relying on His life and love to work in you and through you?

Name some spiritual fruit (evidence of Christ's love) in your relationships.

WE TWO BOYS *together clinging,*
ONE THE OTHER
NEVER LEAVING,

UP AND DOWN *the roads going,*

NORTH *and* SOUTH
EXCURSIONS
MAKING.

— Walt Whitman, "Leaves of Grass"

There's hardly a better example in the Bible of true friendship built on the foundation of godly commitment than the story of Jonathan and David. They were supposed to be bitter rivals, but instead, they chose to be loyal friends. There's a lot we can learn from their famous friendship and what it teaches us about living together with one another in Christ. Pray for your friends by name. Pray that you can help each other grow closer to God. Pray that your friendships would be strengthened as you grow stronger in your faith, regardless of what life brings your way.

together // lesson 3 day 2 // 179

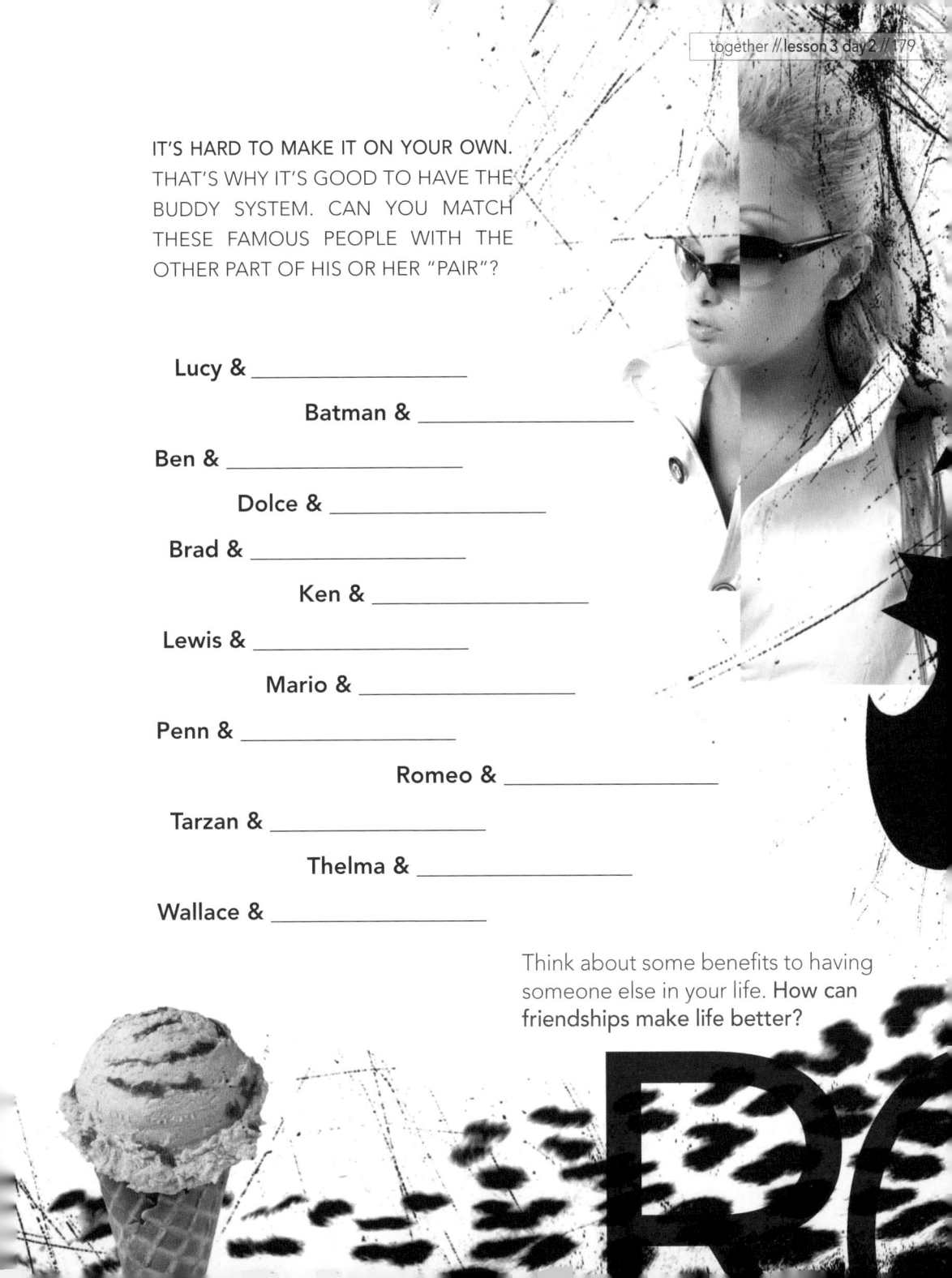

IT'S HARD TO MAKE IT ON YOUR OWN. THAT'S WHY IT'S GOOD TO HAVE THE BUDDY SYSTEM. CAN YOU MATCH THESE FAMOUS PEOPLE WITH THE OTHER PART OF HIS OR HER "PAIR"?

Lucy & _____

Batman & _____

Ben & _____

Dolce & _____

Brad & _____

Ken & _____

Lewis & _____

Mario & _____

Penn & _____

Romeo & _____

Tarzan & _____

Thelma & _____

Wallace & _____

Think about some benefits to having someone else in your life. **How can friendships make life better?**

Van Halen (1982)
M&M's
WARNING: ABSOLUTELY NO BROWN ONES.

Taylor Swift (2008)
A bag of Twizzlers
Two pints of Ben & Jerry's
One stick of butter
A jar of Pace picante sauce (mild)

Jennifer Lopez (2001)
DRESSING ROOM REQUIREMENTS:
WHITE ROOM
WHITE FLOWERS
WHITE TABLES AND/OR TABLECLOTHS
WHITE DRAPES
WHITE CANDIES
WHITE COUCHES

CRAZY CONTRACTS

CELEBRITIES CAN GET PRETTY DEMANDING BEFORE ENTERING INTO A CONTRACT. SURE, YOU CAN'T BLAME THEM IN SOME WAYS; THEY'RE LIVING ON THE ROAD. THAT GETS TOUGHER THAN WE THINK SOMETIMES. BUT COME ON. SERIOUSLY? SOME CELEBRITIES ARE PRETTY REASONABLE BUT FOR OTHERS, "PICKY" ISN'T EVEN THE RIGHT WORD. (VAN HALEN INSISTS THAT THE M&M'S DEMAND WAS TO MAKE SURE PROMOTERS ACTUALLY READ OVER EVERYTHING CAREFULLY, NOT BECAUSE THEY HAD SOME ROCK STAR PHOBIA OF BROWN CANDY.)

THINK ABOUT THIS: AREN'T YOU GLAD GOD DOESN'T MAKE YOU JUMP THROUGH CRAZY HOOPS BEFORE HE AGREES TO COME INTO YOUR LIFE? THERE ARE NO UNREASONABLE DEMANDS JUST TO PROVE YOU ARE PAYING ATTENTION. NO LIST TO CHECK OFF TO EARN HIS APPROVAL. HE HAS VOLUNTEERED TO ENTER INTO RELATIONSHIP WITH YOU! THANK GOD FOR HIS COVENANT WITH YOU.

HERE'S ANOTHER THOUGHT: DO YOU HAVE A ROCK STAR MINDSET? ARE YOU A DIVA? ARE YOU COMING UP WITH YOUR OWN CRAZY DEMANDS THAT YOU EXPECT GOD TO MEET BEFORE YOU'LL AGREE TO ENTER COVENANT WITH HIM? PRAY FOR HUMILITY AS YOU THANK GOD FOR HIS COMMITMENT TO YOU.

COVENANT

So what's the deal with this word *covenant*?

A wedding is a great picture of covenant today. (Though, unfortunately, this covenant doesn't always last.) Some neighborhoods, apartments, and condos have covenants concerning what is expected from residents' property. (Though there will always be tacky or noisy neighbors.) Even iTunes has a covenant of sorts, requiring you to agree to a code of conduct for your downloads. (Though nobody reads it.) You get the idea.

A covenant is like a contract. But it is more personal than we typically think about a contract being today. It is a deep commitment. Let's look at a few super-important pictures of covenant in Scripture.

GENESIS 6:17–22
Who entered a covenant with God?
Who initiated the covenant?
What did God promise?
What was the response?

GENESIS 17:1–7, 10
Who entered a covenant with God?
Who initiated the covenant?
What did God promise?
What was the response?

EXODUS 24:4–8
Who entered a covenant with God?
Who initiated the covenant?
What did God promise?
What was the response?

There are other covenants as well, most playing a part in this overall promise of God to His people. He would save them and be their God if they would be His people, trusting and obeying His Word. The Lord proved His faithfulness over and over again throughout Scripture. But unlike God, people aren't so faithful. They constantly broke their promises, sinning against God. They repeatedly offered sacrifices for forgiveness. This couldn't go on forever. God had a better way in mind all along. These promises were leading up to something much greater. . . .

READ JEREMIAH 31:31–34
Who will initiate the new covenant?
What does God promise?

At last, God fulfilled all of these promises, initiating a new covenant through JESUS. Christ told His disciples that His body would be broken and His blood poured out for the forgiveness of their sins. He promised them that the new covenant would be initiated at the cross. He was the world's salvation, sparing people from God's wrath toward sin for all of eternity. He was the promised King of kings who would bless all nations having faith like Abraham's. He was the perfect fulfillment of the Law given to Moses, the Word become flesh, and His blood cleansed all who would trust in Him.

To tie everything together, read **HEBREWS 9:13–15**. Whew! That was a lot of big, spiritual language. But hopefully after looking at those other covenants, it makes better sense. If trusting God in the old covenants and sacrifices worked for the time, yet people kept breaking the rules, how much greater is the new covenant through Christ? It is an eternal promise of salvation and abundant life as part of God's family for all who trust in Him.

Wow. So you are free. Saved. In relationship with a God who is more than faithful. He was committed to you through Christ before the beginning of time, despite your sins against Him. That is good news. That should affect everything about our lives. Everything should reflect His covenant with us.

together // lesson 3 day 5 // 182

SO

SO, IF HAVING THIS COVENANT RELATIONSHIP WITH SOMEONE IS SO IMPORTANT, THEN **WHO IS YOUR JONATHAN?** WHO IS THAT PERSON YOU CAN ALWAYS COUNT ON? THAT PERSON WHO WILL STICK UP FOR YOU, NO MATTER WHAT? ALWAYS HAS YOUR BACK? PRAYS FOR YOU? ENCOURAGES YOU? NEVER MAKES HIM OR HERSELF FEEL BETTER BY TEARING YOU DOWN? DO YOU HAVE A FRIEND LIKE THAT? ARE YOU A JONATHAN TO ANYONE?

Use the space to write about it. If you have a Jonathan, write down what makes that person a Jonathan to you. If you don't have this type of friend, write about the ideal friend.

DEVOTION

A best friend is someone you can spill your guts to. You tell each other everything. You've been through a lot together. A true friend has your back. But what if they actually needed some guts . . . literally. What if they needed an organ?

In December 2009, a police officer from St. Louis drove across the country to give a total stranger his kidney. Why? He received a kidney for his wife in return. His wife couldn't receive his kidney. Family members weren't matches for the transplant, either. In fact, she didn't match 95 percent of the country's population. But the officer was willing to do anything he could for the woman he had committed his life to.

Tom Otten wasn't the only person looking to save the life of a loved one. Thirteen other people were in similar situations trying to find rare matches for friends and family. So Tom donated his kidney to someone, and someone donated a kidney to another person, and then another . . . until six days and 26 surgeries later, 13 people had new kidneys from someone they didn't know, including Tom's wife. It was a record-setting organ swap. Wow!

If you remember from last week, Jesus said that there is no greater love than to lay down your life for your friends (John 15:13). Ultimately, we know He was talking about how He would sacrifice His life on the cross, but we need to follow that example by being committed to our friends in sacrificial love, too. So how do we do this?

Read 1 John 3:16–18. If your Bible says "brothers," that means friends. Christ-followers should consider their friendships to be relationships as close as family. This bond within God's family is actually greater than physical blood and natural birth; it is a bond through the blood of Christ and spiritual rebirth.

John then explains how you can do this today (since it is unlikely that you will end up literally dying to save your friends). Verses 17–18 clarify that to really be a friend is a commitment to love sacrificially. You help them with anything they might need if you have a way of doing so. Period. It's not enough to talk a good game and share stories or secrets. Best friends share life. They share everything. They do something about it, taking action that shows their commitment. Will you give even if it hurts?

Are not lifelong friendships **BORN AT THE** *moment* **WHEN AT LAST YOU MEET ANOTHER HUMAN BEING WHO HAS SOME INKLING** (but faint and uncertain even in the best) of that *something* which you were born desiring, and which, *beneath the flux of other desires* and in all the momentary silences BETWEEN THE LOUDER PASSIONS, NIGHT AND DAY, YEAR BY YEAR, from childhood to old age, you are looking for, WATCHING FOR, listening for? YOU HAVE NEVER HAD IT.

— C.S. Lewis

A great friend helps bring out that part of you that knows there is something more to life than what you normally experience. You are committed to each other through all of the "ups" and "downs" of this crazy life. After David became king, he was probably feeling pretty good. And then, one day, he was out in the field, shooting an arrow or something, and a memory of his dead friend Jonathan flickered across his mind. He missed his best friend. He wondered if there was anyone left in Jonathan's family, any way to keep that relationship going, even just in memory. And there was: Jonathan's crippled son, Mephibosheth. The way David treats Mephibosheth directly mirrors the covenant God has with humanity. Thank God for his faithfulness to you. Pray that you would be a reliable friend to others.

FOLLOW-THROUGH

Follow-through. It's critical in sports. Looking the part and going through all of the right stances and motions are worthless if you don't have follow-through. Sure, you'll make contact and get things moving, but things quickly head in the wrong direction without follow-through.

It's the same in relationships. You have to make the commitment, putting yourself in the right place at the right time, but you have to back it up with your ongoing actions. You can't just call someone a friend and never show up or keep your promises. You have to be there. You have to have follow-through. You may really hit it off at first, but without follow-through, things spin out of control and get ugly. Is there a friendship in which you need to step up your level of commitment? Do you have follow-through? Think about it.

DEVOTION

Did you see *To Save a Life*? It was another film in the recent wave of faith-based "movies with a message." In this case, a youth pastor from California wrote a script that crammed just about every issue a teenager might face into a two-hour movie. People either loved it or hated it.

Here's the gist: Jake and Roger were best friends as kids, but once they got to high school, Jake was the king of the school (super-popular, hot girlfriend, stud athlete). But Roger was the social misfit that didn't fit in anywhere. You know as well as anyone that the unspoken rule as a teenager is not to hang out with freaks and geeks. They'll drag you down the social ladder, and you'll become everyone's doormat. Right?

So, that's what happened. Despite good times back in the day, Jake abandoned Roger. Eventually the forgotten friend lost all hope and snapped. At the end of his rope, Roger took his own life. Shocked and devastated, Jake spends the rest of the movie seeking other hopeless and hurting people, vowing never again to be too cool to reach out to others in need. Leaving people out was no longer an option for Jake.

Read 1 John 4:19–21. The only rule that should matter in our relationships is verse 19. We show love to others because Christ showed love to us. We are misfits. We are far from perfect. But God loves us and reached out to us. He initiated a relationship with us by sending Jesus to save us. If we truly love God, then we'll follow Christ into a hurting world seeking out those in need of love.

You can't hate people, ignoring or making fun of them, because God loves them, too. They're no less deserving of a "good life" than you.

Think back, from earlier, to the story of David and Jonathan's son. David was literally king, not of a high school but of a kingdom. And his best friend from back in the day had a son who was literally abandoned after things turned bad for the royal family. Since his own family had died in war and David was the new king, Mephibosheth was a social outcast. Now, kings don't bring the family of former kings into their palace on friendly terms. (They would be considered enemies and usually killed.) On top of that, Mephibosheth was crippled, and kings simply didn't associate with poor commoners or people with physical deformities or mental handicaps. It was the cultural expectation to be surrounded by perfect people in your perfect life as king. But King David refused to forget about his friendship to Jonathan and followed through on his commitment. Not only did he make sure his friend's son was cared for, David brought him into his home, loving him like a son, and always had a place for him at the table.

This is exactly what God did for you, too. Do you love others the way Christ loved you first? Like David, do you invite outcasts to sit at your table and join your group? Or are you caught up in having cool friends like Jake in the movie, shunning the "Rogers" in your world? Scripture says you don't love God if you don't love the people around you. So do you?

together // lesson 4 day 4 //187

We've had **promises kept** to us and promises broken. One elates you; one breaks your heart. And we've done the same to others. In the "Kept" section, write down promises you've kept and promises others have kept to you. In the "Broken" section, write down promises you or someone else has broken.

Do you feel like you've had **promises broken** or kept by God? How does this make you feel?

(Sometimes we may feel like God is letting us down, but He is always faithful. Often we simply need to be patient for His perfect timing. Other times we may need to reevaluate our understanding. Maybe we've had unrealistic expectations. Ask God to help you trust Him completely, thanking Him for His perfect faithfulness.)

PROMISES
KEPT   BROKEN

together // lesson 4 day 5 // 188

SOMEONE WHO WILL HELP YOU WHEN YOU CAN'T HELP YOURSELF

SOMEONE TO FIGHT FOR YOU

MAN'S BEST FRIEND

SOMEONE TO SERVE SELFLESSLY

SOMEONE TO LOVE

SOMEONE TO TELL THE MONSTERS TO SCRAM

WHAT DOES LOYALTY MEAN TO YOU?

BFF

BFF. Let's be honest. Have you had the same best friend forever? Or have you had a falling out, moved away, or simply moved on to other interests and other circles of friends?

Hopefully you do know what it's like to have at least someone in your life that you can count on. But even if you don't have someone like that in your life at this time, the important thing is that YOU are that kind of person to others. That is part of what loving like God loved us is all about. Faithfulness. Commitment. Follow-through. You know that God is there for you at all times, and He can be trusted to keep His word.

Read the Scriptures below to see the ways God has always loved us and/or how we should love others. Write a summary in each blank of what the verse says about godly love. Then say a prayer asking Him to help you love others like He has loved you. Also, thank Him that His love for you really is "forever."

Exodus 34:6

Numbers 23:19

Jeremiah 31:3

Luke 6:35

Luke 6:36

Luke 6:37

Luke 6:38

1 Corinthians 13:1

1 Corinthians 13:2

1 Corinthians 13:3

1 Corinthians 13:4

write a prayer:

together // lesson 5 day 1 // 190

WE ARE
**EACH OTHER'S
BUSINESS;**

*WE ARE
EACH OTHER'S
harvest;*

we are EACH OTHER'S
**MAGNITUDE
and BOND.**

— Gwendolyn Brooks

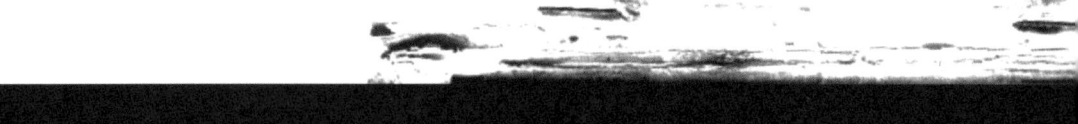

Through His covenant with us (His people), Jesus broke down the barrier between Jews and Gentiles. This may not sound like much to you today, but these two separate groups had nothing to do with each other. Both groups pretty much ignored the other, sticking to their own cliques, looking down on the others as weird and inferior.

Besides that, you are probably one of the "Gentiles" benefiting from this deal. Before Christ, if you were not Jewish, you were an outsider. You were not part of God's people. Sorry. But now, you reap the reward of this radical shift in history. From that point on, life changed forever. God was gathering people from all different "groups" into one big happy family (though sometimes still dysfunctional, let's be honest).

So with that in mind, thank God for including you in His new group. Pray too that you wouldn't exclude others, thinking you're better than anyone else. Make it your business today to see the value and similarities in others instead of the differences.

together // lesson 5 day 2 // 191

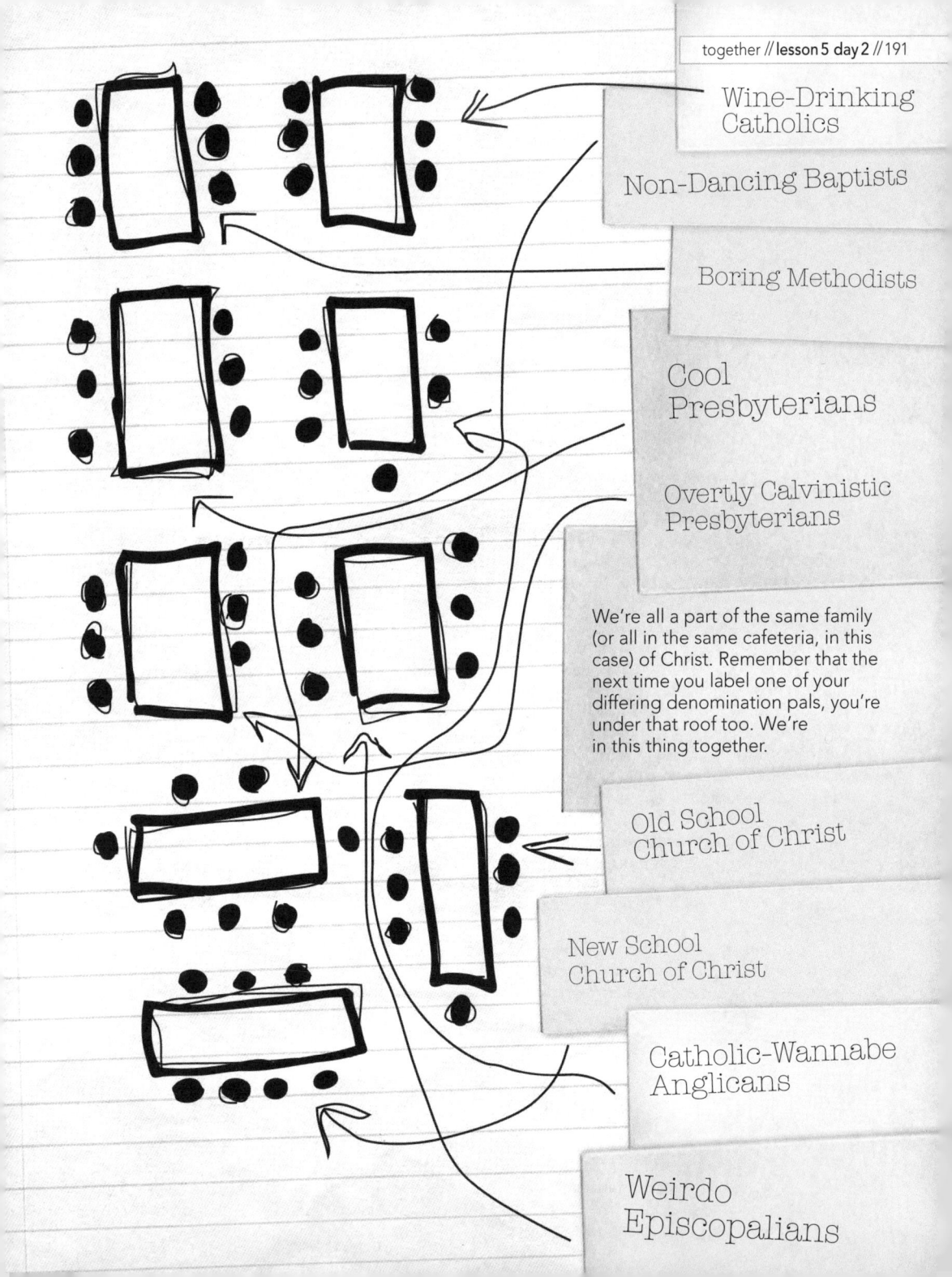

Wine-Drinking Catholics

Non-Dancing Baptists

Boring Methodists

Cool Presbyterians

Overtly Calvinistic Presbyterians

We're all a part of the same family (or all in the same cafeteria, in this case) of Christ. Remember that the next time you label one of your differing denomination pals, you're under that roof too. We're in this thing together.

Old School Church of Christ

New School Church of Christ

Catholic-Wannabe Anglicans

Weirdo Episcopalians

DEVOTION

Asimo. Have you seen Honda's little spaceman-looking robot? Decades in the making, the little helper is a technological wonder. What appears to be a white-suited visitor from outer space is a bi-pedal humanoid (meaning it walks on two feet like a human) that can obey simple commands. And what's more amazing than the life-like movement, is that these commands are not spoken or typed into a computer. You simply think about what you want it to do!

That's right. Asimo is a mind-reading humanoid robot. This isn't some sci-fi fantasy; it's real technology. Don't worry; you don't have to implant any electrodes into your brain. (Whew! That's a relief.) You simply have to put on a helmet that measures brain activity. The humanoid then moves its hands, arms, and legs upon mental command. The other command Asimo understands is moving the tongue . . . but it obviously doesn't have a face, so it touches where the tongue would be if it weren't a futuristic robot. According to the official Web site, the hope is to create a partner in daily tasks, a robot companion that functions in society and lives in harmony with humans. Lives? In society? (This might sound cool at first, but it gets creepy if you think about it.)

With that in mind, read Philippians 2:1–6. The writer, Paul, is encouraging Christ-followers to come together and get along. Apparently, petty jealousy and division was common in this community. Go figure. Paul says that when Christ came, He brought us together. And the key to unity is humility. That doesn't mean having a low self-esteem, it means having a high-esteem for others, seeing their needs as more important than your own preferences. Jesus was the ultimate example of humility. Even though He was God, the Creator of the universe, Christ became a man. He walked and talked with us. He died on the cross to save us and glorify God. And one day, every knee will bow and every tongue will confess that Jesus Christ is Lord.

But for now, how should we act in our relationships? We put on the mind of Christ. If we are all in tune with His attitude, then we'll all be united. Together, we'll be likeminded with Christ and therefore share the same mind, love, spirit, and purpose with one another. That purpose is to look out for others so that they may know the glory of God.

So how do you function in your society (at home, school, church, or wherever)? Are you a servant of Christ and of God's people? Do you help others see the glory of God by confessing Christ as the Lord? Do you put on the mind of Christ and let His attitude guide every step you take? Not in a creepy robot way, but in a way that you choose to let His thoughts become your thoughts and His will become your motivation. Think about it.

together // lesson 5 day 4 // 93

An **army** of ants
A **barrel** of monkeys
A **bed** of oysters
A **bloat** of hippo
A **bloom** of jellyfish
A **bob** of sea lion
A **bundle** of frogs
A **byke** of ants
A **cackle** of hyena
A **cartload** of monkeys
A **cauldron** of bats
A **clowder** of cats
A **congregation** of alligators
A **consortium** of crab
A **court** of kangaroo
A **crash** of rhinos
A **dazzle** of zebras
A **fluther** of jellyfish
A **gaggle** of geese
A **heard** of buffalo
An **intrusion** of cockroaches
A **kindle** of kittens
A **leap** of leopard
A **litter** of puppies
A **lump** of toads
A **marmalade** of ponies
A **mischief** of mice
A **mob** of goats
A **murder** of crows
A **pack** of dogs
A **parliament** of owl
A **party** of dolphin (female)
A **peep** of chickens
A **pipe** of eel
A **prickle** of porcupine

A **pride** of lions
A **quiver** of cobras
A **rangale** of deer
A **rafter** of turkeys
A **risk** of lobster
A **romp** of otter
A **school** of fish
A **skulk** of foxes
A **sleuth** of bear
A **smack** of jellyfish
A **smuck** of jellyfish
A **sneak** of weasels
A **snuggle** of kittens
A **squad** of squirrels
A **squirm** of worms
A **stretch** of giraffe
A **swarm** of bees
A **thunder** of hippo
A **tower** of giraffe
A **troop** of gorillas
An **unkindness** of raven
A **wisdom** of owl
A **yoke** of oxen

WHATEVER YOU CALL IT, YOU WERE MADE FOR COMMUNITY.

WE ARE THE BODY OF CHRIST

Seven years. That's how long gum is rumored to stay in a person's stomach if swallowed. Of course, by the time you're older than age 7, you begin to realize such talk is crazy. Once you begin to question the validity of this scientific "fact," the appendix is likely brought into the argument, right? According to urban legend, with no known function, the human appendix (a small, finger-like dangly thing on the end of your large intestine) is used to store your gum. Once the gum has served it's time in bubble gum belly prison, it is then released and allowed to exit your digestive system. (No need to explain that). This is, of course, ridiculous. Like your body has a filter that only grabs chewing gum and gives it a seven-year sentence. It is true, however that we don't know what purpose the appendix serves.

Ever feel like you were "the appendix"? Just some extra worthless thing hanging around with no real use to anybody, especially to God. What purpose could you have for God? But the Bible states clearly that together we are the Body of Christ. Each of us plays an important part. As the Church, the community of faith, the Body of Christ has no worthless parts. There is no appendix.

Check out the following verses and answer the questions for each. Once you've finished, pray for God to give you a unified spirit, thanking Him for the unique parts that everyone plays . . . including you. Ask Him to grow you up into maturity.

1 Corinthians 12:12–13
Christ has removed all labels and made us into one family—one body. What labels get put on people today, even in church, dividing them into separate groups?

1 Corinthians 12:14–20
There is no greater or lesser important part of Christ's Body. Certain people may have a more noticeable role in the Church, but everyone is a part of the same Body. Have you ever wished that you had a more or less visible part to play among God's people? What gifts or talents do you tend to be jealous of or look down upon?

Ephesians 4:1–7
What word appears over and over?
Write down all of the things Christ-followers have in common.
Write down the different attitudes you should have as a result.

Ephesians 4:11–14
OK, in super-simple terms, you could think about these categories of gifts/roles in the following way:

Apostles = "Goers" and "Doers" who go out to do new things for Christ.
Prophets = "Rebels" and "Messengers" who stand up against what's wrong and speak up for what's right.
Evangelists = "Lookers" and "Talkers" who see opportunities to share the life-changing gospel.
   *An evangelist doesn't have to be a public speaker, but simply someone who often has Christ come up in conversation.
Pastors = "Helpers" and "Leaders" who care about people and want to make sure their needs get met.
Teachers = "Learners" and "Sharers" who like to pass on what God has taught them.

So which best describes the way God has made you?
All of these different gifts have the same purpose, what is it?

Ephesians 4:15–16
Who is the head, holding everyone together and empowering the different parts to serve their purposes?

What is the result when everyone works together, unified and lead by Christ?

AT THAT MOMENT, the curtain of the Temple was torn from top to bottom. The earth shook and the rocks split.

The Kodesh Hakodashim, or Holy of Holies, was the most sacred place for someone of Jewish heritage. Deep inside the Temple in Jerusalem, the 15-by-15-foot room contained the very presence of God. It was kept completely dark, and only once a year (on the Day of Atonement… what we now call Yom Kippur) could the High Priest enter to make a sacrifice forgiving the sins of the people. In the Second Temple, the Temple Jesus would have attended, the Holy of Holies was separated from the Holy Place by a thick, 60-foot curtain.

The moment that Jesus died was a dramatic one. The Son of God was dead. There was an earthquake. And mysteriously, the veil separating God from His people was ripped from the top to the bottom. Think about it… from the highest point of a thick, heavy, embroidered fabric came a 60-foot gash, splitting the veil in two. It was as if God had grabbed the top of it with His holy hands and just tore right through it. Through this symbolic tearing of a curtain, Jesus made possible unity between God and His people as well as unity among the people. You didn't have to be Jewish; you didn't have to be a man; you didn't have to be a priest; you didn't have to be the High Priest. Anyone could meet with God. Gentiles, women, children—anyone. There is no more veil. There is no more distinction. He wants all to come and see His goodness.

Thank God now that you have unlimited access to Him anytime of every day!

together // lesson 6 day 1 // 196

one day
you will do things **FOR ME**
THAT YOU HATE.

THAT IS WHAT IT MEANS TO BE **FAMILY.**

— Jonathan Safran Foer *(Everything Is Illuminated)*

Not terrible, sinful, hateful things, but things you would never choose to do on your own. These are the kind of things you do for the people you love and who love you. You are committed to each other. You're family. So, if that means you have to do something gross, inconvenient, boring, embarrassing, or maybe even painful… well, you do it. Because you're family.

That's not always easy. For better or for worse. We get who we get, and there's no getting out of your family for the most part. Even when your little brother drives you insane or your older sister doesn't give a moment's notice to you. Even if your dad would rather be golfing or you can't get a second away from your mom.

And what does Scripture say about family? Submit. Yeah, submit to them. Even when it's hard. You may think it makes you look weak. You may hate it and feel awful. You may have the best family in the world or you may feel like you've got the worst one in history. Doesn't matter. Submit. Love unconditionally. So how do you do this without going crazy? Start by praying about it now. Do something today that you wouldn't normally choose to do. Love your family sacrificially today.

SIGNS OF RESPECT

R-E-S-P-E-C-T. Submission has its roots in respecting others. And let's face it: some people aren't really worthy of respect. But that is not up to us to decide. Respecting everyone, including the person who least deserves it, is part of the submitting process. This process changes your heart and makes you more like Christ, who submitted in the ultimate form by dying for you and me—people who certainly didn't deserve it.

How can you show respect in your daily life? What is disrespectful? Pray for God's help in showing respect to everyone today.

RESPECT

RELATIONSHIPS 101

So, we are all part of the Body of Christ. We need to be unified. We need the mind of Christ, characterized by humility. You've got that by now. Hopefully you've been thinking about this the past week. But you may have started to wonder if there are any more specific steps you could take with God's help. Maybe you've run into some situations where you just don't know what the attitude of Christ looks like. Sure, you get "why" you should be humble in your relationships (because Christ loved us first), but "how" gets tricky at times.

Grab your Bible and open it to **Romans 12. Read verses 3–8.** This is just another reminder that we're all in this thing together! Pray that God would help this truth sink in like never before; it is so important.

Paul, the writer of Romans, goes into some very practical ways to live this out. He gives some simple steps (but that doesn't mean easy). Writing things down can help you remember them. So, for the rest of this page you are simply going to write out each thing he says to do. Every time a new action is described, write it by the next star. Pretty much every time you see a comma, semi-colon, or period in these verses, that indicates a new action. There are a certain number of stars with each verse number below to help you. Got it? Then get to it!

Read Romans 12:9–21. Write down each thing Paul instructs you to do as a humble Christ-follower. Then pray that God would help you in each of these specific areas.

9
*
*
*

10
*
*

11
*
*
*

12
*
*
*

13
*
*

14
*
*

15
*
*

16
*
*
*
*

17
*
*

18
*

19
*
*

20
*
*

21
*
*

together // **lesson 6 day 4** // 199

WHEN AN ARCH is used in architecture, it's a tricky thing. How do you make stones curve in mid-air without falling into each other and collapsing the entire structure?

Architects came up with the idea for a **keystone**—a central stone, larger than the surrounding ones, which forms the apex of the arch. This keystone locks the other stones in place, as they bow to one another to create the arch.

Do you see where we're going with this? The keystone is Christ. He holds all things together. We ultimately submit to Him. But while we do so, we also bow our heads to others. And when we are all humble and willing to be used by the Keystone, we create beautiful arches in the buildings of our lives.

Look for keystones today and each time you notice one, pray that you would submit to Christ and support others as they trust Him too.

keystone

DEVOTION

Remember Chinese finger traps? The first time you stuck your little pointer fingers in one as a child, so innocently, you never suspected it would grab hold of you. YOINK! Like quicksand, the harder you struggled, attempting to assert your will to be free and to prove your strength, the tighter it got. You probably laughed at first. But you then may have panicked a little. Would you ever be able to point at things or press buttons again? You'd be "that kid with his fingers stuck together" for the rest of your life. How do you ride a bike, or pick up a bowl of Coco Krispies to drink the chocolate milk out of the bottom, or put on your favorite t-shirt if you're trapped in this sneaky little toy? (On the bright side, maybe you can get out of homework and brushing your teeth . . .)

But what was the secret? Your natural reaction was to pull away and use more force, but freedom was found when you relaxed and gently brought your fingers together. There's a great lesson to learn in the children's gag gift. . . . Grab your Bible.

Read 1 Peter 5:5–6. Peter was one of Jesus' closest disciples. He had a reputation for being "a little too big for his britches," to borrow an old expression. (What? You don't say "britches"?) At one point in his life, right after confessing Jesus as the Savior and Son of God, Peter basically told Jesus to stop all this crazy talk that sounds like He's going to die soon. Well, Jesus put Peter right back in his place, to put it mildly. But Peter eventually learned a valuable lesson. Be humble, respectful of everyone—but especially people older than you, and trust God.

God doesn't put up with pride and big egos. That's our natural response as humans. We think we know best or that we need to prove we are right. So we try to force our wills by acting rude, forceful, and disrespectful. Something inside of us just naturally resists the idea of submitting to someone else (who may very well know better from experience the key to our little situation). "That would be giving in. That's weak," we think. But it's not; it's the secret to freedom in God–honoring relationships. It frees us from worry and conflict, among other things.

Humility through Christ frees us from sin, if you think about it. What is sin after all? It is thinking we know better than God. It is disrespecting Him, ignoring His commands, and asserting our own will to prove our own ability. Hmmm . . . pride is such a sneaky little trap. So pray that God would free you from pride in your heart and in your relationships. Pray for patience and just relax. Stop trying so hard to be in control. Trust that when you loosen up and humble yourself, giving God and others greater respect, that He will bless you with a new found freedom to enjoy your relationships.

together // lesson 6 day 6 // 201

THE WORLD HAS BIG IDEAS ABOUT STRENGTH AND POWER. GET RICH AND IMPORTANT, OWN A LOT OF STUFF, AND RELISH YOUR HIGH POSITION AS A PERSON OF STATURE. IN WHAT WAYS DO WE SEE THE WORLD DEFINING STRENGTH?

WORLD vs. GOD
STRONG

BUT **GOD'S STRENGTH** IS TRUE STRENGTH. WE KNOW THE BIBLE SAYS THAT WHEN WE ARE WEAK, THEN CHRIST IS STRONG. AND GOD'S STRENGTH MAY NOT LOOK LIKE STRENGTH TO THE WORLD, BECAUSE DARKNESS IS AFRAID OF THE LIGHT AND DOES NOT KNOW IT. WHAT ARE WAYS THAT SEEM TO BE WEAKNESS, BUT ARE ACTUALLY FEATS OF GOD'S STRENGTH?

CHOSEN

So, we're created for relationships. But once we're in a relationship with God and each other, what does life look like together? As the global community of God's people, we are a family. He is our Heavenly Father. We are His children. That makes us brothers and sisters in Christ. You and that older person. You and that annoying little child. You and that perfect girl or that weird guy. You and them. . . . All of us. We're all in this thing together. All over the world. And we will be recognized by our actions. Our lives should be noticeably different. God has handmade and hand picked each one of us. He put us together. For a purpose.

Unique.

Set apart.

Chosen.

- **Lesson 1: What If?**— pg 204-209
- **Lesson 2: The Need to Be Needy**— pg 210-215
- **Lesson 3: True Community**— pg 216-221
- **Lesson 4: Give Yourself Away**— pg 222-227
- **Lesson 5: Swimming Upstream**— pg 228-233
- **Lesson 6: Carry Each Other's Burdens**— pg 234-239

TO WHAT ARE YOU LOYAL?

WHAT IS YOUR YOUTH GROUP OR YOUR GROUP OF FRIENDS COMMITTED TO? (YOU CAN TELL BY WHAT MOST INFLUENCES YOUR DECISIONS.)

PRAY THAT YOU AND YOUR FRIENDS WOULD SURRENDER TO CHRIST AND PLEDGE ALLEGIANCE TO HIS KINGDOM.

DEVOTION

"You're just a kid. You'll understand when you grow up."

Anyone ever say something like that to you? Bet it ticked you off, didn't it? Sure, there are things to learn, but that doesn't mean you're clueless. It's good to admit that you always have room to grow and learn, respecting people older than you; but you already have a pretty good grasp on some things. And here's the real kicker: sometimes being young is an advantage in matters of faith. You have less to lose, less worries, and less experience to jade you and kill your optimism and hopefulness. You believe that the world can be changed. And it can.

Read 1 Timothy 4:12–16. The Apostle Paul has poured his time and wisdom into this younger guy named Timothy. Paul believed not just in Timothy's potential to be a great leader but also in his ability right then and there. Timothy was given a list of things to which to devote himself, spiritual disciplines or godly characteristics. But what is the point of being a good follower of Christ? His life is to serve as an example to others in his community. People both young and old in his circle of influence should be inspired and motivated to live out their salvation due to Timothy's example.

Christ is calling you to devote yourself to these things, too. With God's help, through Christ's Spirit inside of you, you can live in a way that makes a difference. The point is not to just be a better person. The point is definitely not to feel better about yourself or think you are better than other people. It's not about "getting it." It's about encouraging others to follow Christ wholeheartedly. Can other people in your church, youth group, or circle of friends look to your example and see how to live by faith? Is your salvation evident to everyone or are you neglecting the gift of God's Spirit in your life. His Spirit gives all of His people the power to follow Him faithfully.

chosen // lesson 1 day 3 // 206

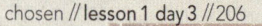

REPENT

**MEANS TO TURN AROUND
GO THE OPPOSITE WAY
REVERSE
180°**

Christ said, "Repent, for the kingdom of heaven is near" (Matt. 4:17).

HOW HAS YOUR LIFE CHANGED DIRECTION SINCE YOU BEGAN FOLLOWING CHRIST?

chosen // lesson 1 day 4 //207

Is there anywhere that seems too "far" for God's grace to reach? Where would it most surprise you to see God's Spirit bring citywide repentance? Pray for that place. Now, pray for revival in your own community (starting in your own life).

So how do you live in such a way that your salvation is evident to everyone? How can you be like Timothy, living out your faith, setting an example for the people around you? How can you and your friends be like the people of Nineveh (not in the God-is-about-to-destroy-you-due-to-your-sinfulness kind of way, but in the immediate and radical response to God's Word kind of way)? Once the Ninevites heard from God, they changed the course of their lives dramatically—every one of them. God's Word changed their lives in a way that was undeniable, easily seen by anyone.

Grab your Bible. (That's always a good place to start, right?) Open it up to James 2.

Before you read, here's a little background on James. He is the leader of the Jerusalem church. More significantly, he is the half brother of Jesus. (Mary was their mom; Joseph was James' dad, but Jesus was the Son of God.) James is writing this letter to explain how faith in God plays out in daily life for Christ-followers. It has actually caused some controversy throughout church history since some people think it contradicts other places in the New Testament, especially the writings of Paul, which teach that people are saved by grace through faith alone. This is absolutely, 100 percent true, and James would agree. James doesn't contradict this at all. (The Bible never contradicts itself since it is all God's Word.) James simply explains that real saving faith doesn't just believing something is true; saving faith does something about it. James teaches us that if we really have faith, then we'll live it out.

Read James 2:14–20. Then, answer these simple questions honestly. (Circle your answers)

Do you call yourself a Christian?   YES   NO

Do you live out what you say you believe?   YES   NO

So, would James (the Bible) say you have real faith?   YES   NO

Wow. Yeah. So if you call yourself a Christ-follower but never act like Christ, then according to the Bible, you're not really following Him are you? No. James explains that even demons know the truth about Jesus. It is not enough for you and your friends to merely know the right things about Jesus and believe that they are true. Honestly, a lot of people that go to church or youth group every week know all of the right answers, but they have no real respect when it comes to obeying Christ and following Him with the way they live. James teaches that demons "shudder," meaning they have respect for God's power, but they don't obey it. Do you?

Think about it. Do you and your friends really respect God's authority in your lives? What do you talk about? What do you do when you hang out? What do you watch, listen to, and laugh about? In the remaining space, write a prayer asking God to help you and your friends live out your faith. Ask for real faith that puts what you know and believe into action every day out of love and respect for God.

chosen // lesson 1 day 6 // 209

Back in the day, people in the Bible would occasionally put on sackcloth (scratchy cloth like burlap bags or potato sacks). Why? This was a way of showing their humility before God. People would replace comfortable clothes with sackcloth as a sign of mourning or repentance (grieving over sin). Sometimes they would shave off all of their hair and rub or sprinkle dust or ashes on their heads. Then, they would sit in the dust, too. This was to show the world a clear outward display of what was happening in their hearts.

What about you? You probably don't wear a potato sack, shave your head, or roll around in the dirt to express your feelings.

So, how do you show that your life has changed? How do you express what God is doing in your heart? How do you and your friends put into action the truth that God has made known to you?

chosen // lesson 2 day 1 // 210

EVERYBODY HAS TO EAT.
SO WHAT ARE YOU HUNGRY & THIRSTY FOR?
(NOT LITERALLY HUNGRY, BUT SPIRITUALLY AND IN LIFE...)

WHAT DO YOU CRAVE?
WITH WHAT DO YOU FILL YOUR LIFE?
DOES IT SATISFY YOU?

DEVOTION

Three days. That's about how long as person can live without water. Three weeks. That's roughly how long a person can survive without food. Now these numbers give and take a little, depending on the person. But one thing is for sure: Humans cannot keep living for long if they neglect to eat or drink. Your body gets hungry and thirsty. They are natural needs. A person's gotta eat and drink. Right?

Read just one verse today. Open your Bible to Matthew 5:6. Read it. **Now, read it again.**

"Blessed are those who hunger and thirst for righteousness, for they will be filled."

This verse falls right in the middle of something called the Beatitudes. You may have heard of them. Basically, Jesus teaches what attitudes His followers should have. Get it? So, if you and your friends are going to be Christ-followers, you have to hunger and thirst for righteousness. It's vital.

What do you do if you're hungry? What about if you're thirsty? You get something to eat or drink, because if you don't, the feeling grows so overwhelming, you can't stand it. (Not to mention, you'll literally die if you don't.) Now think about this: while you and your friends probably make plenty of fast food runs or raid the kitchen when the munchies strike, what about the hunger Christ is talking about here? How long do you let yourselves go without intentionally seeking out the spiritual nourishment you need? Chances are you go a lot longer between spiritual feedings than you do between physical meals.

Why is that?

Jesus promises that when you hunger and thirst for righteousness (meaning doing His good works in faith) then you will be filled. It is truly satisfying. It gives strength and life and energy. Once you taste and see that the Lord is good, you'll want to share Him with your friends, too. Just like that favorite new snack or drink. Share what you're learning. Invite others to join you in what you're doing. Live out your faith together. Everyone who hungers and thirsts for godly lives, who craves Christ instead of the things of this world, will be satisfied. They will be full. They will be happy (which is what some translations say instead of "blessed").

Don't you want to be happy? Blessed? Healthy? Filled with Christ? Satisfied in life? Then don't go one more day without the spiritual nourishment you need. Hunger and thirst for more of Him and live out your faith today.

PULL YOURSELF UP BY YOUR BOOTSTRAPS

Ever hear that expression? It summarizes good old-fashioned hard work and independence. If you just believe in yourself and never give up, you can do anything you set your mind to. And you don't need help from anyone to do it. Our culture takes great pride in being tough and self-sufficient.

But this stands in stark contrast to biblical community. The Bible says that God's people (the Church) need Him and each other. We put our faith in Him, not in our own abilities, and we trust that He can do anything He wants to do with us, through us, and in spite of our inability.

This is what the LORD says: "Let not the wise man boast of his wisdom or the strong man boast of his strength or the rich man boast of his riches . . . " —Jeremiah 9:23

"My grace is sufficient for you, for my power is made perfect in weakness." Therefore I will boast all the more gladly about my weaknesses, so that Christ's power may rest on me. —2 Corinthians 12:9

chosen // lesson 2 day 4 // 213

I need Jesus.
i need Jesus.
I Need Jesus
I NEED JESUS
I NEED JESUS
I need Jesus!
I need Jesus.
I need Jesus
I need Jesus

**Who helped you see your need for Jesus?
How do you help others see their need for Christ?**

All right. So what's the deal with this word, "abide" anyway? It's probably a safe bet that you rarely or never hear the word used except for in the Bible. So what does it mean? The Greek word is "meno." It means to remain or stay. This can be in a place, a time, or a condition.

To abide or remain in a place basically means: dwell, be present, don't go anywhere, and to continually be held or kept from leaving.

To abide or remain in a time basically means: continue to exist or live, endure, last, or survive.

To abide or remain in a state or condition basically means: stay unified, the same, and never change or become different.

So what does this have to do with your life in relationship with God and His people? Look up John 15 and read verses 4–9.

How many times did you read the word "abide" or "remain" in these verses?

Jesus couldn't be any clearer. His point is obvious. If you want to experience life, stick with Him. He's the only way to truly live a meaningful life.
Stay in Him.
Stay with Him.
Don't leave Him.
He won't leave you.
Live and exist in Him.
Remain unified with Him.
Continue to remain dependant on Him for your life.
Never let anything change your relationship with Him.

According to what Jesus says in John 15:5, what can you do apart from Him?

So this really all boils down to one simple fact: You need Jesus—big time. We all do.

Notice in John 15:9 Jesus shifts from saying abide in Him to abide in His love. How many times do you read the word "love" in verses 9–17?

Christ defines love as spending your life on the people you care about and obeying His Word. Are you doing these things? That's what life abiding in Christ looks like. He chose you to abide in Him. He has chosen you to live a life that brings great glory to God. Jesus tells you to pray for the things that He would pray for (That's part of what it means to pray in his name.) and that God will answer those prayers. Right now, He is saying to pray that you would love your friends with all of your life and remain obedient to Christ for all of your life. So start obeying Him now by praying for these things: obedience, love, and a life of abiding in Christ.

chosen // lesson 2 day 6 //215

You can't grow.

You can't be productive (or "fruitful").

You can't even live

without being rooted in Christ.

Do you try to live life through your own
power and ability?

Do you even try to live your "Christian" life
without abiding in Christ?

Pray for the Spirit of Christ to produce
spiritual fruit in your life
and relationships
today.

THINK

ABOUT YOUR YOUTH GROUP & YOUR CIRCLE OF FRIENDS...

WHAT IS AT THE CENTER OF YOUR RELATIONSHIPS?
WHAT IS YOUR PURPOSE FOR GATHERING?
ARE YOU UNITED WITH A COMMON GOAL?
DO YOU HAVE A GAME PLAN, EVERYONE PLAYING HIS OR HER PART,
TO LIVE VICTORIOUSLY FOR THE SAKE OF CHRIST AND HIS KINGDOM?

DEVOTION

Frodo. You may know him as Elijah Wood's character from the movie trilogy of the early-2000s. This stumpy little hero is the main character of J.R.R. Tolkien's epic masterpiece *The Lord of the Rings*. Frodo Baggins is a young hobbit entrusted with a mission that will either save or doom everyone: destroying a ring the gives ultimate power to anyone who wears it. This ring was forged long ago and has been lost for generations until finding its way to the pure-hearted hobbit. You've probably read the books or seen the films (or at least heard of the story). Part way through his journey, Frodo and his companions officially become a special group called the Fellowship of the Ring. This is more than just a gang of friends or a club of mythical woodland creatures. The fellowship is a unique relationship centered around a mission involving the life-changing power of the ring Frodo carries. Without delving into any more of the story line, keep this concept of fellowship in mind as you grab your Bible.

Read 1 John 1:1–7. These seven verses have an epic feel don't they? John, the author, shared from personal experience something that is truly life changing. He wrote that this Word of Life has existed since before time began but that the mystery has been revealed and made known to him. He and his fellow disciples had journeyed with the Son of God, Jesus Himself. Since that time, John's life had never been the same and neither had any of the disciples' lives.

Over and over he used the word "fellowship." As in the story above, this fellowship is more than just a gathering of friends. As Christ-followers, walking in the Light of Truth, we share a unique mission and purpose in life. Our fellowship with God and each other is a specific relationship centered around Christ. John says that he wants to share this good news with everyone so that they can also join the fellowship and have their joy made complete.

Think about this today: A relationship with God and with His people is not just casual friendship or passing acquaintance. Your fellowship is intentional. It has purpose. You have a mission. You should be careful about how you live because you have been entrusted with the truth of God, the world-changing power of the Word of Life. You share the common bond of the blood of Jesus and forgiveness of sins with all who follow Christ. What will you do with this truth? Will it be the guiding force in your life? Will you invite others to join the fellowship?

TOGETHER

Matthew 18:20—For where two or three come together in my name, there am I with them.

Mark 10:9—Therefore what God has joined together, let man not separate.

Acts 1:14—They all joined together constantly in prayer.

Acts 2:44—All the believers were together and had everything in common.

Acts 2:46—Every day they continued to meet together in the temple courts. They broke bread in their homes and ate together with glad and sincere hearts.

1 Corinthians 1:2–3—To those sanctified in Christ Jesus and called to be holy, together with all those everywhere who call on the name of our Lord Jesus Christ—their Lord and ours: Grace and peace to you from God our Father and the Lord Jesus Christ.

1 Corinthians 11:33—So then, my brothers, when you come together to eat, wait for each other.

1 Corinthians 14:26—What then shall we say, brothers? When you come together, everyone has a hymn, or a word of instruction, a revelation, a tongue or an interpretation. All of these must be done for the strengthening of the church.

2 Corinthians 6:14—Do not be yoked together with unbelievers. For what do righteousness and wickedness have in common? Or what fellowship can light have with darkness?

Ephesians 2:22—And in him you too are being built together to become a dwelling in which God lives by his Spirit.

Ephesians 3:6—This mystery is that through the gospel the Gentiles are heirs together with Israel, members together of one body, and sharers together in the promise in Christ Jesus.

Ephesians 3:16–19—I pray that out of his glorious riches he may strengthen you with power through his Spirit in your inner being, so that Christ may dwell in your hearts through faith. And I pray that you, being rooted and established in love, may have power, together with all the saints, to grasp how wide and long and high and deep is the love of Christ, and to know this love that surpasses knowledge—that you may be filled to the measure of all the fullness of God.

Ephesians 4:16—From him the whole body, joined and held together by every supporting ligament, grows and builds itself up in love, as each part does its work.

Colossians 1:17—He is before all things, and in him all things hold together.

Colossians 3:14—And over all these virtues put on love, which binds them all together in perfect unity.

1 Thessalonians 4:17—After that, we who are still alive and are left will be caught up together with them in the clouds to meet the Lord in the air. And so we will be with the Lord forever.

1 Thessalonians 5:10—He died for us so that, whether we are awake or asleep, we may live together with him.

Hebrews 10:25—Let us not give up meeting together, as some are in the habit of doing, but let us encourage one another—and all the more as you see the Day approaching.

3 John 1:8—We ought therefore to show hospitality to such men so that we may work together for the truth.

chosen // lesson 3 day 4 // 219

HOW TO HAVE TRUE
COMMUNITY

Fill in the top section of each column with your own definition of each word. Imagine you were explaining this to a friend, and write what these three things mean using your own words.

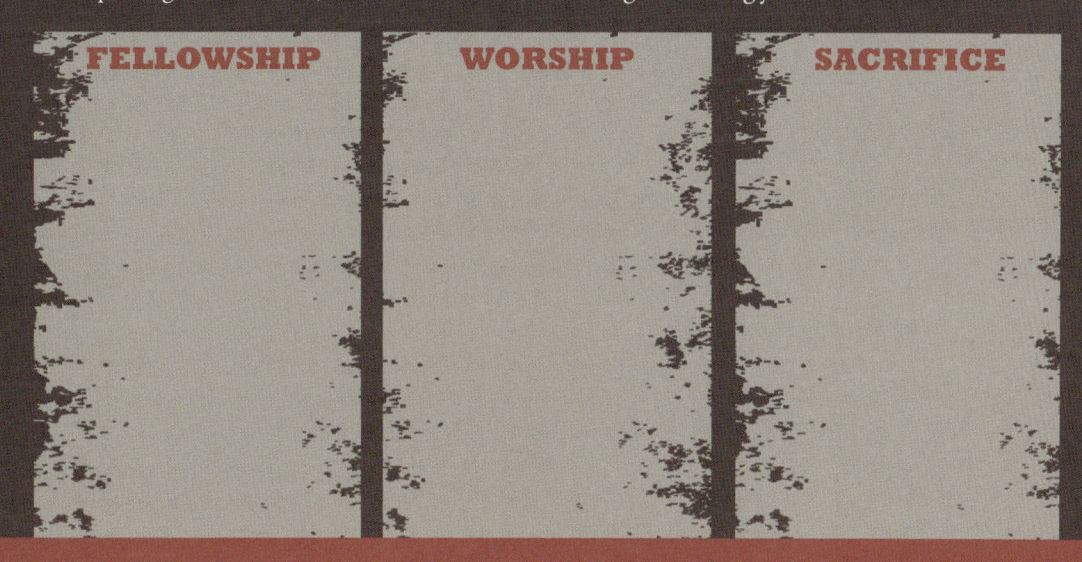

FELLOWSHIP

WORSHIP

SACRIFICE

Now, in the bottom half of each column, write examples of how you and your friends can do these three things. How can you fellowship? How can you worship together? How can you live sacrificially? Use this space to brainstorm. Then, talk to your friends about actually doing some or all of these things.

THE O.C.
THE ORIGINAL CHURCH

Let's take a closer look at the very first community of Christ-followers: the first church. They were in Jerusalem, from all around the ancient world. These Jewish believers had traveled to the city for an annual religious festival called Pentecost. About six weeks earlier, Jesus had been crucified and resurrected and had been appearing to His disciples for 40 days. Now, the Holy Spirit had been given to the Church, enabling people to preach the gospel. Peter stood up and preached a Spirit-filled sermon that resulted in 3,000 people believing in Christ and being baptized.

OK. Read Acts 2:42–47. You're probably familiar with these verses by now. But now you will pay extra attention to certain words in verse 42.

"They" The first word reminds us that this was something the community was doing. The things described apply to everyone in this first church. As you read about these things, think about your own church and/or youth group. Think about your own group of friends.

"devoted themselves" In the Greek, it is easy to see that this means they are continually doing the things it is about to describe (this is a regular part of the lives of the community of faith).

"the apostles' teaching" Look up Matthew 28:19–20. After Jesus was resurrected, He told the apostles to go make new disciples by teaching people to obey everything He had taught them... So when Acts 2:42 says the first church was devoted to the apostles' teaching, it is the same thing as Jesus' teaching. In this blank, write a time you will commit to reading your Bible each day (This book can help, too.) _____ Now write the name of someone you will talk to about the things you are reading. Since the idea is to be in community, whom will you ask to keep you accountable to spending time in God's Word? _____

"the fellowship" Remember, this means an intentional gathering of people for a purpose and with a mission. You should be intentional about spending quality time with other believers, encouraging each other to live out your faith. Write a time each week you can spend getting to know other people better. _____ Also, write the name of someone you would like to know better, someone whom you think could help you grow stronger in your faith. _____

"the breaking of bread" This can mean either eating together, simply sharing a meal, or taking communion. The Bible talks about both of these being a regular part of the original Church's life. Now, you may not have as much control over when your church has communion, but you can have a worshipful attitude in your daily meals. Let's be honest, lunch conversations can have a pretty big impact on your day. Name some friends you will eat lunch with during the week. _____

"prayer" This is talking about worship in general. It could even include songs. (When you sing in church, the hope is that you are making the words your own personal prayers.) Write the name of a friend or several friends you will commit to praying for and praying with every week. _____ Remember, this is about community (the original church) not just your own private prayer time. So decide now to share your prayer requests and to pray for your friends.

Now, verses 43–47 reveal that when the original church was continually devoted to those things they experienced God's power in awesome ways (literally), and God added more and more people to their community all the time. Pray that God would fill you with His Spirit and give you a heart for community. Pray that you would have a mentality of "togetherness," sharing your life with the people around you... continually devoting yourselves to the apostles' teaching, fellowship, breaking bread, and prayer.

chosen // lesson 3 day 6 //221

IS YOUR COMMUNITY ALL FLUFF & NO MEAT?

*How much substance is there to your youth group?
Your church? Your friendships?*

*Are you being fed the Word?
Are you hungry for God's Word, true
worship, fellowship, and sacrificial living?*

DINER

chosen // lesson 4 day 1 // 222

Do you ever wish that you could just stay at the high points in life?

Have you ever been at a low point and then someone helped you back up?

Pray that God would help you develop a healthy balance between your expectations and your realities . . .

What you have and what you can share . . .

Where you need help and where you can help others.

DEVOTION

"Jenga!" Yes, it's a real word. The Parker Brothers skill game is named after a Swahili word meaning "to build." Players shout this when the Jenga tower tumbles over, spilling 54 wooden blocks onto the table. The game is simple. Players alternate turns, using one hand to remove a block from the lower part of the tower and then replace it on top without causing the whole thing to crash. All blocks are identical in size, so the key is balance. As long as the players can keep the weight evenly distributed, then the tower grows higher and the game gets more exciting. If anyone is clumsy or uses poor judgment in placing the block, everything collapses.

While Jenga can be a fun personal challenge (The world record is 40-2/3 levels high) and a boredom killer when hanging out with friends (especially if you write stupid dares on the blocks), Jenga can actually teach us an important lesson.

Read 2 Corinthians 8:9. Paul explains that Jesus humbled Himself, giving up His royal position in heaven to come to earth and save us. This is a truth that you're probably familiar with and grateful for. You're glad Jesus came to earth, was born to a poor teenage mom, was raised by a blue-collar carpenter dad, taught a bunch of ordinary fishermen before He suffered a criminal execution, and was buried in a borrowed tomb. But you know He got up. God raised Him from the dead! And now we can all experience abundant and eternal life in Him!

The fact that Christ became poor so that we might be made rich with Him is more than just spiritual truth; it is a practical example to follow in our lives. That's where Jenga comes in . . .

Read verses 13–15. As a follower of Christ, your stuff is not your stuff and your life is not your life. Paul said that God has allowed some people to be rich and others are poor but that those who have enough should share it with those who don't. Then, someday it will inevitably be the reverse situation. You take turns and the goal is balance, just like in Jenga.

We're all made in God's image, so you're no more or less deserving of comforts or even necessities in life than the next person. You just may happen to be in a better position at the moment. So take what God has given you in the moment and give it to someone else, balancing things out. If any of us start getting greedy, the "tower" gets lopsided and life comes crashing down. You've probably noticed this in the world or in the news lately.

You have things. However much or little, you have plenty of things. There are other people who have hardly anything. So, share. Show the love of Christ by forfeiting your claim on wealth and comforts for the sake of someone else. This isn't just a nice thing to do; it is the Christlike thing to do. It brings glory to God. It's a way to practically live out the spiritual truth that changed your life and may change someone else's life as a result of your generosity. Begin praying about material things you can use, share, or give away. Begin praying about talents, abilities, or passions you can use to share the love of Christ with the people around you. Remember, Christ did it for you.

Now it's your turn.

chosen // lesson 4 day 3 // 224

My "Abundant" Life

Use the following spaces to brainstorm, list, take inventory, or map out your "budget" and spending habits.

How much money I am given or earn each week/month:

Things I spend money on each week:

How much money I spend on those things:

Total amount I spend each week:

Things that I own but rarely or never use:

Things I have a lot of:

How I can use these things to show the love of Christ:

In 2009, the Lincoln penny celebrated its 100th birthday.

About 1,000 pennies are made every second by the U.S. Treasury.
(How many thousands of pennies have been made in the amount of time it has taken you to read these random facts?)

It costs the government more to make a penny than it is worth.
(As of 2009, it cost about 1.4 cents to make a one-cent penny.)

Where do all of these pennies go?
A lot are spent. Many are lost. Often they are just left on counters for the next person to spend. Some are thrown away. The rest are piling up in a jar or cup somewhere. Oh yeah, and don't forget about railroad tracks and those souvenir machines that flatten pennies...

So, how many unwanted pennies do you think are abandoned every day? What would they add up to?

What do you do with your pennies?

What COULD you do with your pennies?

Think about it. Pray about it.

Jesus said it doesn't take much; you just have to give from your heart and spend your life faithfully. Trust God with what you have. Get creative about finding a way to use what most people don't want to meet other people's needs.

What difference could you make with pennies?

Jesus sat down opposite the place where the offerings were put and watched the crowd putting their money into the temple treasury. Many rich people threw in large amounts. But a poor widow came and put in two very small copper coins, worth only a fraction of a penny.

Calling his disciples to him, Jesus said, "I tell you the truth, this poor widow has put more into the treasury than all the others. They all gave out of their wealth; but she, out of her poverty, put in everything— all she had to live on."
—Mark 12:41–44

All right. Look up John 3:16 or say it from memory. You've done this before, but do it again for a refresher. You will compare this verse to another verse almost just like it. Fill in the blanks below.

_____ showed His love
by _____ His only Son
so that we would not _____
but instead have _____.

Look up 1 John 3:16 and fill in the blanks below with the same words as above.

We show _____ love
by _____ our lives
so that others would not _____
but instead have _____.

So, as we've seen before, we're supposed to follow the example of Christ by living out practically the spiritual truth of the gospel. Because of God's love, Christ gave His life for us. And WE should be willing to give anything in our lives for those same people whom God loves. If we're part of His family, then we'll share what we have with other family members, right?

Back up a little and see how John described life. He said there are only two options in life, only two families you can be a part of. Fill in the blanks that go with 1 John 3:10.

You are either a child of _____ or a child of the _____.
Anyone who does not _____ or _____ is not a child of _____, but a child of the _____.

Assuming you would prefer to be a child of God instead of a child of the devil, let's see what it means to practice righteousness and love your neighbor. Read verses 11–18. So murder and hate are obviously the opposite of love. But in verse 17, John revealed a shocking truth . . . LOVING YOUR BROTHER MEANS YOU CAN'T IGNORE HIS NEED.

Put another way: To not help someone is the way a child of the devil would act.

To see someone and help meet that need if you're able is to show the love of God, the love of your Father who loved you and gave His very best for you.

Using the blanks in verse 17, fill in your own name, making it a reminder and prayer. Pray that you would do more than call yourself a follower of Christ. Pray that God's love would fill you up and move you to action, loving your brother.

If _____ has material possessions and sees _____ brother in need but has no pity on him, how can the love of God be in _____?

GOD HAS BLESSED AMERICA

About half of the world lives on less than $2 a day. (Meaning, if you get $15 a week allowance or work two hours a week at a minimum wage job... you have more income than half the planet. That's not even taking into account the food, water, shelter, clothing, education, and other stuff that is just for fun in your life.)

If you worked a minimum wage job for nine or ten hours a week, you would earn more than what 80 percent of the world's population has to survive.

North America has only 5–6 percent of the world's population, but over 30 percent of the world's wealth. Think about it this way: If you were in a room with 20 people and there were three cheeseburgers, you would get one and the other 19 people could split the other 2 burgers. Three blankets? You get one; they share the other two. You get the idea. That means there are some seriously hungry people out there... and they're cold, too.

So how will you be a blessing today, and every day? What will you use or give to bless someone today?

Did you know that adult salmon really do swim back upstream to the place of their birth? You've probably heard about this rebel-with-a-cause, current-defying fish.

Two species in Idaho, the chinook and sockeye salmon, journey over 900 miles! An overwhelming desire for their home is hardwired into their brains somehow, causing them to endure incredible resistance and persevere through seemingly impossible conditions.

It is simply what these fish do. They're salmon. They swim upstream.

What about you? As a follower of Christ, He has set you apart. Made you holy. Filled you with His Spirit. Giving you what should be an intense longing for your true home—your heavenly home with your Heavenly Father. As you grow more mature in your faith, is your behavior influenced by this desire for a life and a world other than the little pond in which you currently swim?

Against all odds, you and your friends have to fight against a culture that is rushing in the opposite direction—running away from God. Don't worry; you'll make it. Go against the flow.

DEVOTION

Jessica Watson was tired of being treated like a little girl. She knew that she had the ability, confidence, and sense of adventure to do something great, something life-changing. So by age 15 she began serious preparation for a trip around the world. As if it wasn't a bold enough dream to travel around the world as a teenager, Jessica planned to do it alone . . . in a boat. Well, technically in a yacht named Ella's Pink Lady. After completing her training, arrangements, and practice runs (including a hard lesson learned from a middle-of-the-night collision with a 63,000 ton freighter), she was ready. The young Australian set off on her solo voyage on October 18, 2009, at age 16. She returned home to Sydney before her 17th birthday in May of 2010. Dodging icebergs, braving fierce winds, and navigating rough waters, Jessica set a world record for being the youngest person to sail nonstop and unassisted around the globe.

With that bold venture in mind, read 2 Timothy 1:7. Paul reminded his young friend Timothy, that God has filled Him with the Holy Spirit. Life would be rough and unpredictable, especially as a Christ-follower. When devoting his life to Christ, going with the flow was no longer an option. The young man would face stormy seas, so to speak, but God had given him the ability to face adversity with confidence.

Your life isn't always going to be smooth sailing, either. Like Timothy and Jessica, you don't have to shy away from the challenges before you. But unlike Jessica, you are not solo and unassisted. Notice that Paul said, "God did not give us . . ." meaning you're not alone. As Christ-followers we have all been filled with His power, love, and discipline. If you were going to sail around the world, you'd better have serious toughness, passion, and discipline. The same is true for a life of following Christ. It is a matchless adventure, literally a life changing experience, and God has equipped you and everyone on the journey with a "spirit of power, of love, and of self-discipline."

You're not just another teenager. You have been given the very Spirit of God. You are filled with the character of Christ to accomplish great things for His glory (not your own fame). So whatever's in your way, whatever daunting task or seemingly impossible obstacle is freaking you out, take courage. Know that fear is not from God. If He has called you to radical steps of faith in obedience, He will see those plans through to completion. He believes in you, maybe more than you believe in yourself, so forge ahead with boldness today. He has given you a spirit of power, love, and self-discipline.

FACE YOUR FEARS

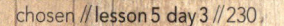

It's not easy to buck the system, go against the flow, swim upstream, fight the power, stick it to da' man, stick out like a sore thumb so embrace your inner rebel as you march to the beat of a different drum.

When you follow Christ, you and all of your friends will be set apart from the world in which you live. You'll be aliens in a strange land. Strangers in a foreign place. Does that scare you? Be honest.

Use the space below to write out the places where you feel most pressured to conform to the ways of the world. Write about the things that the culture and your friends value or get involved with that you know go against your faith.

What are your greatest fears when you think about living out this life of faith in relationship with God and His people? What scares you about being different from the world around you?

Write all of those fears in the space below.

Now, just be honest about these fears. Give them to God in prayer. Pray for His Spirit to replace your fearful spirit with His Spirit of power, love, and self-discipline. (remember yesterday?)

chosen // lesson 5 day 4 // 231

DO PEOPLE EASILY RECOGNIZE YOU AS BEING "DIFFERENT"?

5

Armor of God, Suit Up.

So, you may have gotten the impression that living for God is like a battle. And you'd be right to have that feeling. Ever heard of the expression "spiritual warfare"? It's the real deal. You've read this week about how life is tough but God puts His Spirit inside you. But He also doesn't just send you into the fight vulnerable and exposed. Just like any good soldier or any good athlete, you'd better suit up before you head into battle. Each day is a cosmic battle in which you are caught in the middle.

So put on your armor.

Grab your sword . . . or if you don't know what that means yet, grab your Bible. Read Ephesians 6:10–12. Answer the question for each verse below.

(v. 10) Where do you find strength? _____
(v. 11) Whose schemes do you need to stand firm against? _____
(v. 12) No matter what it looks like, your struggle is not against whom? _____ It is against [

Awesome. So no matter what you're facing, those struggles and attacks are a spiritual battle. No matter how badly someone has hurt you or how hateful or violent a person has been to you, they were being used as weapons of mass destruction in your life. They are not the enemy. They were used by the Enemy to get to you. Warning: Now that you've identified your Enemy, you'd better suit up, because the Enemy is about to bring the heat your way.

Read verses 13–18. Fill in the blanks below.

(v. 13) Put on the _____ armor of God. Not some of it, or just your favorite or the most comfortable parts. You need every single piece of armor to fight the good fight.
What are you supposed to do once you've put on the armor of God? _____

So what is the armor?
(v. 14) the belt of _____
     the breastplate of _____
(v. 15) the boots of _____
(v. 16) the shield of _____
(v. 17) the helmet of _____
     the sword of _____

(v. 18) And once you've put on the armor, you do what? _____ When? _____

So pray right now, thanking God for equipping you for the spiritual battle. Pray that your faith would bring you alongside others, and together your shields would join to form a mighty wall that no attack from the devil can penetrate. Pray that you would never rely on your own strength, but that you would trust the one weapon He has given you in spiritual warfare: God's Word. (That doesn't mean you beat people up with the Bible; remember your battle is not against people, it is spiritual warfare.)

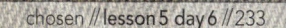

PRAY THAT YOU WOULD BE CLOTHED IN RIGHTEOUSNESS.

So let us put aside the deeds of darkness and put on the armor of light.
—Romans 13:12

Clothe yourselves with the Lord Jesus Christ, and do not think about how to gratify the desires of the sinful nature.
—Romans 13:14

TAKE OFF YOUR MASK.
GET BELOW THE SURFACE.
DOES ANYBODY KNOW THE "REAL" YOU?
DO YOU REALLY KNOW YOUR FRIENDS?

BE TRANSPARENT.

PRAY FOR COMPLETE HONESTY
IN YOUR RELATIONSHIPS.

DEVOTION

Band-Aids. Who didn't love Band-Aids as a child? They were awesome. They were battle scars and fashion statements. If you were really lucky you had some awesome cartoon character or design stuck to you like a temporary tattoo. Some children beg for their favorite Band-Aid, just because they like to wear them. Maybe you were even this child. You thought Band-Aids had healing powers. Just wearing one made you feel better.

But something happens as you get older. The bright and colorful cartoons of those kiddie Band-Aids don't look so cool anymore. In fact, they look embarrassing. So you get the plain, old-school kind, or maybe the clear kind. (Though who are we kidding? They're far from invisible.) You try to hide these wounds, flaws, and scars. You don't want anyone to see what ugly thing has happened, bringing pain or embarrassment into your life. You want to hide it until it heals on it's own. Most people want their imperfections covered up, never revealing the wound underneath…

Read James 5:13–18. Prayer is powerful. It heals. You may not have ever experienced a literal healing as a result of prayer, at least not that you would acknowledge as miraculous, but the Bible is clear about this. Prayer is powerful. James says that in good or bad times God's people need to pray.

Take a close look at verse 16.

Read it again.

Remember, James was writing to communities of Christ-followers. He was not instructing some ritualistic confession to strangers. James was saying that in your circle of trusted relationships, the friends and spiritual leaders in your life, be honest about everything. Even sin. Especially sin. When you try to hide sin and wait for it to just heal on it's own, it grows into a deadly sickness, poisoning both you and the community around you. So James said to confess our sins to each other and pray for each other. Nobody is saying you have to parade it around, showing it off. But, there's no need to feel embarrassed or grossed out by your own sin or anybody else's. If you care about each other and if you desire to have a healthy relationship with your community and with God, then you have to pray. In the good times, bad times, sick times, and when you've fallen into sin. Confess. Pray. Be healed.

Brothers, if someone is caught in a sin, you who are spiritual should restore him gently. But watch yourself, or you also may be tempted. Carry each other's burdens, and in this way you will fulfill the law of Christ. If anyone thinks he is something when he is nothing, he deceives himself. Each one should test his own actions. Then he can take pride in himself, without comparing himself to somebody else, for each one should carry his own load. —Galatians 6:1–5

Think about life as a hike. It is a journey. Christ is leading the way. We are following in His footsteps. You are responsible for your own "stuff." Don't expect anyone else to pick up your slack. Your sin is on you. No matter what the culture tells us, what you choose is nobody's fault but your own.

BUT . . . Like any great hike with friends, people will share the load as well. This benefits everyone when each person expects to carry his or her own "burden" and also volunteers to help everyone else in the group with their burdens.

So know that you are ultimately responsible, BUT also know that we need to help each other. In helping others with whatever weighs them down, we are fulfilling the Law of Christ. . . .

He wants to free you and your friends up from the sin that weighs each of you down. He does this through prayer and other people.

And remember, Jesus promises:

For my yoke is easy and my burden is light—Matthew 11:30

chosen // lesson 6 day 4 //237

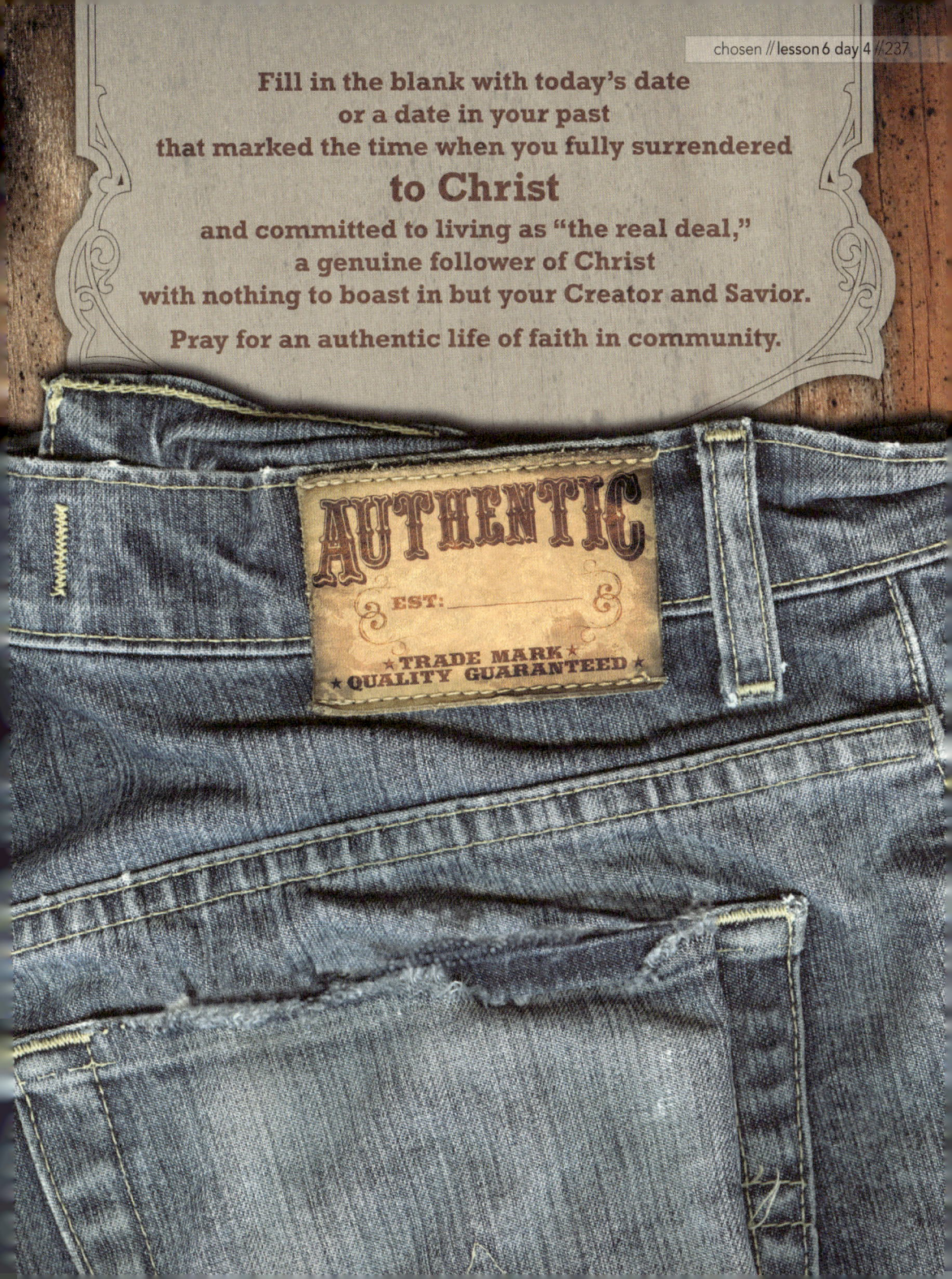

Fill in the blank with today's date
or a date in your past
that marked the time when you fully surrendered
to Christ
and committed to living as "the real deal,"
a genuine follower of Christ
with nothing to boast in but your Creator and Savior.

Pray for an authentic life of faith in community.

AUTHENTIC
EST: _____
★ TRADE MARK ★
★ QUALITY GUARANTEED ★

How important is honesty? So what if you're not completely real? What's the big deal if you tell a little white lie, or maybe you don't tell the whole truth? Who's it hurting if you mislead people or try to make yourself look better?

Well, let's look at two very different examples of honesty, generosity, and faith in the original church. Think back to Jerusalem, just a short time after Peter's big sermon at Pentecost. (Remember the whole tongues of fire and 3,000 people getting saved and baptized thing?)

Compare the two stories by reading the Scriptures below and filling in the blanks:

Acts 4:32–37
All the believers were _____ in heart and mind.
They shared _____ they had, considering _____ their own possession.
What was the name of the man who sold a field, giving everything away? _____
Where did he lay the money? _____

Acts 5:1–10
A husband and wife _____ to test the Spirit of the Lord.
They kept _____ of what they had, since it was their own possession.
What was the name of the man and woman who sold land, lying about giving everything away? _____ and _____
Where did they fall when they lied about the money? _____

Wow. So . . . yeah. God takes it pretty seriously to say the least. On the one hand, you had a community that was one in heart and mind. On the other, you had a couple in whom Satan filled their hearts. On the one hand, Joseph/Barnabas laid his gift at the Apostles' feet. On the other, Ananias and Sapphira fell dead at the Apostles' feet. Why? Both stories involve selling land and giving money to the church to help the poor. But the difference is that Ananias and Sapphira lied. Peter even says that they didn't have to give all of the money away. It was their choice. But we can assume that since these two stories are back to back, that the married couple wanted to look good in front of everyone, gaining the respect that Barnabas probably received. They sort of did a good thing, but they were not sincere. They were trying to look good in front of the church . . . maybe trying to impress others. But God knows our hearts.

Peter says that when we lie or try to look like something we're not, were not lying to men, we're lying to _____.

I don't know about you, but I'd rather live in the Acts 4 scenario than in the Acts 5 scenario. Are you more like Barnabas or Ananias and Sapphira? Think about it. Honestly. Would you rather experience life in a community full of awe, united in Christ, sharing and being real with each other? Or would you test the limits, pretending to be something you're not, killing relationships and worship?

It's your life. How you spend it is up to you.

WHO ARE YOU FOOLING?

Maybe your parents. Maybe some adults. Maybe your friends. Maybe. You may even try to fool yourself. But you can't.

And you're not fooling God.

Stop trying so hard.
Be real.

Pray that God would free you from feeling like you have to impress others. Pray that you would find freedom and confidence in His sight, knowing that you don't have to impress Him, either. God loves you. He has chosen you. He has brought you into His family. So get real with God. Get real with yourself. Get real with your friends. Get real with your family.

It's not only a relief. It's a great joy to truly know and be known, love and be loved.

ALL ABOUT YOU:
Living a Life of Worship

Worshiping God takes many forms. It can be singing. It can be silence. It can be technical. It can be messy. It can be alone. It can be in community. It can be whatever God wants it to be. Why? Because, worship is all about God. As long as He's the focus, almost anything can be an act of worship. It's that simple.

In this section, we will discuss what it means to worship, Who we worship, and why we worship Him. This is your chance to get real with God and let Him be the center of your attention. If you really want to get to know God and experience Him in worship, here's a tip: Start each time of worship (including every time you read a page of this book for the next six weeks) by telling God: "It's all about You." It'll change your whole perspective. Try it. You'll see...

- LESSON 1: Knowing The One We Worship — pg 242-247
- LESSON 2: Worship - It's His Call To Make — pg 248-253
- LESSON 3: An Audience of One — pg 254-259
- LESSON 4: Not Confined To A Place — pg 260-265
- LESSON 5: Sacrifice - A Primary Ingredient — pg 266-271
- LESSON 6: Worship Is A Forever Thing — pg 272-275

all about // lesson 1 day 1 // 242

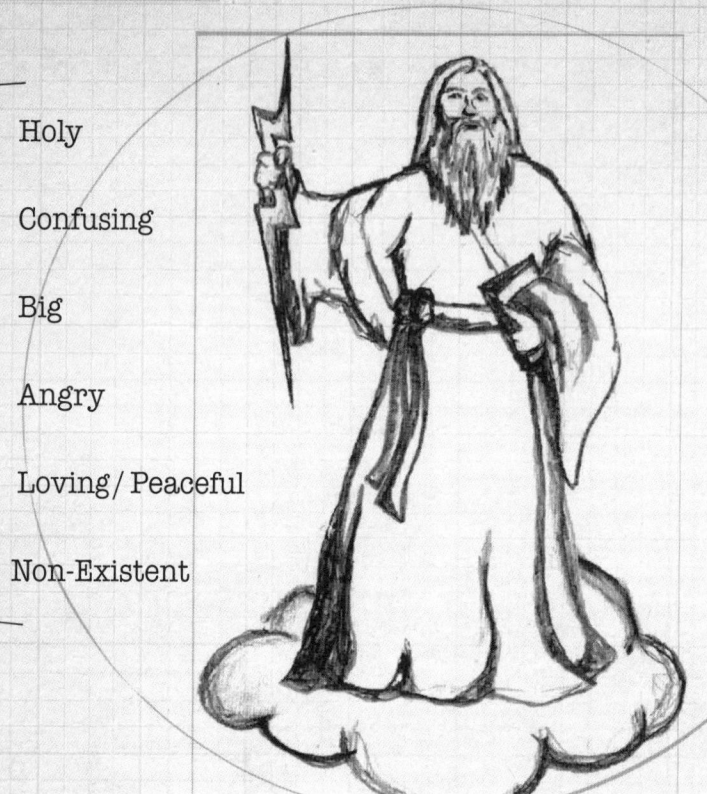

- Holy
- Confusing
- Big
- Angry
- Loving/Peaceful
- Non-Existent

- Old Man with a Beard
- Merciful
- Distant
- Constant

KNOWING THE ONE WE WORSHIP

It's hard to feel excited about something when you don't know a lot about it. You know those tech geeks that get so amped up when Apple introduces a new gadget? They bombard you with how amazing it is, down to the tiniest detail. "The CPU's are really improved on this model, as opposed to the last version when the RAM wasn't even 248k!" Then they laugh, and you laugh because you think you should. And it's awkward.

But they love it. They are excited about it, and they can tell you anything you want to know about it. This is how it is with anything in life. The more you know, the more you can fall in love with it. The more you love it, the more you want to know...

Why would God be any different? We have weekly services devoted to praising something we may or may not know much about. The more we know about God, His character, who He is, and why He loves us, the more we know about how to worship Him and why we worship Him.

The world tells a conflicting story about who God is, if it acknowledges Him at all. Take a moment to pray that God would show you his character, so that you might worship Him better, so that you can make His name known.

Think about WHO God is. Think about the attributes with which people label God. (Some are above) Would you add any? Take any away?

all about // lesson 1 day 2 //243

Today, a name may not mean much more than the fact that someone's parents liked the way it sounds. Think about it. Do you know what your name means? Chance are, you don't. We don't have symbolic or descriptive names anymore, such as: "Brave and mighty warrior princess," or "One who sits on the sofa eating cheese puffs."

In biblical times, names were loaded with meaning. You can usually tell a lot about somebody in Scripture once you know the meaning of his or her name. This is especially true in relation to God. The names used for God reveal a lot about His character. And when you get a better understanding of who God is, you will respond to Him in more meaningful worship.

Today, spend some time getting to know God. Look up the verses and write the different characteristics/names for God in the space provided. Think about how knowing God in these different ways affects your worship of Him.

GENESIS 1:1

GENESIS 16:13

GENESIS 22:14

EXODUS 17:15

EXODUS 31:13

DEUTERONOMY 32:4

1 SAMUEL 17:45

PSALM 23:1

PSALM 91:1–2

ISAIAH 9:6

ISAIAH 54:5

JEREMIAH 8:18

JEREMIAH 23:6

JEREMIAH 32:37

MATTHEW 1:23

JOHN 14:6

JOHN 14:17

REVELATION 22:13

WHAT'S IN A NAME?

all about // lesson 1 day 3 //244

HOW DO YOU SEE GOD?

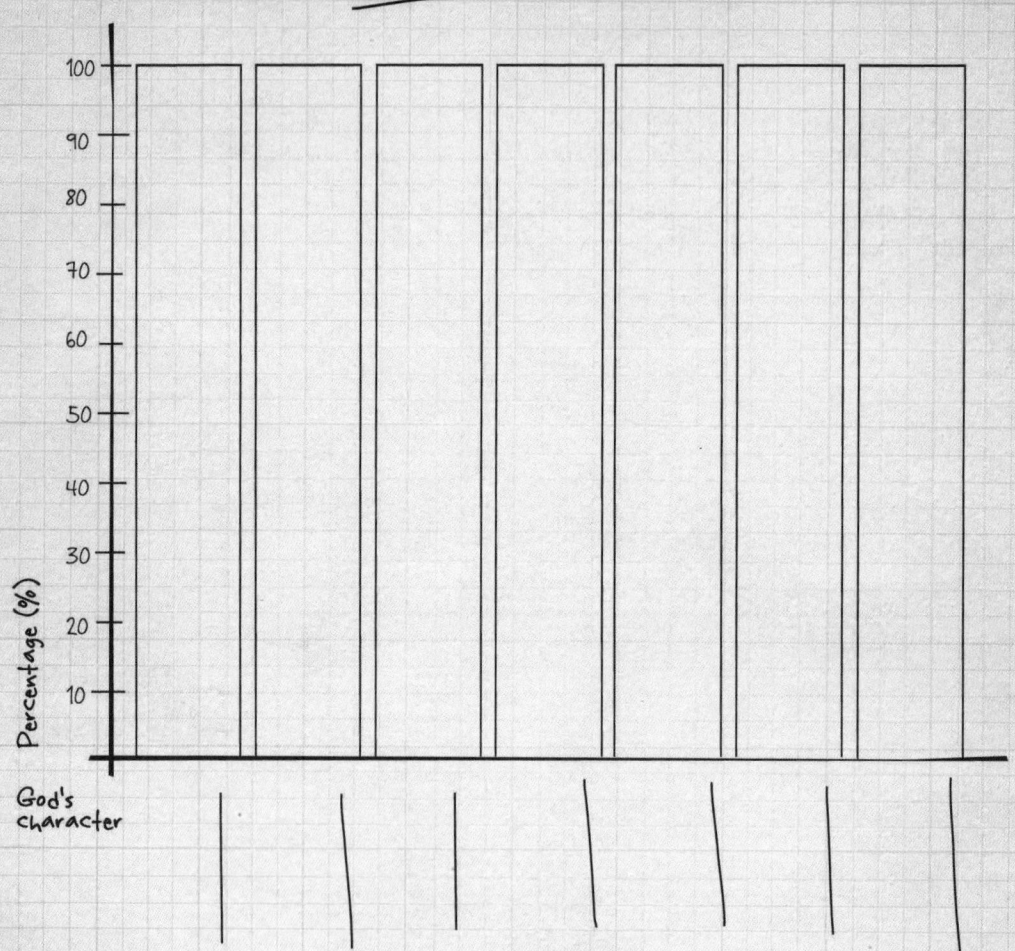

Percentage (%) — 100, 90, 80, 70, 60, 50, 40, 30, 20, 10

God's character

Before we can deal with who God really is, we have to take a look at our preconceived notions about Him. We get these ideas (no matter how right or wrong they are) from parents, friends, Sunday school teachers ... and the list goes on. So take a minute and think about who you think God is. Don't just go straight to the "Church" answer, but really consider what you think. Write what you consider God's top seven character traits and give Him a percentage. Do you think He's good? How good do you think God is ... 75 percent? Maybe more or maybe less? After you've finished filling in your graph, take a moment and think about why you believe these things about God. Tomorrow we will take a look at who God really is, regardless of what you think.

all about // lesson 1 day 4 // 245

WHO GOD REALLY IS

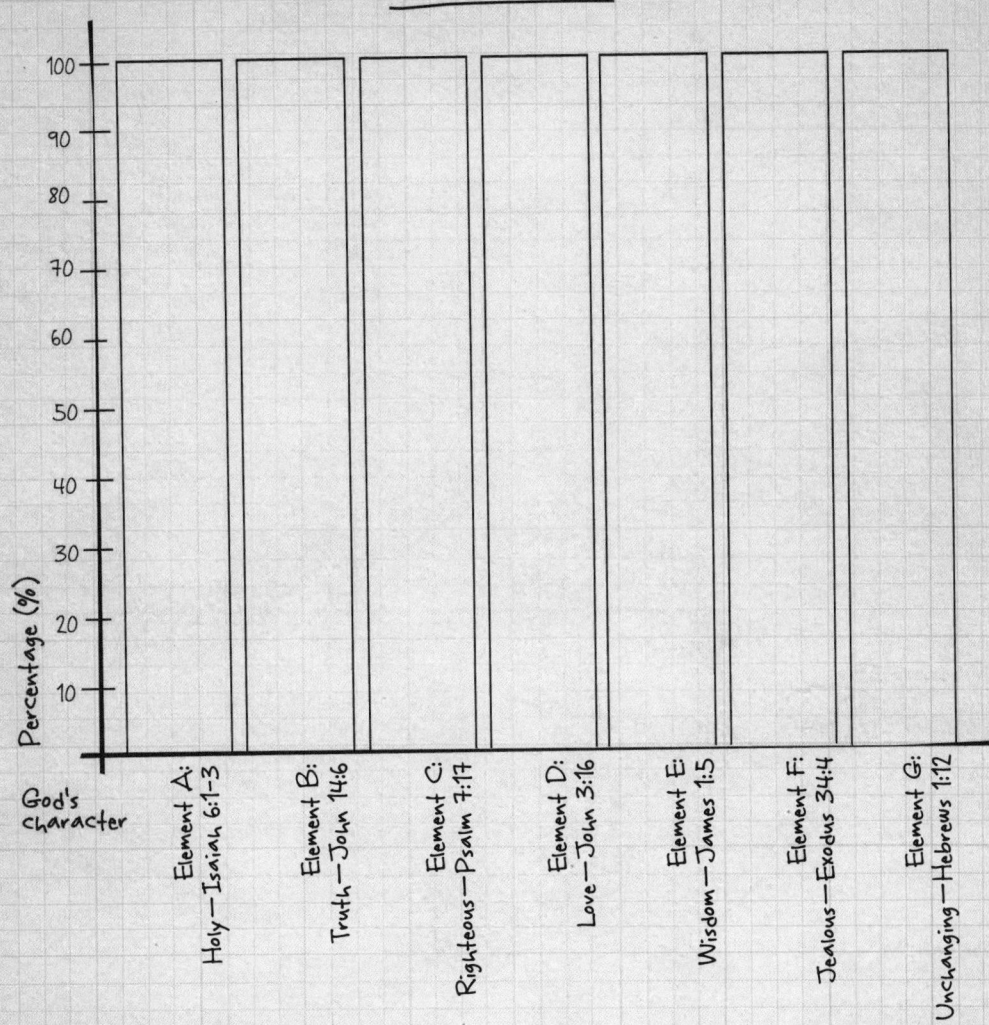

Bar chart with y-axis labeled "Percentage (%)" from 0 to 100, and x-axis labeled "God's character" with the following bars (all at 100%):

- Element A: Holy—Isaiah 6:1-3
- Element B: Truth—John 14:6
- Element C: Righteous—Psalm 7:17
- Element D: Love—John 3:16
- Element E: Wisdom—James 1:5
- Element F: Jealous—Exodus 34:14
- Element G: Unchanging—Hebrews 1:12

Yesterday we took a look at what you thought about God and why you thought those things about Him. Today, we will look at who God really is based on what the Bible tells us. First, shade each bar completely, making each attribute 100 percent.

How do these two charts differ from one another? How are they similar? Grab your Bible and look up the Scriptures that accompany the new chart. What do you think about what the Bible says? Do you agree or disagree?

linked // lesson 1 day 5 //246

GOD REVEALED

BURNING BUSH
To Whom: Moses, Leader of the Israelites, Stuttered, Afraid
Why: To reveal that God was about to bring His people out of Egypt
Specifications: 50000°F | O2 + Heat + Fuel = Fire | Fire typically burns its host, not so in this case. Bush did not burn up.

THE ANGEL OF THE LORD
To Whom: Shadrach, Meshach, Abednego, King Nebuchadnezzar and the court
Why: To protect them from the fiery furnace and display His glory
Specifications: Furnace heated seven times hotter than usual | Casualties: = three guards | three men put in the furnace; four men seen walking around | fourth man looked like a son of the gods according to King

PILLAR OF FIRE/ PILLAR OF CLOUD
To Whom: The Israelites, Blunderers and Blusterers
Why: To guide them through the desert
Specifications: By day, a Pillar of Cloud | By night, a Pillar of Fire. | Each manifestation ensured the Israelites could travel at any time of day.

DOVE
To Whom: Jesus and the people witnessing His baptism
Why: To show that God was pleased with Jesus
Specifications: Doves were considered acceptable as burnt offerings. | Doves can weight anywhere from .77 ounces to 8.8 pounds.

THINK ABOUT IT: God has revealed Himself in so many ways to so many people. How has God revealed Himself to you?

JESUS CHRIST
To Whom: The world and all its people
Why: To show them the Way, the Truth, and the Life
Specifications: The Greek meaning of "Christ" (Christos) means "the Anointed One." | Jesus' baptism is considered the beginning of His public ministry | Immediately following His baptism, Jesus was led into the desert where he fasted for 40 days.

DEVOTION

Have you ever been in the presence of someone amazing? That girl or guy you've got a crush on? A celebrity or athlete? Someone famous, influential, or admired? Most of us have had times in our lives when we've met somebody and simply felt overwhelmed, not knowing what to do or say. We were dumbfounded in his or her company; nothing seemed worthy of mention. After all, what could we possibly say or do that would seem as significant as he or she were in our eyes. So we do one of two things: The first option is to remain in silent awe, soaking in every moment. The second option is to try and force a response—one that is probably an embarrassing and bumbling attempt to interact with this lofty personality. Don't you wish you just knew how to act in those situations?

Have you ever felt that way about God? Like you don't know how to interact with Him? Like He is so otherworldly that He couldn't possibly relate to your life or care about you? Well fortunately, God proves over and over in Scripture that He has deep concern for our lives and goes to great lengths to have a personal relationship with us! We also see pictures of how to best respond to God when He makes Himself known to us.

Grab you Bible and open it to Exodus 3. You're probably familiar with this story. It's a classic. Read verses 1—18. Did you notice that Moses was out shepherding alone? God just showed up in this literally awesome way and said: I want to be known. I know everything about My people and I care about them. God revealed Himself in a new way. This was a new level in the relationship between God and humankind.

Like many other stories in Scripture where people "meet God," Moses immediately responded in awe. But God told him exactly what to do, and Moses obeyed (removing his sandals to show humility and respect). How could Moses possibly put into words this indescribable experience for other people? Moses asked God how to refer to Him. God introduced His personal name for the first time: YHWH or Yahweh. This name essentially means, "I AM WHO I AM." (What else can you really say about God, right?) Moses wouldn't be able to put a nice neat label on God; He was simply too big. So God said, you can know Me as the One who is God. The LORD. (Whenever you see LORD written in all capitol letters, this is the translation for YHWH. Lord means, "master.")

Finally, notice God's purpose for rescuing His people in verse 18. That's right. The LORD said He wanted to free His people from oppression so that they might know and worship Him. Wow. So if He has saved you through Jesus Christ, He wants to be known and worshiped by you, too.

Today, think about the ways God has revealed Himself to you. Probably no bushes in your yard have burst into flames, but hopefully you've had at least a moment in your life where you came to a new level in your personal relationship with God. He knows everything about you and cares about every little detail in your life. The LORD will reveal Himself in amazing ways. When He does, don't force a response. Let Him direct your response. He's the Master, Lord, and God. He is who He is. And He wants to be known and worshiped. So get to know God and worship Him in obedience to whatever the LORD says.

all about // **lesson 2 day 1** // 248

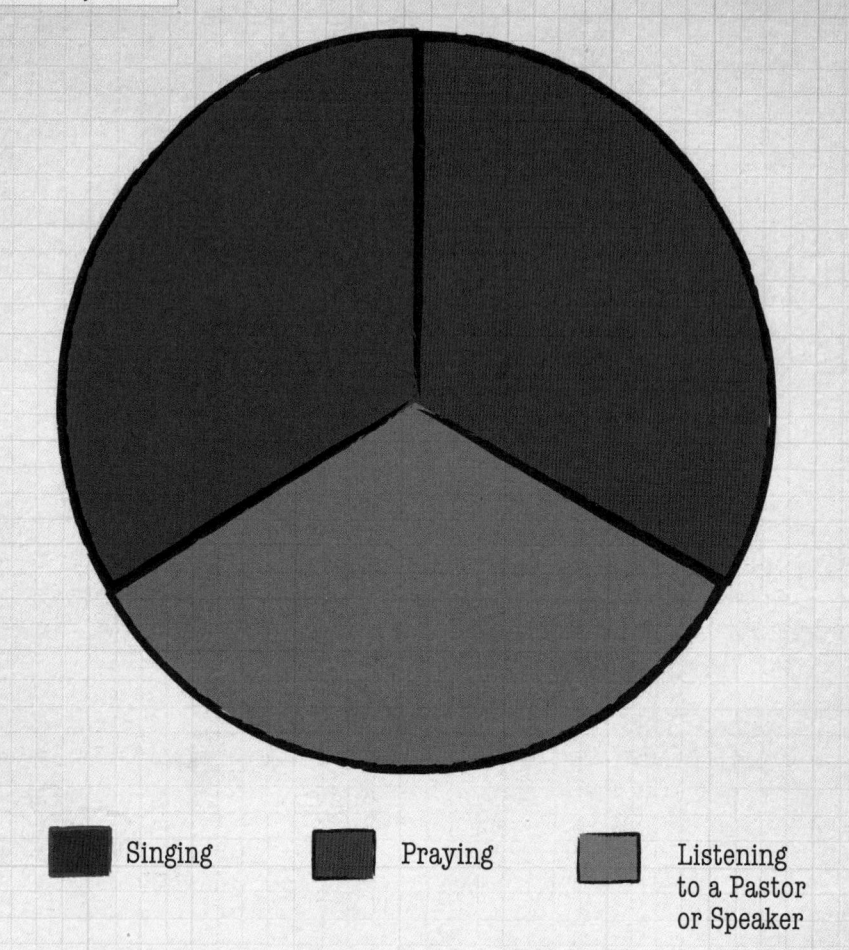

■ Singing   ■ Praying   ■ Listening to a Pastor or Speaker

WORSHIP:
IT'S HIS CALL TO MAKE

Does this pie chart look a little dull to you? Why do we constantly limit ourselves to the same ways of worship? In this section, we will take a look at all the different ways we can worship God with our hearts, souls, and minds. And it's more than just going to church every Sunday morning.

all about // lesson 2 day 2 // 249

Always rise to a standing position when visitors enter the room, and greet them after your elders do so.

Always give way to the younger child. It is your duty to look after them instead of fretting them.

PROPER ETIQUETTE

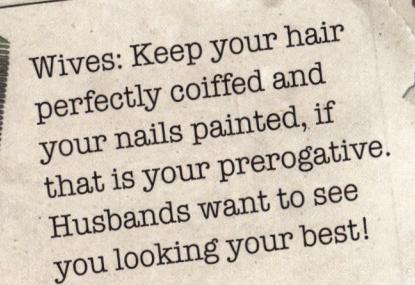

Wives: Keep your hair perfectly coiffed and your nails painted, if that is your prerogative. Husbands want to see you looking your best!

It is only acceptable to call on people between 3:30 to 5:00 p.m., unless an appointment has been arranged.

In every situation, there's proper etiquette to follow. Although the above practices are a bit outdated, the way we approach God in worship is timeless. Think about the ways you approach God. Do you adhere to timeless traditions of humility and prayer? Or do you neglect the proper avenues in which to set your mind and heart on God alone?

After a dinner party, the hostess must lead her lady guests to another room. This is where the ladies can attend to their makeup while the men talk about important issues.

DEVOTION

You must be at least this tall to ride this ride.

You've seen those words before. At one point in your life—maybe even now—that phrase has held an absolute authority over you. It didn't matter who you were or with whom you were hanging out. It didn't matter who your parents were or how much money your family did or didn't have. It didn't matter what you knew, where you shopped, or how good you were. If you didn't measure up, you weren't getting through that gate.

It might not seem fair, even though deep down you know that the standard was set by someone who knew a lot more about the experience than you did. Whoever designed the ride most likely determined the requirements. Like it or not, deep down, you know it's for your own good.

Of course, once you've crossed that threshold of the predetermined height, there's no turning back. When you're in, you're in. You eagerly follow the rules (buckle up tight, pull the shoulder cage into the locking position, keep your hands inside the car at all times, etc.) because they don't feel like rules. They're simply the necessary guidelines for enjoying an experience unlike anything in your ordinary life. You probably see where this is going, so grab your Bible.

Read Matthew 5:23—24. Jesus reminded His audience of God's standard for worship: If we want to come before God, the Creator of the universe, then our hearts better be right. Christ taught that there is no such thing as "compartmentalized worship." Basically, you can't worship a holy God with a pure heart while ignoring other areas of your life that need attention. Now, of course this doesn't mean you have to be perfect before you can worship God. But it does mean that if you want the incomparable experience of truly worshiping the God who is unlike anything in this world, you must eagerly follow His guidelines for living in right relationship with Him. (This includes living in right relationship with other people, too.)

God is the absolute authority. He knows best. His standard is not some unfair rule; it is the perfect design. To say, "It's worth it," is the understatement of the century. So right now, if there is sin in your life, confess it and repent. If there are apologies you need to make, swallow your pride and apologize. Don't allow anything in this world to become a hindrance, distracting your attention from worshiping God wholeheartedly!

all about // **lesson 2 day 4** // 251

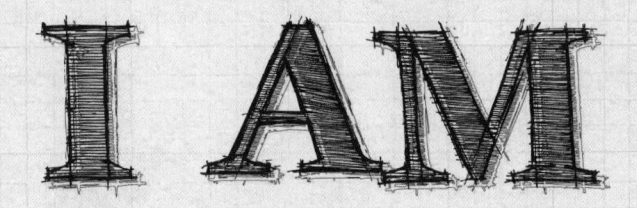

I AM

HOW HAS GOD WORKED IN YOUR LIFE? WHO IS HE IN YOUR LIFE? WHETHER YOU LOVE GOD AND WORSHIP HIM WITH ADORATION OR YOU WRESTLE WITH HIM DAILY, HIS PRESENCE HAS CHANGED YOUR LIFE. MEDITATE ON WHO GOD IS IN YOUR LIFE, THINKING ABOUT THE WORDS THAT PERFECTLY DESCRIBE HIM. USE THE SPACE PROVIDED TO WRITE OUT THESE WORDS.

Jesus wasn't afraid to come right out and say things. Often, what He said would seem radical or shocking. But when we understand that He is God and that He fulfilled the Law, most of what He said was a restatement of what God had been saying all along. In fact, Jesus summed up all of the many detailed laws in the Old Testament by quoting just two verses. Read Matthew 22:36—40. Love God. Love People (Deut. 6:5; Lev. 19:18).

OK. So worshiping God means loving Him. That's what life is all about.

Look at how Jesus worded the essence of worship and life in relationship with God. Read John 14:15. Write this verse down in the blank provided.

_____

_____.

That may sound a bit jarring at first. It doesn't seem to fit the world's definition of "love" does it? But it does perfectly echo the heart of every law in the Old Testament. Story after story and commandment after commandment deals with this very thing: people who truly love God will obey what He says. That is the very definition of a lifestyle of worship.

Don't worry; this isn't some legalistic deal in which you must keep all the rules to prove your love for God. Now read verses 16—21. Whew! This is not only a relief, but also a super-incredible promise. Jesus said that to love Him is to obey Him, but you know as well as anyone that when left to your own strength, temptation gets pretty strong and the willpower to obey God often fails. So Christ promised that after He is crucified and raised from the dead, He will return to heaven and send the Holy Spirit to be with all of His followers.

What does Jesus call the Spirit of truth in verse 16? _____.

Your Bible may translate this name as "Counselor" or as "Helper." So God's Spirit will help you know the right thing to do and provide you with the strength to keep His commands. God isn't simply saying, "Do what I say or you don't really love Me." He's saying, "Not only will I tell you the best way to live, but I'll actually help you every step of the way." Why? Because God loves you! Worship, love, life, and obedience . . . it's all about Him. He's the point of it all, and He's the One making it all possible.

Read verse 21 again. Fill in the blanks.

If you keep Christ's commands, then you love _____.

In order to keep His commands, you will be given help by _____.

If you love Jesus, you are loved by _____.

Think about that today. Jesus promises to show Himself to you. He promises to love you. He promises to help you. So will you love Him? Will you obey Him? Will you worship Him?

WORSHIP = LOVE = OBEY

Act, CLAP, Cook, Counsel, Crawl, CRY, Dance, Discover, Endure, Enter, Examine, Fast, FEEL, Find, Meditate, Mentor, MOVE, Observe, Point, Play, Pray, Prepare, Read, RECONCILE, Resolve, Rise, Run, Salute, Scream, Sell, Serve, Shield, Sing, Skip, Smell, Speak, Spin, Start, Surrender, Swim, SWING, Tackle, TASTE, teach, THROW, TOUCH, Train, Translate, Trounce, Try, Understand, Unite, Vanquish, WALK, Write, YELL

There are so many ways to worship God. We limit ourselves to singing for the most part. But your LIFE is worship, therefore every breath you take is worship, giving back to God what He has given you. Pray that God would make you mindful of every move you make on this earth, that you would glorify Him to make His name known.

all about // lesson 3 day 1 // 254

_____
_____
_____
_____
_____

WHO IS THE OBJECT OF OUR WORSHIP?

Let's be honest. A lot of things draw our attention and affection (a.k.a. our worship). This isn't meant to make you feel bad; this is just a visual to help you recognize the "idols" in your life.

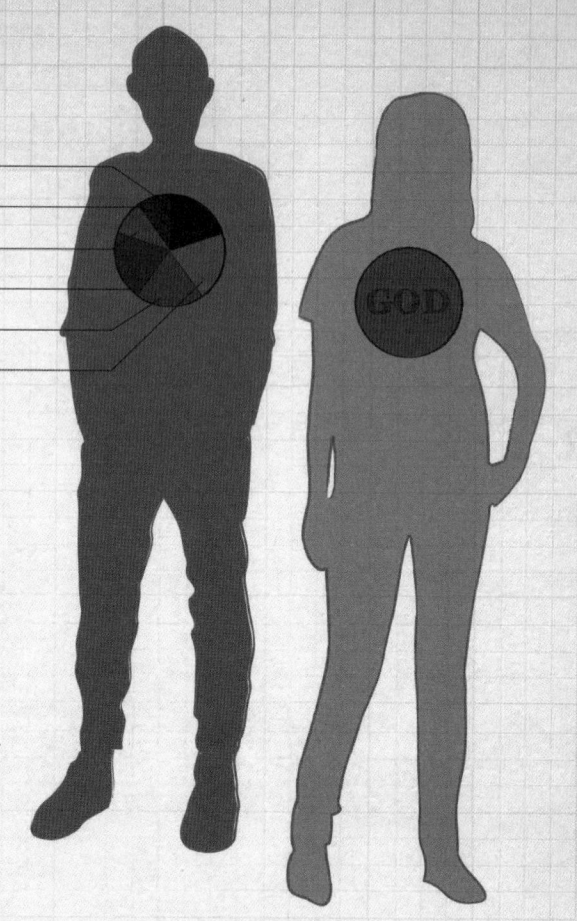

On the blank graph above, label the sections with different things that you worship (meaning things you sometimes value more than God, or things that influence your decisions more than your belief in God).

There's only One who is worthy of our worship and worthy of our praise. That's God. No one or nothing else—boyfriends or girlfriends, movies or books, the attainment of knowledge—NOTHING is more worthy of our devotion and affection than God. And He deserves all of it. Every last bit.

And God wants all of you. He doesn't want 99.9 percent of you. HE WANTS IT ALL. ALL is crucial. It's all or nothing.

The world tells us that we can worship God and still worship other things. We can worship God and a college education. We can worship God and the hope of getting married. We can worship God and money. We can worship God and ourselves. But the Bible says this isn't so. No man can serve two masters. Pray that you would give God all of your worship today.

all about // lesson 3 day 2 //255

REVERSE AUDIENCES

An audience of ONE is the goal for worship. Take a quiet moment in prayer and think about the way you worship. Do you hope others will see you and marvel at your spirituality? Did you sign up to go on that mission trip because the cute guy or girl from your youth group is going? Do you raise your hands on Sunday morning so that everyone will smile and say, "That young person really loves the Lord"?

Any worship that is true worship is done for One, and One alone. Ask God to reveal your worship motives. Do you show off to make your own name great, or is everything done to show others how great God is?

EVERY TRIBE AND TONGUE

Open your Bible to Revelation 15:4. In fact, read that chapter. Do one better and read the book of Revelation. It's weird, but it's a great read and the ending... well, you won't find a better one.

Revelation makes mention several times to all the nations of the world worshipping God. There will be a day when we worship alongside Kenyans, Filipinos, Iraqis, Ukrainians... You get the picture. A time is coming when everyone in relationship with Christ will share that common link for eternity—an ongoing bond through worship. And everyone who had not placed their faith in Jesus... they'll see the Truth. There will be no denying the only One worthy of worship. Everyone who has ever lived will face the supreme reality of Christ.

After you finish reading the book of Revelation (you can totally do it), think for a bit about what it will be like to see the world bow down and worship Christ. What do you hear? What do you see? Can you imagine the scene?

Write it down. Journal it out. Think about it. Imagine it. Savor it.

DEVOTION

Cheeming Boey. If you recognize his name, it is undoubtedly because of his unique talent. The young artist in California draws with a Sharpie on Styrofoam cups. His illustrations transform overlooked (and often looked down upon) disposable items from everyday life into timeless works of art. Literally timeless . . . permanent ink on non-biodegradable cups. What started as doodling in a coffee shop has resulted in a new artistic expression—not to mention that one of his cups can be sold for a couple hundred bucks! The black and white designs range from simple cartoons, to intricate portraits or fantastic scenes. Boey's art is proof that seemingly ordinary things can be used in extraordinary ways.

Grab your Bible and read Exodus 31:1—5. Since you may not be very familiar with Bezalel (He never made the cover of Bible People Magazine's most popular craftsman issue.), a little background on this passage of Scripture may be helpful. Up until this point in Exodus, God had given five chapters worth of super-detailed instructions on how to build the Tabernacle. The Tabernacle was essentially a portable tent version of the Temple back before the Israelites took possession of the promise land. The significance of the Tabernacle was HUGE, so don't miss this: It represented God's constant presence among His people and reminded them of their need to be thoughtful and intentional in their worship of Him. Who could forget the holiness of God when there were such elaborate steps taken to ensure that this place of worship was distinct from everything around it?

Verse 2 says that God chose Bezalel by name, meaning He specifically picked him to be a part of His work in making God's presence known to His people through this place of worship. This craftsman wasn't a Levite of the priestly class. He wasn't a guy you might expect God to use for some great role in His plan. He was a regular guy with regular skills, but God filled Him with His Spirit and those ordinary skills were used for extraordinary things! Seemingly common pieces of wood, stone, and metals were transformed into intricate works of art decorating the tent in which the presence of God dwelt among His people!

If something as common as a Styrofoam cup and a Sharpie pen can be transformed in the hands of a bored illustrator, how much more can your God-given talents be used in the hands of your loving Creator? So, what are your talents? What do you love to do? You may or may not be the next great preacher, teacher, singer, or other high-profile role in God's Church, but whether on stage or behind the scenes, you're a major part of His plan and His work in the world. No matter how ordinary you may feel or how insignificant your talents may seem, God has personally chosen you to make His glorious presence known. He has called you to worship Him with the unique personality and abilities He has given to you. You are a custom design—nobody can worship Him the way you can. No price tag can be put upon your unique expression of worship! Everything can be beautiful. Everything can be an act of worship.

all about // lesson 3 day 5 // 258

HOW DO YOU PREPARE FOR WORSHIP?

THE PRINCIPLES OF CAUSE AND EFFECT RULE OUR LIVES. YOU DON'T WAKE UP IN TIME FOR SCHOOL, SO YOU MISS THE BUS. THEN YOU MISS AN IMPORTANT TEST, WHICH CAUSES YOU TO FAIL A CLASS, THEREFORE ENSURING YOU WILL NEVER GET INTO A GOOD COLLEGE, FORCING YOU TO LIVE AT HOME WITH YOUR PARENTS UNTIL YOU'RE 49.

OK. MAYBE THAT'S A LITTLE DRAMATIC.

IN THE STORIES BELOW, FILL IN THE BLANKS WITH SOME ABSURD AND OUT-THERE CAUSES AND EFFECTS. YOU KNOW, JUST FOR FUN.

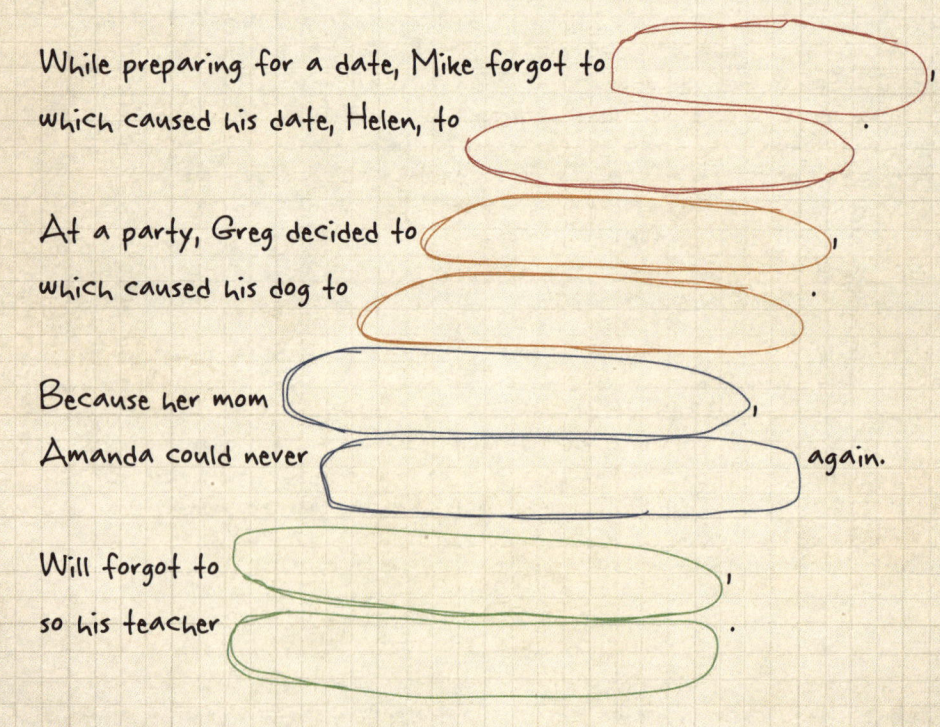

While preparing for a date, Mike forgot to _____, which caused his date, Helen, to _____.

At a party, Greg decided to _____, which caused his dog to _____.

Because her mom _____, Amanda could never _____ again.

Will forgot to _____, so his teacher _____.

NOW, HERE'S AN EXAMPLE...

THE EFFECT OF NOT PROPERLY PREPARING YOURSELF FOR A WORSHIPFUL EXPERIENCE IS NOT BEING ATTUNED TO THE HOLY SPIRIT. COULD YOU JUST GO OUT AND RUN A MARATHON WITH NO TRAINING? OF COURSE NOT, YOU HAVE TO PREPARE. IT'S THE SAME WITH WORSHIP.

SO, HOW WILL YOU PREPARE YOURSELF FOR WORSHIP?

all about // lesson 3 day 6 // 259

Last week, you studied a passage of Scripture that included "the Shema." That is a Hebrew word meaning, "hear," taken from the first word of the verse below. Fill in the missing word...

"Hear, O Israel: The LORD our God, the LORD is _____" (Deut. 6:4).

In the Hebrew language, this verse could be translated like you read it in your Bible, or it can also be read as "The LORD is our God, the LORD alone." So, there is one true God, and there is no one else like Him. So now, let's spend a little time focusing on just a few of the things that make God unique. Look up the Scripture passages below and write in the blank whatever each verse gives as an exclusive characteristic of our God.

1 KINGS 8:39	You alone _____
NEHEMIAH 9:6	You alone _____
PSALM 4:8	You alone _____
PSALM 76:7	You alone _____
PSALM 86:10	You alone _____
ISAIAH 37:16	You alone _____
REVELATION 15:4	You alone _____

So now, take a few minutes to draw or write your praises to God. He is the only One worthy of worship. Express the things that make Him special in your life. In your own way, worship Him for being the one and only true God. Or if you don't want to write or draw, then dance, sing, or simply think and pray about the uniqueness of the LORD.

YOU ALONE

all about // lesson 4 day 1 // 260

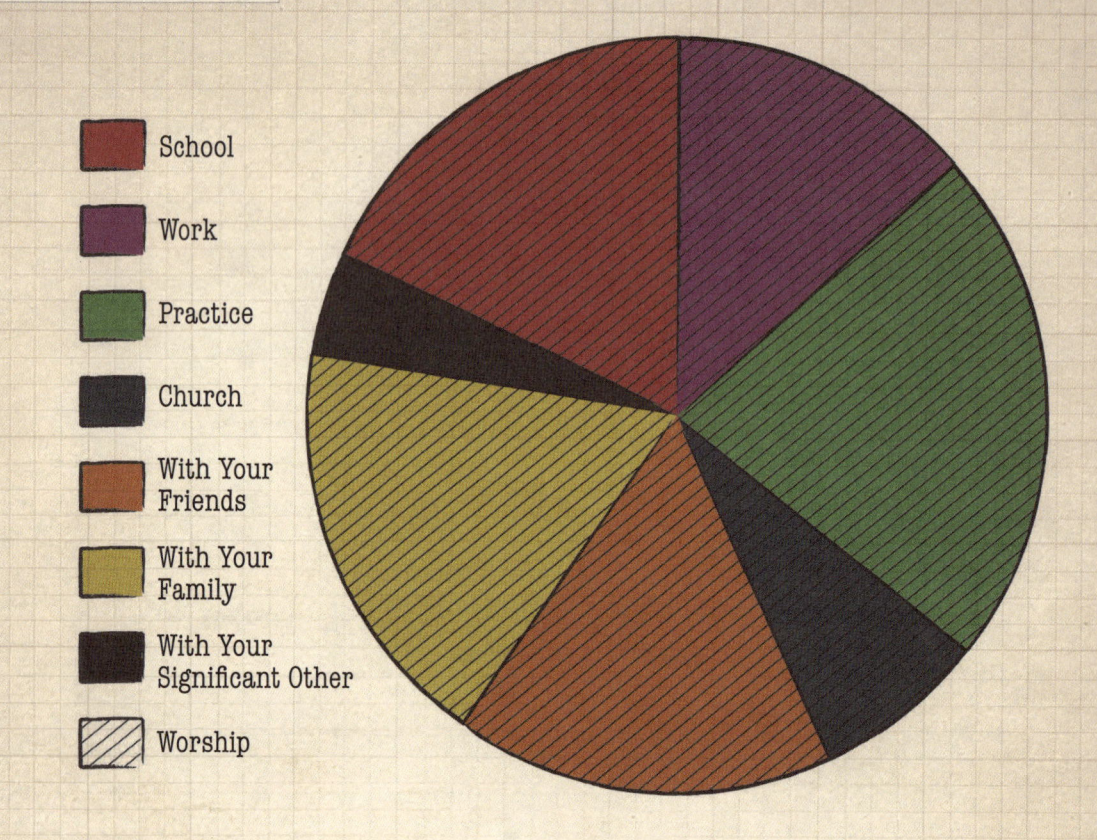

- School
- Work
- Practice
- Church
- With Your Friends
- With Your Family
- With Your Significant Other
- Worship

WHERE DO YOU WORSHIP?

Where do we worship? Church, right? Well, yes . . . but not only at church. True worship in spirit and in truth is not confined to a certain place or time. Where can you worship? Everywhere.

WOMAN AT THE WELL

What if one day, you went to get a Coke from the vending machine and there was a guy there? And although you had never seen him before, he knew everything about you. He knew about the time you cheated on that math test. He knew about the time(s) you went a little too far with your girlfriend or boyfriend. He knew your secret fear of disappointing a parent. Everything.

Weird, right? Kind of creepy? A little nerve-racking? Take a look at John 4:4-30. Put yourself in the woman's shoes. What do you think she journaled about that night as she went to bed? Are you as eager as this woman to introduce others to Christ so that they too can experience Him in a powerful and personal way?

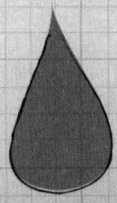

DEVOTION

Joe Tucker hops into his car after a long shift, cranks the music up, and starts checking the text messages on his cell phone. The parking ticket stuck under his wiper blade flaps in the wind as he pulls away from the fire hydrant he had blocked. Narrowly avoiding another driver, he swerves into the opposite lane before speeding through a red light. After jumping a curb to dodge an elderly nun pushing a baby carriage in a crosswalk, Joe screeches to a stop, parking in a handicap space. It's no big deal—he'll only be gone for a minute. Joes slams his car door into the vehicle parked in the next spot. He doesn't wait for the crossing signal, choosing instead to hop through oncoming traffic Frogger-style. He bursts through the door, ringing the bell just before the DMV closes. "Who do I have to pay to renew my license?" Joe shouts. "Mine has been expired for a month!"

"Yes sir, Officer Tucker," an attendant replies, "I'd be glad to take care of you. How was your day at the Department of Public Safety?"

"Huh? Oh . . . just call me Joe. I'm off duty."

How ridiculous would it seem to live in blatant disregard to the very thing you devote yourself to during certain hours of the day? It would seem outrageous for someone in law enforcement to assume he could ignore the law simply because he wasn't "on the clock." But how many people live their so-called faith this way? They show up for worship services at the scheduled times, sing, and do the "church thing" for a couple of hours, before resuming lives that in no way resemble the Christ they claim to follow. What if this book narrated your day before or after attending a worship service? Would your speech, actions, entertainment, and relationships seem equally void of praise for the God you worshiped as our imaginary officer friend's life was void of any real respect for the law he enforced?

Read Psalm 113:1—3. This psalm is the first in a collection of praises traditionally sung during Passover. Psalms 113 and 114 were sung before the ceremonial meal at which God's people would remember God's faithfulness to them in delivering them from slavery in Egypt. Psalms 115-118 were sung after the meal. The verses you just read open the time of celebration with a reminder that not only during the annual holiday or at mealtime, but also at all times, God's people should be prayerful, thankful, and worshipful with their lives.

So from the moment you get up each morning until the time you fall asleep, do you remain consistent in praising the God who saved you? Do you only pray before meals or think about salvation during holidays, such as Christmas or Easter? Do you act like a completely different person when you're not at church? Think about those things. If God has truly set you free from the bondage of sin and given you a new life of freedom in Christ, His praises should fill your heart, mind, and actions all day long. Worship should be like the song you can't get out of your head, even if you tried. Today, live like worship isn't something reserved for church buildings on certain days of the week. Today, make sure you are the same person both inside and outside of the church building. No more living in a way that contradicts the time you spend worshiping at church events. Whether at church, school, home, or hanging out . . . from the rising of the sun until it sets . . . praise the name of the Lord. Be consistent. Live worshipfully. All the time. Everywhere.

all about // **lesson 4 day 4** // 263

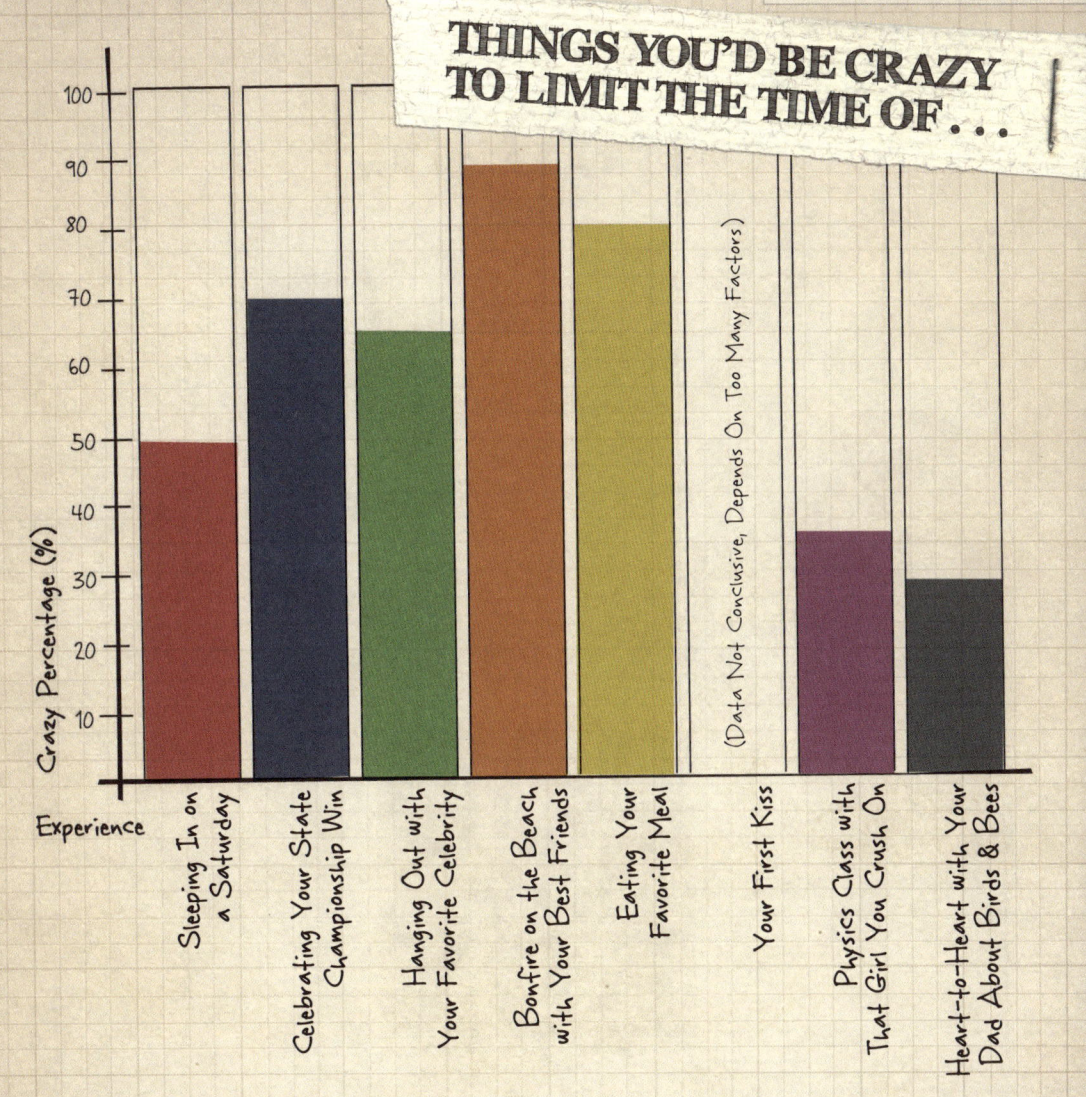

THINGS YOU'D BE CRAZY TO LIMIT THE TIME OF...

Crazy Percentage (%)

Experience	%
Sleeping In on a Saturday	50
Celebrating Your State Championship Win	70
Hanging Out with Your Favorite Celebrity	65
Bonfire on the Beach with Your Best Friends	90
Eating Your Favorite Meal	81
Your First Kiss	(Data Not Conclusive, Depends On Too Many Factors)
Physics Class with That Girl You Crush On	36
Heart-to-Heart with Your Dad About Birds & Bees	30

TAKE A LOOK AT THE GRAPH ABOVE. IT'S ALL ABOUT SAVORING THE MOMENT. YOU KNOW, THOSE MOMENTS WHEN YOU WISH YOU COULD JUST PUSH "PAUSE" ON LIFE AND MAKE IT LAST FOREVER?

DO YOU FEEL THAT WAY ABOUT WORSHIP? DO YOU EVER WISH YOU COULD JUST SIT IN YOUR CHURCH PEW AND SING TO GOD FOREVER? DO YOU EVER LEAVE A BIBLE STUDY AND THINK, *TWO HOURS JUST WASN'T ENOUGH?*

IF WE'RE WILLING TO PUSH THE PAUSE BUTTON ON A SLIMY, BRACES-FILLED, AWKWARD FIRST KISS, WOULDN'T WE EVEN MORE SO WANT TO PAUSE ON THE MOMENTS IN LIFE WHEN WE ARE ABLE TO GLIMPSE GOD'S PRESENCE AND DELIGHT IN HIM? PAUSE NOW AND WORSHIP HIM IN SILENCE.

all about // **lesson 4 day 5** // 264

GOD IS...

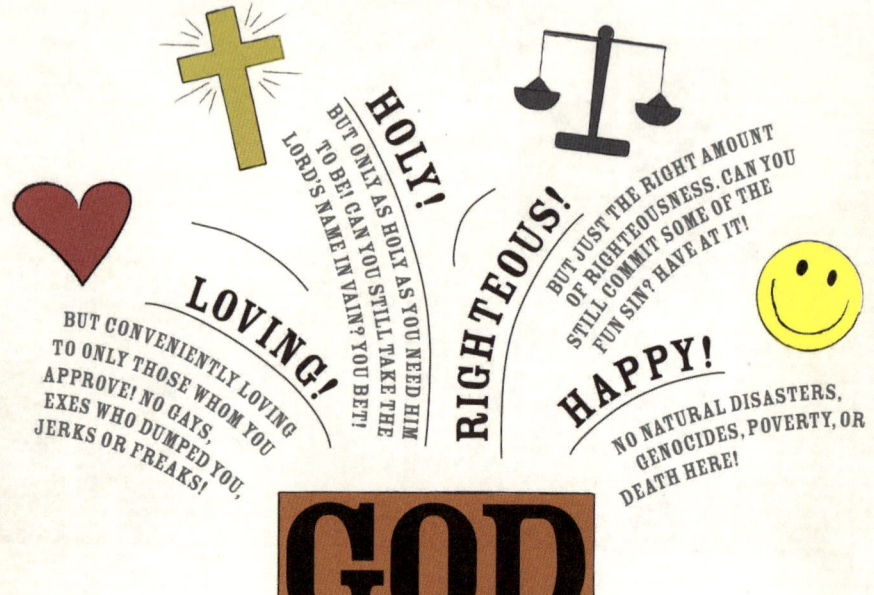

HOLY! But only as holy as you need him to be! Can you still take the Lord's name in vain? You bet!

RIGHTEOUS! But just the right amount of righteousness. Can you still commit some of the fun sin? Have at it!

LOVING! But conveniently loving to only those whom you approve! No gays, exes who dumped you, jerks or freaks!

HAPPY! No natural disasters, genocides, poverty, or death here!

GOD IN A BOX

GOD IN A BOX! THE NEWEST WAY TO CARRY GOD AROUND TO FIT YOUR EVERYDAY NEEDS!

Call now to get your God in a Box! Operators are standing by. 1-800-GDNA-BOX! Supplies are limited! Hurry! Act now and get a second God in a Box ABSOLUTELY FREE!

THINK ABOUT IT: How often DO YOU put God in a box?

When Jesus was 12 years old, He journeyed to the Temple of Jerusalem with His family. The young boy's understanding of God amazed the religious leaders who were unaware that they were conversing with the very One they worshiped. Emmanuel was His name, meaning "God with us." After starting back home without their firstborn son, Mary and Joseph found Jesus in the sacred place of worship. The Son of God asked His earthly parents, "Why were you searching for me? Didn't you know I had to be in my Father's house?" (Luke 2:49—50)

In much of the Old Testament and New Testament, the Temple is God's house. It was seen as the place in which the presence and glory of God dwelled. The Temple represented a holy space, separated from the world around it. Everything within the Temple had been cleansed, and all the activities of those within the Temple reflected the fact that they were worshiping in the presence of a holy God. Keep that in mind, as you look at the next several passages of Scripture. God didn't always have a mailing address, so to speak. He didn't always reside in a permanent building . . . and He doesn't today. So before you simply say, "He lives in heaven," look at the different places God has lived throughout history. Read the Scripture and fill in the blank with the name of each place God resides.

_____ **Read Exodus 25:8—9.** The LORD proceeded to give Moses intricate instructions for every detail of the Tabernacle (also known as the Tent of Meeting, because it was literally a tent where God would meet His people). The Tabernacle was an ornate tent, made from the finest materials, and measured 45 feet long, by 15 feet wide, and 15 feet tall. Every time the Israelites traveled, they would roll up the Tabernacle and carry along with it all of the furnishings, including the altar and ark of the covenant, to the next place they would make camp. **To get an overwhelming idea of how detail-oriented God was about the Tabernacle, take the time to read chapters 25—31.**

_____ **Read 1 Kings 5:5.** King Solomon had now been given detailed directions for constructing a "permanent" house for God, now that His people had settled in their own kingdom. If the King had a palace, it seemed right that God should have an even greater house. The Temple was not only for the people's own worship and a tangible way to honor God; it was also a way to display to all the world the greatness and beauty of the one, true God. The massive Temple was made of stone and the interior was completely covered in gold; it was twice as large as the Tabernacle, measuring 90 feet long, 30 feet wide, and 45 feet high. **To get a sense of it's overwhelming beauty read chapters 6—7.**

_____ **Read 1 Corinthians 6:19—20.** Finally, Paul teaches that the Spirit of God no longer dwells in tents or buildings. He dwells in the lives of His people. People come in all shapes and sizes, but God is just as concerned about every detail of your life and the holiness of your body as He was with the Tabernacle. He is displaying His beauty and glory through permanently dwelling in you as His Temple. Your life is not insignificant, neither is what you do with your body. You are the Temple, and your life is an act of worship!

You no longer have to travel great distances to spend time in the Temple like people in King Solomon's time or even Jesus' family. You no longer have to carefully take God with you, like in the time of Moses. You have the best of both worlds and more! Not only does God go with you, but also He is permanently dwelling in you. Today, you have the Spirit of Christ inside of you. That means you have been made holy, set apart from the world around you, and everything about your activities should reflect the mysterious truth that the holy God of the universe is with you every step you take. That transforms everything about your life into an act of worship, because everything you do is done in the presence of God.

Think about that today. You may recognize Psalm 84:10 from a popular worship song; it says that one day in God's presence (in the courts of His Temple) is better than 1,000 years anywhere else. Knowing that YOU are now God's Temple, how will you live in His presence today? This one day lived worshipfully aware of His presence will be worth more than 1,000 years spent doing anything else!

GOD'S HOUSE

all about // lesson 5 day 1 // 266

YOU'RE THE LAST PERSON ON EARTH. The zombie apocalypse has destroyed everyone. What do you need to survive?

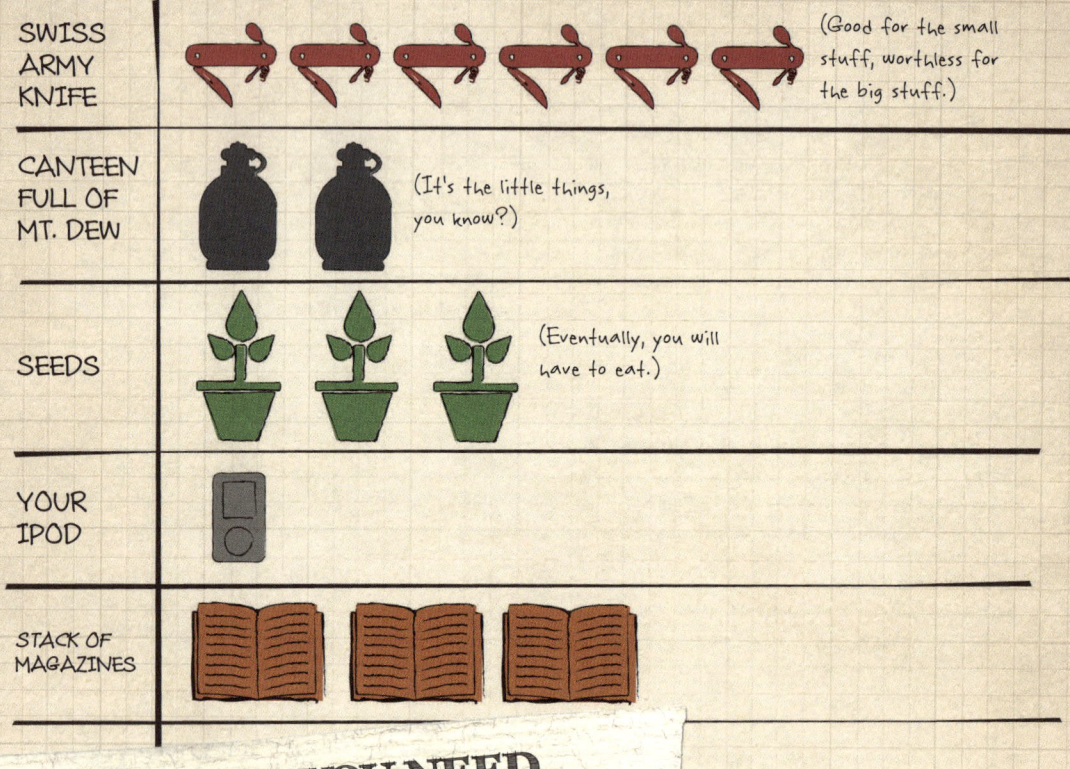

SWISS ARMY KNIFE	🔪🔪🔪🔪🔪🔪	(Good for the small stuff, worthless for the big stuff.)
CANTEEN FULL OF MT. DEW	🫙🫙	(It's the little things, you know?)
SEEDS	🪴🪴🪴	(Eventually, you will have to eat.)
YOUR IPOD	📱	
STACK OF MAGAZINES	📖📖📖	

WHAT DO YOU NEED FOR WORSHIP?

What would you add to the ultimate survival kit?

OK, so that was fun. Worship works the exact same way... minus the zombies. There are certain things you need for worship. You need grace. You need humility. And most importantly, you need sacrifice—an attitude of sacrifice; no lambs, please. Jesus took care of that part for you. Pray now, asking God to teach you this week about what role sacrifice plays in worship. I think you'll be surprised.

DEVOTION

What's the most incredible thing you've heard about a person doing to express his or her love for someone? Maybe you've personally experienced a great display of devotion and affection for someone. The perfect prom date, a parent taking a second job to pay for your involvement in that extra activity, JumboTron proposals, chick-flick sappy endings, a surprise party with all of your favorite people and things, or simply doing or saying the perfect words at the time they were most needed . . .

So what do these different acts of love all have in common? The point is not how elaborate or expensive the gesture may be; it's not even how much time or even effort went into the act. The point is the intention and motivation behind each expression of love.

Read Hosea 6:6. This doesn't mean God doesn't desire sacrifice. (By now you've seen pretty clearly that faithful sacrifice is vital in worship and in a relationship with God.) What this means is that going through some empty routine is meaningless. God doesn't want your religious routine if it is hollow. He wants your actions to be fueled by a heart for Him.

The Book of Hosea was written during a time of material wealth but spiritual poverty in Israel, much like our own culture today. The lack of sincere worship among God's people is characterized by Hosea's marriage to a prostitute named Gomer. The tension in their relationship reflects the spiritual condition of God's relationship with His people. Despite Israel's unfaithfulness, God lovingly pursues a relationship. Jesus quoted Hosea 6:6 on more than one occasion in reference to the religious leaders during His ministry. The heart of the message during both Hosea's and Jesus' time is that God isn't interested in empty religious routines. God desires a heart of worship. Yes, sacrifice is a key part of the relationship, but the intent of the heart is what makes the sacrifice an act of worship.

So, commit to living with a pure heart. Let your affection be set entirely on Jesus who is faithful even when we don't deserve His love. He forgives you. He loves you. He pursues you daily. Let that truth fill your heart with joy and praise for His grace and mercy. Your worship is not mere duty (something good Christians must do at church, singing songs and reading their Bibles); it is an act of passion and devotion to the One loving you in a way infinitely greater than anyone in this world ever could. God has displayed His love perfectly through the sacrifice of Jesus Christ. When seen from this perspective, sacrifice is a joy to act in love instead of something painful to give up. Not only will you not mind letting go of things or going out of your way to express your love for God, you also will find greater satisfaction in giving those things to God than you ever could have by hanging on to them. Live sacrificially. This is your act of worship. This is your expression of love to the One who loves you.

all about // lesson 5 day 3 //268

Do not offer animals bought with the wages of a harlot or the animal exchanged for a dog.

Do not burn honey or yeast on the altar.

Do not eat sacrifices offered with improper intentions.

Do not eat the meal offering of a High Priest.

Do not eat the meat of minor sacrifices before sprinkling the blood.

Do not decapitate a fowl brought as a sin offering.

Do not omit the salt from sacrifices.

Do not work the consecrated animals.

Do not leave the fat overnight.

Do not leave the meat of the holiday offering of the 14th until the 16th.

Do not allow an uncircumcised male to eat from the offering.

Do not forget to offer the wave offering from the meal of the new wheat.

Do not forget to break the neck of a calf by the river valley following an unsolved murder.

The old sacrificial system was... how should we say it? A little confusing, perhaps? A little complicated, maybe? Do you think that sometimes, even in modern day, we make worship just as complicated? We must have the right music (no organs and no hymnals, thanks); we can't worship in a place that's not air-conditioned; maybe we want candles, etc. Ask God to show you where you are over-complicating your worship.

all about // lesson 5 day 4 // 269

OLD VS. NEW
(The Sacrificial System)

Jesus Christ sacrificed Himself once and for all, making us blameless before God, so that God would be glorified. The good news is that we don't have to sacrifice any more goats or other animals in order to be cleansed of our sins. Christ took care of that with His death and resurrection.

The new worship "system" isn't cluttered or complicated. It's all about one thing: Jesus. Simply thank God right now for Christ's sacrifice on your behalf, making worship and relationship with God possible.

By now, you should have a pretty good grasp of the fact that sacrifice and holiness was a BIG deal when it came to worshipping God and being in right relationship with Him. The Old Testament is at least as full of specifics regarding how and when to do what kind of sacrifice as it is with the details of the Tabernacle and Temple you read about last week. So you probably don't understand when a dove is acceptable verses a sheep or during which month you should bring grain etc. But that's OK for now. You've also seen that you're on this side of the cross, so all of those specifics don't apply to your daily life. So let's look at a few things that do apply to you and your worship through sacrifice.

Read Genesis 4:1-16. The world's first brothers were Cain and Abel. Chances are, you would say this story is about murder. (Which it is.) But notice that this is the very first story in the Bible after Adam and Eve sinned and were expelled from Eden. After their sin and before their son's sin, the story begins with the original family worshipping God through sacrifice. One brother brought a sacrifice that pleased God—the other brother's sacrifice was not acceptable. Scripture doesn't tell us exactly why the sacrifice wasn't acceptable until later, but we get a major clue in verse 7 when the LORD tells Cain to fix his attitude. Obviously sin got a hold of him as God warned and he killed Abel—How is Abel's sacrifice described in verse 4? What clue does that give you as to what makes a pleasing sacrifice? _____

Read Hebrews 11:4. What did Abel's sacrifice have that Cain's did not? _____

Now read Hebrews 11:17. Another story from Genesis is the epitome of faith making a sacrifice pleasing to God. In fact, God was so pleased by the faith of Abraham in his willingness to sacrifice his son, Isaac, that God did not even allow Abraham to suffer the loss of his son. All God wanted was the act of faith, not the literal sacrifice!

Turn back to Genesis and read 22:1-18. Ultimately, there would be another beloved Son. And like Abraham said in verse 8, God would provide for Himself the lamb for the sacrifice. Jesus Christ, the Lamb of God. Like Isaac, Jesus would willingly submit to the will of His Father, laying down His life. Unlike Isaac, God would allow Christ to die as the ultimate sacrifice. His righteous blood would be shed like Abel's by the hand of sinful men. But unlike Abel's blood, which cried out to God to condemn the brother who sinned against Him, Jesus' blood forgave you of your sins, making you His brother when you cried out to God in faith!

Did you follow all of that?

God gave His very best for you. He gave Himself as Jesus Christ, who literally lived and died for you. Through faith in His great sacrifice you have been given a new life. Will you follow Christ, living by faith until the day you die?

Will you give your best in faith like Abel? Or just the leftovers you can spare like Cain? (Don't try to justify this attitude as "At least I'm doing something!" because so was Cain—and you saw how that story turned out—God was less than pleased with the attitude of His so-called sacrifice.) Today, be like Abraham and give anything and everything to show your faith in God (even when you don't understand).

PERFECT SACRIFICE

Grandma Edna's Worship Pie

3 heaping cups of Sacrifice (strain blood beforehand)
2 cups of Humility
2 cups of Scripture
1/2 cup of Prayer and Meditation (mix prior)
4 tbsp. of Grace
2 tbsp. of Service

Mix with hand mixer on high for 2 minutes. Pour mixture into a Trinity piecrust. Bake at 355 until top is golden brown. Allow time to cool, then serve.

So obviously, sacrifice isn't the ONLY element to worship. Worship is a rich, enduring phenomenon that we experience continually through our lives. What do you think of the worship "recipe" above? What ingredient might you increase? What would you take away? Would you add any extra ingredients? Share your "ingredients" below:

all about // lesson 6 day 1 // 272

"Forever—is composed of Nows."
—Emily Dickinson, Forever—is composed of Nows

"My music will go on forever." —Bob Marley

"We'll stay forever this way. / You are safe in my heart. / And my heart will go on and on."
—Celine Dion, "My Heart Will Go On"

"Liberty, once lost, is lost forever." — John Adams

"Nothing lasts forever."
—Sidney Sheldon, Nothing Lasts Forever

Forever is such a long, long time. Actually, forever is sort of OUTSIDE of time. As in . . . you can't measure or mark it. When we're in forever there is no time.

Many people have a lot to say about the idea of forever. It's the great "what if?" What if forever exists? What if THIS isn't it? What if we go on and on?

God shows us in the Bible that one day we will worship Him forever. But what does that mean? Will we get bored? Will we get a sore throat from all the singing?

Forever is such a long, long time. So let's figure out what it's all about . . . if you're brain can handle it. What lasts forever?

"I used to believe in forever. But forever's too good to be true."
—A.A. Milne

"The grass withers and the flowers fall, but the word of our God stands forever." —Isaiah 40:8

"If you can do it for joy, you can do it forever." —Stephen King, On Writing: A Memoir of the Craft

you are here

Read Genesis 1:1-5. Before anything existed... God existed. Before there was ever a day. Before there was even light, there was God. Pause now, take a second and look around wherever you are. If possible, find a window or go outside. You are surrounded (whether you're able to see it now or not) by God's creation. You, yourself, are God's creation. He made you and everything around you for a reason. Thank God now for all He has created.

Now read John 1:1-5. Wow. That sounds remarkably similar to what you just read in Genesis, although it brings everything to a whole new level. In the beginning, God spoke Creation into existence, separating light from darkness... Now the Word and Light are personified. In the Gospel of John, Jesus is the Word and the Light. He is the creator of all things and giver of life. Reread John 1:1-5 but say "Jesus" each time instead of "the Word" or "Him." So Jesus is the Light. In Him is life. Everything in heaven and earth was created by and for Him. And He has chosen to make Himself known to you! He has given you His Word and He has (hopefully) opened your eyes to the truth of eternal life with Him. Pause now to thank Christ for bringing you life in this dark world.

Finally, read Revelation 21:1-5. The Book of Revelation truly takes it to the furthest level imaginable! Honestly, it freaks some people out. But it shouldn't; this is incredible stuff! An incredible hope and promise is present in the midst of what can seem confusing with the prophetic imagery. Your hope is found in Christ and the promise of this new heaven and earth. If you are a child of God through faith in Christ, you will someday experience a perfect reality with Him for all eternity. Read those verses again. WOW! Our worship becomes more than just a time of singing. Our relationship with God becomes more than just His invisible Spirit inside of us. Beyond this life, you will literally live with God! Forever! THAT is something to get excited about. Nothing bad, negative, or painful will exist in God's glorious presence for the rest of eternity. All of God's people will be united as one, like a beautiful bride, to exist in perfect relationship with Christ, dwelling with Him forever. "Happily ever after" is the biggest understatement in human history. Here's something else cool . . . Remember all of the talk about light in Genesis 1 and John 1? **Check out verses 22—23.** Take the rest of your time to just praise God for inviting you into such an incredible eternal reality.

In these three passages of Scripture, you've seen the broadest picture of life. You've seen where it all started, what happened in "the middle" to change the course of history and forever change the relationship between God and humankind, and where it is all headed for those who worship God. So now, in light of the past and the future, how will you worship God in the present? How will you live today knowing where you're headed for eternity?

all about // lesson 6 day 3 //274

LIFE SPANS

See? Forever is a really long time. Thinking about YOU in the scope of forever puts a little perspective on things. How do you feel now that you've seen this timeline? How do you fit in eternity?

Posidonia Oceanica (sea grass): 100,000 years

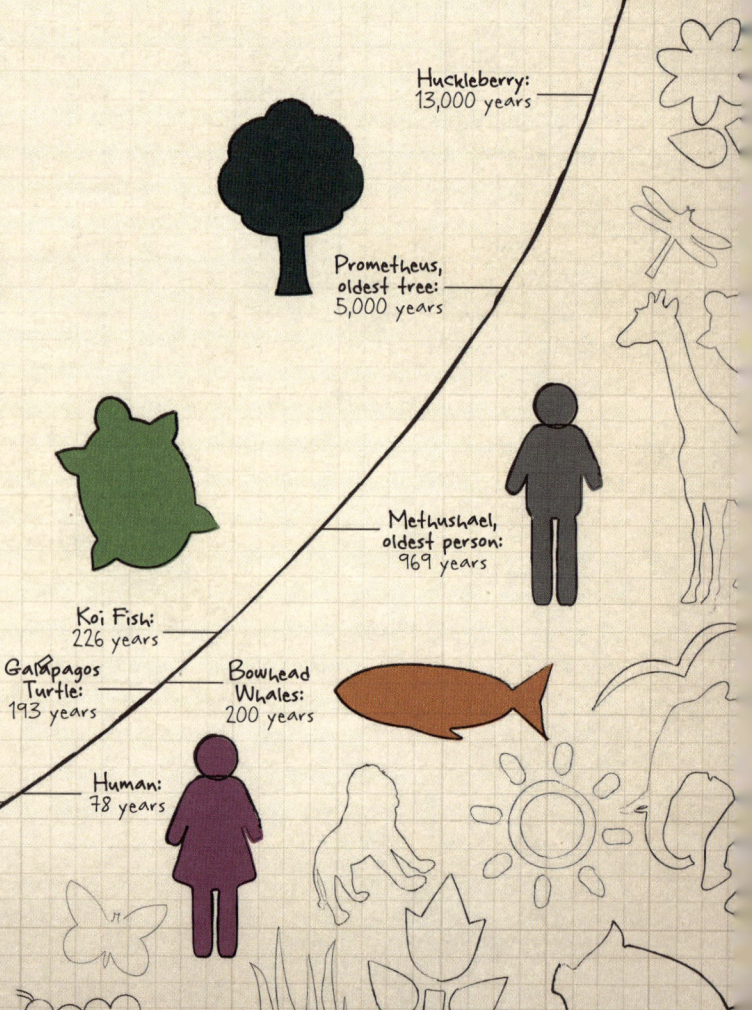

Huckleberry: 13,000 years

Prometheus, oldest tree: 5,000 years

Methushael, oldest person: 969 years

Koi Fish: 226 years

Galapagos Turtle: 193 years

Bowhead Whales: 200 years

Elephant: 70 years

DEVOTION

Rob Dyrdek, pro skateboarder and MTV reality star, has broken over 20 world records for skateboarding as well as a few for eating (powdered donuts and bananas). His most famous record came in 2009: the world's longest skateboard. It was a dream come true for Dyrdek. Dwarfed by the mammoth deck, Rob looked like a posed action figure standing on the 36-foot board. But no matter how many records he sets or how much wealth or celebrity he gains, anything in this world ultimately comes to an end. Records are broken (Dyrdek broke someone else's records and some of his have already been broken by yet another person.). Celebrity is fleeting (Can you name five other reality show personalities from five years ago?). And money burns holes in pockets (Spending it on things like . . . giant skateboards.). So even things that are bigger than life have limits. There's nothing we can do or imagine that is big enough, fast enough, long enough, or worth enough to last forever. So what lasts? Is anything really worth all of our time and energy or is life just a matter of having fun while we can?

Read Revelation 22:12—13. Christ said that what we do in this life does matter. It does have a lasting reward. But the reward is not fame, wealth, or glory for our own lives. The reward is the priceless experience of eternal life in the midst of God's glory. The only thing that ultimately matters and stands the test of time (and beyond) is our worship. Right before these verses an angel commanded John (the writer of Revelation) to "Worship God." That is the only worthy response when He reveals His greatness.

When Jesus said that He is the Alpha and Omega, those are the first and last letters of the Greek alphabet. Essentially, He is the A-Z; meaning, Jesus is everything. He is the starting point of anything meaningful, and He is the ultimate goal and final say in our existence. Christ promised this when speaking about the new heaven and earth, life beyond the world, as we know it. He made it plain: The way you live now, what you choose to do with your life, has eternal significance . . . either consequence or reward.

So is your life all about Christ? Do you seek His fame and glory, making His greatness known through your actions? Do you have big dreams of eternal life with the One who is worth more than anything in this world? His glory is too great for words. His plans for the future are larger than life. He will never be outdone. Only He is eternal, and only what is done to honor Him will have eternal reward. Praise Him now for being what life is all about. He is the beginning and end and everything in between. What you do in this life echoes into eternity.

all about // lesson 6 day 5 //276

HEAVEN'S JUST ONE LONG CHURCH SERVICE

Heaven's just one big worship service! Whoo hoo! Sounds like a great time, doesn't it? Can't wait to sing, "This is My Father's World" for eternity? Hope that Mrs. Pritchett's lovely off-key soprano screech will be far from you on the holy risers of heaven? Just itching to dust off your uncomfortable shoes and clip-on tie for the occasion of worshiping God forever? Too bad! Thankfully, heaven is not some sort of eternal, stuffy worship service. So, what is it? Check out the Scriptures below:

John 14:2 • Revelation 14:13 • 2 Peter 3:13 • Revelation 21:1-2

How do these Scriptures compare to the way you picture our heavenly home?

MIND-BOGGLING CONCEPTS OF FOREVER

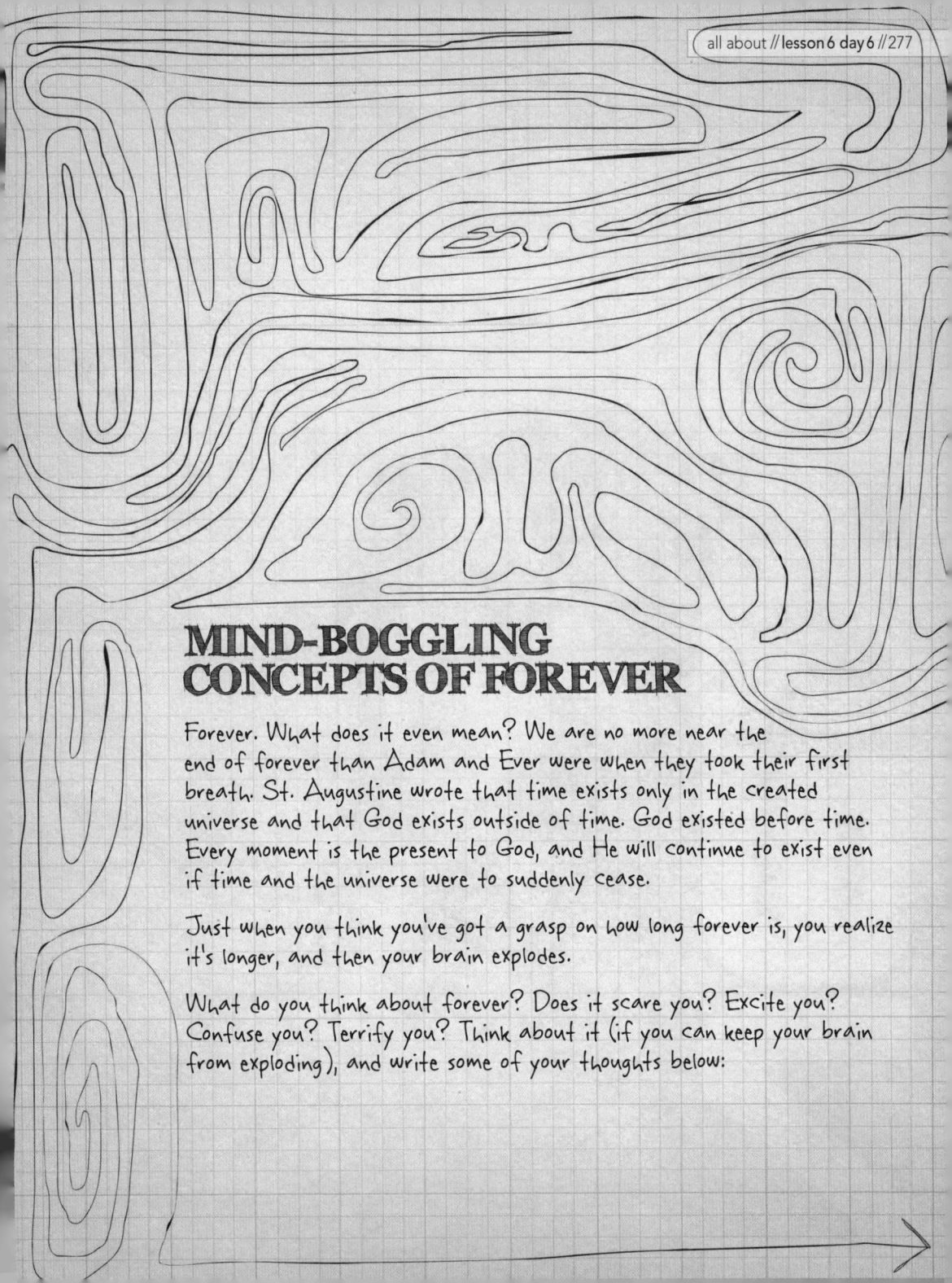

Forever. What does it even mean? We are no more near the end of forever than Adam and Eve were when they took their first breath. St. Augustine wrote that time exists only in the created universe and that God exists outside of time. God existed before time. Every moment is the present to God, and He will continue to exist even if time and the universe were to suddenly cease.

Just when you think you've got a grasp on how long forever is, you realize it's longer, and then your brain explodes.

What do you think about forever? Does it scare you? Excite you? Confuse you? Terrify you? Think about it (if you can keep your brain from exploding), and write some of your thoughts below:

next

EVER WONDER WHAT COMES NEXT? What does the future look like? What is beyond this world? God has promised that Christ is coming back to the earth someday and then His people will live eternally with Him. Not in some sugary-sweet cartoon heaven, but an everlasting home in perfect relationship with our Heavenly Father. Don't go filling your mind with scenes of fluffy clouds and little angels with glowing halos, strumming harps as they float into forever. We're talking a powerful new reality in the future that should radically impact your life in the present day. What you do now has eternal consequence.

LESSON 1: The God Of The Future—pg 280-285
LESSON 2: His vs. Mine—pg 286-291
LESSON 3: Living In Today—pg 292-297
LESSON 4: What Is To Come?—pg 298-303
LESSON 5: What Is God Waiting For?—pg 304-309
LESSON 6: Be Ready—pg 310-315

next // lesson 1 day 1 // 280

THE FUTURE

THINK ABOUT IT. WHAT COMES TO MIND? DOES IT SCARE YOU? EXCITE YOU?

Is there anything about the future that is 100% certain? Anything you know for sure will happen?

What if you knew somebody who DID know the future—everything about the future, not just some things? Would you seek that person out? Would you pay attention to what that person said? Would it feel less like "obeying" and more like "trusting" when you did what that person told you to do? Would you experience a sense of peace, hope, and confidence in this world no matter what your current situation happened to be?

I think you get the idea: GOD is "that person." So are you seeking? Paying attention? Trusting? Are you peaceful and confident?

DEVOTION

What do you think of when I say the word *Infinity*? Do you think of a luxury car? A phrase Buzz Lightyear says? A number that only Chuck Norris and Tim Tebow have counted to…twice? Or do you think about God? The truth is that we really cannot fathom infinity. We are only finite in our knowledge. But God is infinite. God's existence is infinite. He never had a beginning and will never have an end. That is really hard for us to imagine because each one of us had a beginning at birth and each of us will have and end in death. Our days are finite and can be counted; God's days are infinite.

Have you ever stared up at the night sky and wondered what was on the other side of the stars? Then wondered what was on the other side of that and then the other side of that. Do you ever picture a giant brick wall out in space somewhere beyond the stars that would be the finish line of space? What about this, "What is beyond that wall?" The cycle is never ending. We cannot fathom forever.

Read Psalm 89:47-48 and see if you can fathom our finiteness and God's eternal nature. In this psalm the psalmist is coming to grips with the fact that his body and life is temporary. Things are not going so well around him and he is pouring out his frustration to God while at the same time showing God his admiration of God's enormity.

Think about how short your life is. Eighty-five, ninety years if you're healthy is about all you've got in your earthly shell. Then think about this, that from eternity past to eternity future, God is God. God doesn't have the same limitations we as humans have. God exists outside of the parameters of time and space. But, God chose to place these limitations on Himself when He became the man of Jesus. In some mysterious, mind-blowing way, God become man. He bridged the gap between limited human existence and God's eternal nature through Jesus' death on a cross and resurrection from the grave.

When we trust Jesus with our life, we enter into part of God's eternal existence because our souls are eternal. Right now, there is an eternal soul in your finite body. We can trust God with our eternal future regardless of how feeble our fleshly soul-closets are. Our future is secure with God because God is in control. He is beyond time and space. People living without God's security have no hope for the future. The best they can hope for is a good life on this earth. But, contrary to that, the best is yet to come for people who've put their faith and trust in Jesus.

LISTEN

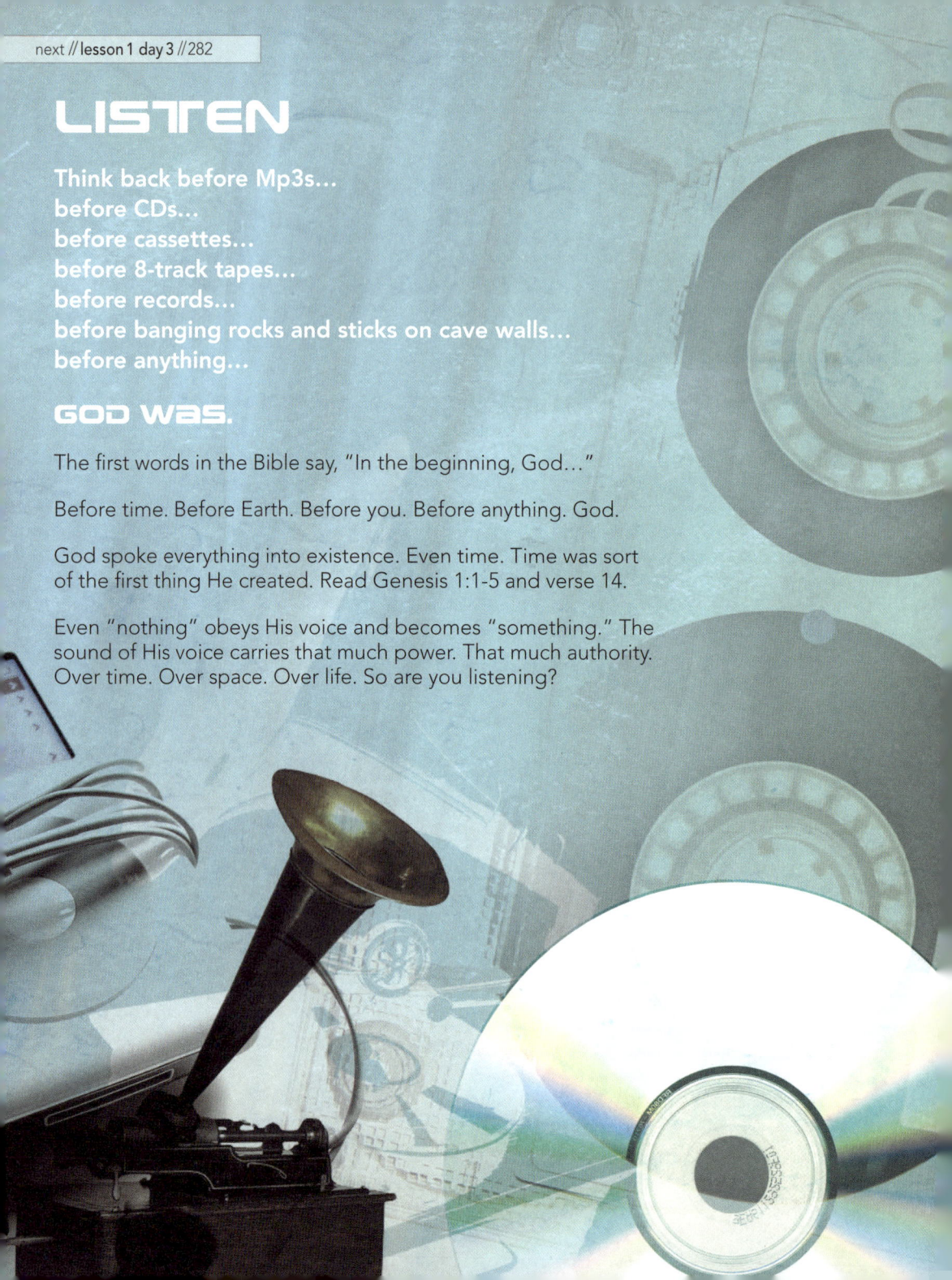

Think back before Mp3s...
before CDs...
before cassettes...
before 8-track tapes...
before records...
before banging rocks and sticks on cave walls...
before anything...

GOD was.

The first words in the Bible say, "In the beginning, God..."

Before time. Before Earth. Before you. Before anything. God.

God spoke everything into existence. Even time. Time was sort of the first thing He created. Read Genesis 1:1-5 and verse 14.

Even "nothing" obeys His voice and becomes "something." The sound of His voice carries that much power. That much authority. Over time. Over space. Over life. So are you listening?

Imagine life is like a raging river. It probably feels this way sometimes. Life is rushing past. Time keeps rolling on, never slowing down. And everything is caught up in the current of time.

Now imagine that you are being swept away, in danger of being hurled off of the edge of a roaring waterfall. What will save you? Where can you find hope and security? To what should you trust your life? Do you cling to other things floating along in the river? Of course not. No matter how secure or valuable these things may appear, they are headed for the same fate as you. Destruction. They may provide temporary relief from your struggle, but at the end of time they will all be destroyed along with anyone who is clinging to them. Everything in this life is caught up in the same current, being swept away with each fleeting moment.

The only way to be saved is to take hold of something existing outside of the flow of time. Now imagine a giant branch reaching out over the river like an outstretched arm. The ancient tree is firmly rooted in the riverbank, outside the wild current of time. The passing waters have no effect on the giant tree overlooking the passing water.

Nothing in this world can offer any real hope. Nothing in this life is worth clinging to. Everything is headed for the same fate at the end of time. Our only hope is found in the outstretched arms of Jesus Christ as God reaches down from eternity to save us from certain destruction. Only He is our Rock and Salvation. Only He is our firm foundation. Only He is the Root, the Branch. Only He is outside of time. Cling to Him alone. Let everything else go; it can only drag you down.

next // lesson 1 day 5 // 284

But do not forget this one thing, dear friends: with the Lord a day is like a thousand years, and a thousand years are like a day.

2 Peter 3:8

STUDY

Many of the psalms are conversations between the writer and God. In this particular one, Psalm 90:1-6, the writer is professing to God what God already knows. He is not telling God these things to inform Him of what He has already done; the writer is confessing to God that he acknowledges what God has done, is doing, and will do.

How many times do we overlook what God has done in our own life? Are there situations, experiences, or even hard times that we need to acknowledge by saying, "That was God working in my life when I _____ (you fill in the blank).

In Psalm 90 verses 1 and 2 we see that God has been with us throughout all generations. That means that before there were people, there was God. We also see that before there was an earth, there was God. This really gives us a good picture of how big our God is since He was God before the oldest thing imaginable. God wasn't created on the first day of creation, or even before creation; God wasn't created at all—God has always existed.

Do you ever place the same limitations on God that you have in your own life? Do you think God sleeps? Did God have to depend on someone or something to give Him life like Adam depended on God? God existed outside of creation because He is the Creator. With God there is no beginning and end; God is the beginning and end.

How does that change the way you think about God for today? Do you think God can handle your problems? Do you think God knows what you are going through?

Read verses 3-6 again. This is talking about the future. Not only is it referring to our future when we face death, but it is referring to God's control over the future. We all face death but God has control over death. Dying is a scary thought but being dead is not the end. Even after our physical death, God is still in control.

How should we live our life today knowing that death is not the end and that our future is in God's hands? I want you to write down 5 things that you are concerned about for the future. For some people, your family might be getting a divorce. For others, you are worried about terrorists. What about college? How am I going to pay my speeding ticket?

After you've written them down picture them in the grand scheme of eternity. Not just your lifetime or your parents' lifetime but all of time. Even before you were born and after you are gone. Got it? The only common thread throughout time and before time is God. Do you think the things you are concerned with for your future are too big for God to handle? I didn't think so.

next // lesson 2 day 1 //286

WHAT PROPELS YOU? MOTIVATES YOU? GETS YOU FIRED UP?

Honestly, what role does God play in your life today and in your plans for the future?

Do you believe that God is the driving force behind history and that He has a plan for the future towards which everything is headed? If so, is He the sole motivation behind the plans for your life?

DEVOTION

Have you ever said the Lord's Prayer? Did you memorize it as a child? You've probably said it at church, maybe before or after a sporting event or class if you attend a Christian school. You've almost definitely said it at one time or another in your life. But, have you ever wondered about the importance of the Lord's Prayer? Is that how we should pray every prayer? Is it a model to follow but not necessarily repeat verbatim each time we pray. There is something special about everyone repeating a prayer together, but there is more to that prayer than just repetition.

Read Matthew 6:9-13. This is a section of verses falling within a larger collection of Scripture called "The Sermon on the Mount" since Jesus usually taught on the side of a mountain (or hill technically). In this particular group of verses in chapter 6, Jesus is teaching his disciples how they should pray. He tells them how not to pray and then recites to them what we now call "the Lord's Prayer."

Focus on verse 10, "your will be done." God has a will that He is going to accomplish on this earth. When we pray "your will be done," we are surrendering ourselves to God's will and forfeiting our own will. Another way to think about this part of the Lord's Prayer is to say, "God let your will be done and make me content with whatever happens." When we pray for God to have His way in our life we need to make sure our heart is ready for God's will to happen. There are things that are in God's will that might not be in yours and you have to be okay with that. You have to have faith that God knows what is best for you and trust that His love will come through in the end.

Whenever you are faced with a tough situation, whether it is a choice about the future or if you are watching a loved one suffer in a hospital bed, our prayer has to be, "your will be done, God." When we are going through hard times and things don't make sense, our prayer has to be, "your will be done, God."

God changes your heart when you pray a prayer like this, "God, work this situation out to where You will receive the most glory and help me to deal with the results." That prayer has the same effect of praying, "your will be done, God," because you are trusting God with the situation and you are showing faith that He will be with you through good and bad. God will help you deal with the results of His will being done when we turn to him for strength.

Try praying that prayer the next time you are faced with some heavy circumstances. God will transform your heart so you can receive His will for your life. When you focus on God's will, you realize that it is less about what you do with your life and more about who God is making you to be.

LIFE FORECAST

OK. You know what a weather forecast is. How about a LIFE forecast?

Draw or write down any of the things that you "foresee" or hope for as part of your future? What would you honestly like your future to look like?

After filling this space with your life forecast, pray about these things. Ask God to help you see clearly what HIS will for your life looks like. Pray for clarity on how you can start preparing now for what He has in store for your future. Ask how these dreams might play a part in His unique purpose for your life. Also pray that He would help you let go of anything that is not part of His plan for your life.

BIG PICTURE

Your life is like an extreme close up. A super, zoomed-in, über-tight shot of a much bigger picture. You're focused on what is right in front of you. It may look confusing at times. It may be hard to see what God is doing in the grand scheme of things. But hang in there. Someday, you'll have His perspective. A heavenly view. Not just bird's eye from the sky, Google Earth view, but angelic, divine, out-of-this-world perspective.

So whatever you're facing. Step back. Pray about it. Even looking back on things over time often reveals a better understanding. But one day… One day it will all be clear. One day you'll be with the One who knows every microscopic detail about your life. He's with you now too. But someday, when you're with Him outside of time, living in eternity, you'll see the big picture. His masterpiece. The beauty of a life spent on His eternal glory.

NOW I KNOW IN PART; THEN I SHALL KNOW FULLY, EVEN AS I AM FULLY KNOWN.
1 CORINTHIANS 13:12

next // lesson 2 day 5 //290

YOUR VISION IS LIMITED.

GOD'S ISN'T.

STUDY

The Book of Proverbs is a book of wisdom. Solomon, the son of King David, usually gets credit for writing (or at least collecting) most of the wise sayings. Solomon was said to be the wisest man in the world and people came from all over to seek his wisdom. Chapter three of Proverbs shares the benefits of living a wise life.

Read Proverbs 3:5-6.

Our plans as Christians should mirror these verses. We should let God direct every step of our life. How can He do that? Are we robots? Puppets? No. We aren't mere puppets on a string; we are children seeking our Heavenly Father's best for our life. Let's look at these two verses.

How does Proverbs 3:5-6 help you understand how to plan for the future?

Based on what you know about Proverbs 3:5-6 and looking back at your passage in James 4:13-15; do you think that making plans is bad? Or should it be done a certain way?

We all have a limited knowledge of tomorrow. Think about it. Do we really know what will happen tomorrow? Do we really even know what we will eat for breakfast tomorrow? No. When we make plans we should make them within the parameters of God's will. God knows what is best for us even if we don't understand why. It is okay to make plans but our hearts should be sensitive to God's direction. Here is how that happens:

When you spend time in God's Word you are more sensitive to His direction. When you are sensitive to God's direction, your attitude changes and you trust His ways instead of seeking your own.

Our attitude should be that we are okay with whatever comes our way. If we make plans but God says, "no" or even "not now," we should be satisfied with that. Planning for the future is more of God transforming your mind through His word so that you consider God's will for your life with every decision you make.

Beside each space below put your plans:
Summer/Spring Break _____
Vehicle you'll drive _____
Where you'll work _____
Where you'll go to college _____
Who you'll date _____

Who you'll marry _____
What career you'll pursue _____
Where you will live _____
The salary you will make _____
Family you'll have _____

Based on these decisions, what plans have you made without seeking God's will? How can you reconsider these things with God's will in mind?

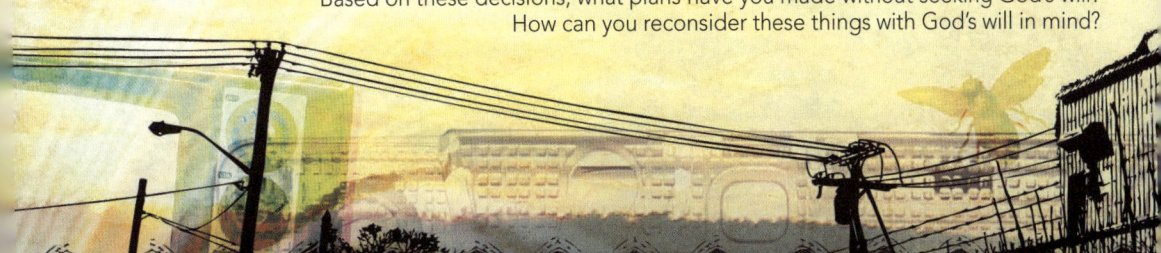

next // lesson 2 day 6 // 291

NOW & LATER

God is in control of the future. Not just the distant, flying car, robots and jet packs future, but also tomorrow. (That's not insignificant!) It's all the same to Him. We shouldn't treat it any differently either.

God is not so busy with the big mysterious future for all of Creation that He doesn't have time for every minute of your future. He's not only in control of your eternal destiny, but He cares deeply about who you marry, where you go to college, what you do this weekend… He cares about TODAY – even the "little" things. He cares about the thoughts popping into your mind right now. He cares about what you do next. So give it all to Him now. Trust Him every minute, giving every thought and action to Him "now" will add up to an incredible "future."

1 DAY

1000 YEARS

next // lesson 3 day 2 // 293

WORRIES

loneliness/isolation
overwhelming pressure
money
family
no one understand
no one agrees
not fitting in
being laughed at
what to wear
where to sit in lunch room
what if I see so-and-so
death
your mom embarrasses you

What worries do you need to give to God?
(circle any that apply to you and/or add things you are stressed about)

next // lesson 3 day 3 //294

WHY WORRY ABOUT TOMORROW?

What are you missing TODAY by focusing all of your attention on the "what if's" of tomorrow?

DEVOTION

Carbonrally.com estimates that 20 billion pounds of clothing are thrown away and dumped into landfills each year. Can even fathom something that overwhelming? The saddest part is that many people once thought life would not be complete without those very clothes. Have you ever been disappointed after returning home from a day full of shopping because you didn't like what you bought? What about all the toys you received as a child? What happened to them? How many times have you seen something on the Internet or TV that you just had to have and after six months or a year you had forgotten all about it? Regardless of what our culture encourages us to believe about material things, what does the Bible say about our possessions?

Read Matthew 6:19-21. Jesus taught his disciples in this passage about the importance of being heavenly minded. He stressed that they needed to build treasures in heaven rather than on earth.

Jesus mentions earthly treasures in verse 19. Those can be understood as material possessions that you have. Below, write down 5 "treasures" that you just had to have at some point. Then out beside them write down how long you used or plan to use each item. Got it? After you've done that, circle the ones that you expect to last 100 years. Probably not many. Right?

When we are focused on gaining all the possessions we can in one lifetime, we are not focused on God. God wants us to use our energies on things that will last. He wants us to invest in Him. He wants us to stop thinking temporarily and start thinking eternally.

In verse 20, Jesus tells the disciples to store up treasures in heaven. We know that a life spent on Jesus has eternal benefit and is of infinite value. Think about the following things today:

What have you done this year that has eternal significance? What about today?

Can you think of 5 people with whom you've shared your faith with this year? What about your lifetime?

If you could put your earthly treasures in one box and your eternal treasures in a different box, which one would be overflowing like a pirate's treasure chest? If you compared the two, which would be larger? Don't waste your life on things that will just end up in the landfill. Don't let your earthly "treasures" out weigh our heavenly ones.

Therefore I tell you, do not worry about your life, what you will eat or drink; or about your body, what you will wear. Is not life more important than food, and the body more important than clothes? Look at the birds of the air; they do not sow or reap or store away in barns, and yet your heavenly Father feeds them. Are you not much more valuable than they? Who of you by worrying can add a single hour to his life? "And why do you worry about clothes? See how the lilies of the field grow. They do not labor or spin. Yet I tell you that not even Solomon in all his splendor was dressed like one of these. If that is how God clothes the grass of the field, which is here today and tomorrow is thrown into the fire, will he not much more clothe you, O you of little faith? So do not worry, saying, 'What shall we eat?' or 'What shall we drink?' or 'What shall we wear?' For the pagans run after all these things, and your heavenly Father knows that you need them. But seek first his kingdom and his righteousness, and all these things will be given to you as well. Therefore do not worry about tomorrow, for tomorrow will worry about itself. Each day has enough trouble of its own.
Matthew 6:25-34

next // lesson 3 day 6 //297

STUDY

In Matthew 6:25-34, Jesus begins by saying, "Do not worry." He then asks five questions and finally wraps up His point by repeating the opening statement, "Do not worry." We can learn a lot from these questions Jesus raised.

1. "Is not life more important than food, and the body more important than clothes?"

Sometimes we forget which is more important; our bodies or the things we cover them with. Some people are more concerned with food and less about the life they are feeding. Sounds ironic but it is true. Jesus asked this question to help His listeners focus on the more important issue. It is easy for the less important things of life to distract us from the main thing—God.

What less important things distract you from God? _____

2. "Are you not much more valuable than they?"

The "they" Jesus is referring to are birds. Jesus didn't die for birds; He died for you. Sometimes we forget the value God places on our life. If we are valuable in God's eyes then do we really think He will neglect us? God doesn't neglect His children. He provides for them.

How do you know that God values you? _____

3. "Who of you by worrying can add a single hour to his life?"

Worrying never helps anything. Often the things we worry about never even happen. God doesn't want us to worry. He wants you to live a life fully dependent on His provision and acting accordingly. Our worrying shows a lack of faith.

Write down 5 things you've worried about already this year. Now, write out beside each one what the outcome was and if it was worth worrying about.

4. "Why do you worry about clothes?"

Have you ever heard the saying, "Don't major on the minors?" Clothes fall into the category of "minors." You should never worry about something as insignificant as clothes. In fact, all material possessions could be put in the place of the word clothes to read, "Why do you worry about_____?" You could fill in the blank with cars, make-up, video games, shoes, cell phones, etc.

There are other things that fall into the "minors" category. Identify some minor things in your life that you've stressed over._____

5. "If that is how God clothes the grass of the field, which is here today and tomorrow is thrown into the fire, will he not much more clothe you, O you of little faith?"

God knows His children need clothes. Not only does He know you need clothes, He knows all of your needs and knows how to meet your needs. Only God can provide for all of your needs because only God knows what the future will bring.

Read verses 33 and 34 again and answer this question, "How can we keep from worrying about our future?"

next // lesson 4 day 1 // 298

HE WHO WAS SEATED ON THE THRONE SAID, "I AM MAKING EVERYTHING NEW!" THEN HE SAID, "WRITE THIS DOWN, FOR THESE WORDS ARE TRUSTWORTHY AND TRUE." REVELATION 21:5

Write, "He makes all things new." (Sure, you could just read it, but it's amazing how you remember things better when you write it. It's easy. Write it. For real.) That's it. Write it down. Write it really big, or write it over and over. See how many times you can fit the phrase into the space provided. Write it in 3-D letters. Whatever. Get creative. How can you write this simple truth in a new and creative way? Then pray about what God wants to transform in your life as He is making you into something new. Something perfect and holy. A new creation, conformed to the image of His Son, Jesus Christ.

"For I know the plans I have for you," declares the Lord, "plans to prosper you and not to harm you, plans to give you hope and a future." Jeremiah 29:11

Restore us to yourself, O Lord, that we may return; renew our days as of old. Lamentations 5:21

He must remain in heaven until the time comes for God to restore everything, as he promised long ago through his holy prophets. Acts 3:21

Be confident of this, that he who began a good work in you will carry it on to completion until the day of Christ Jesus. Philippians 1:6

And the God of all grace, who called you to his eternal glory in Christ, after you have suffered a little while, will himself restore you and make you strong, firm and steadfast. 1 Peter 5:10

next // lesson 4 day 3 //300

WRITE YOUR OWN PSALM

In the Bible, the Book of Psalms is a collection of songs and poetry expressing honest feelings about God. The authors wrote about all kinds of different topics and emotions. Now you get to do the same thing!

Write a song or a poem, praising God for His sovereignty over the future. (Remember, His sovereignty over time includes what will happen in 1000 years and also the very next moment).

DEVOTION

Suppose a man walked into a doctor's office and said, "I feel sick." The doctor said, "Tell me what is wrong." The man replied, "I have a headache. My nose is runny. I have a rash on my arm. I cough all day. And I feel weak." The doctor grabbed a plastic bag and started putting things in the bag one by one. When he was finished, he handed the bag to the man and said, "This should do it. Here is a Tylenol for your headache, a tissue for your runny nose, a band-aid for your arm, a cough drop for your cough and an energy drink to make you feel stronger."

This man would not be satisfied after he takes all the "medicine" his doctor prescribed. His problems would not be fixed because his illness was not even addressed. The doctor didn't do anything to help the man. He only treated the symptoms. When you treat the symptoms you don't get to the heart of the disease. Symptoms are a result of something else; they aren't the actual problem.

Read 1 Corinthians 15:54-58. Here Paul is teaching the church at Corinth about the power of God over sin and death. Although Paul lived in Corinth for a while, he eventually moved on to start other churches. However, the Corinthians still sought his wisdom and teaching from time to time. This is one of those times. They had some questions about the resurrection of the physical body and the spiritual body. Paul gives them some powerful words as he shows them that Jesus defeated death and sin. Jesus addressed the disease and not just the symptoms.

There are symptoms to sin as well: death, suffering, war, pain, sadness, injustice… The list goes on and on. All of these are symptoms to the greater disease of sin. God does not want to just treat these symptoms. Although He could do away with war, that would not be the answer. God could do away with pain but that would only be a temporary fix. God defeated the disease of sin.

God is the victor. He has won the battle over sin and one day He will restore the earth to how it once was before sin entered like a cancer and corrupted everything. One day we'll all be healed forever – free from sin and all of its symptoms.

next // lesson 4 day 5 // 302

THIS WORLD IS NOT YOUR HOME.

STUDY

Mankind has been in need of restoration since Adam and Eve sinned in the Garden of Eden. Before sin entered the world, God and man had a perfect relationship. Genesis even says God walked in the garden and spoke with Adam. Our hope for the future is that we will someday experience perfect communion in God's presence, not just in an earthly garden, in a new paradise. God is bringing His people back into fellowship with Him but Satan's goal is to hinder that from happening.

Read Romans 16:17-20. Paul provides a list of things to watch out for when guarding against Satan's attempt to break up unity. A dysfunctional church community discourages people from hearing the gospel because they are so distracted and disgusted by the fighting, false teachings, and lives that look no better or sometimes even worse than those of people who don't claim to have a relationship with the Savior.

Here are things Paul said to watch out for:

Look out for people who cause divisions.
Christ came to unite God's people and restore our relationship with God and each other. People who cause divisions disrupt peace and make the church look foolish to outsiders. When that happens, Satan wins a small victory (temporarily).

Look out for people who put obstacles in your way contrary to the teaching you've learned.
Sending mixed signals to the world about the truth of God's Word calls the whole message of the gospel into question for many people. If your heart desires to see your friends and loved ones experience eternity in heaven, then be on the watch against anything that could confuse or deceive them regarding life in relationship with God.

Keep away from them—they are serving themselves and not the Lord.
Paul isn't saying not to share the gospel with people in need of life-change. He is saying that we don't let anyone distract our time and focus from the hope of a life spent for the sake of Christ instead of one spent on selfish pursuits.

Be wise, (or excellent) about what is good.
Fill your mind with God's promises instead of the world's lies. Since God is all-knowing and all-powerful, we should trust His wisdom on how to live today.

Be innocent of evil.
Start living now as if you were already in that perfect state of community with God. Remember how sneaky the devil was back in the garden? Don't even let temptation hang around, or eventually you'll find a seemingly good reason to sin against the God who loves you and has set you free from Satan's power.

Verse 20 should rock your socks off! Why? Paul says that the God of peace will soon crush Satan under your feet. What an awesome image of God's power. He is in control. The future is in His hands. Satan is not equally powerful. This is not just a promise for the future, but it changes how you live today. Knowing that Satan and sin have no power over you eternally, live in that freedom today. Walk and talk with God daily, filling your mind with His Word. Don't let anyone or anything keep you from trusting God and sharing His hope with a world in desperate need of His truth.

next // lesson 5 day 1 // 304

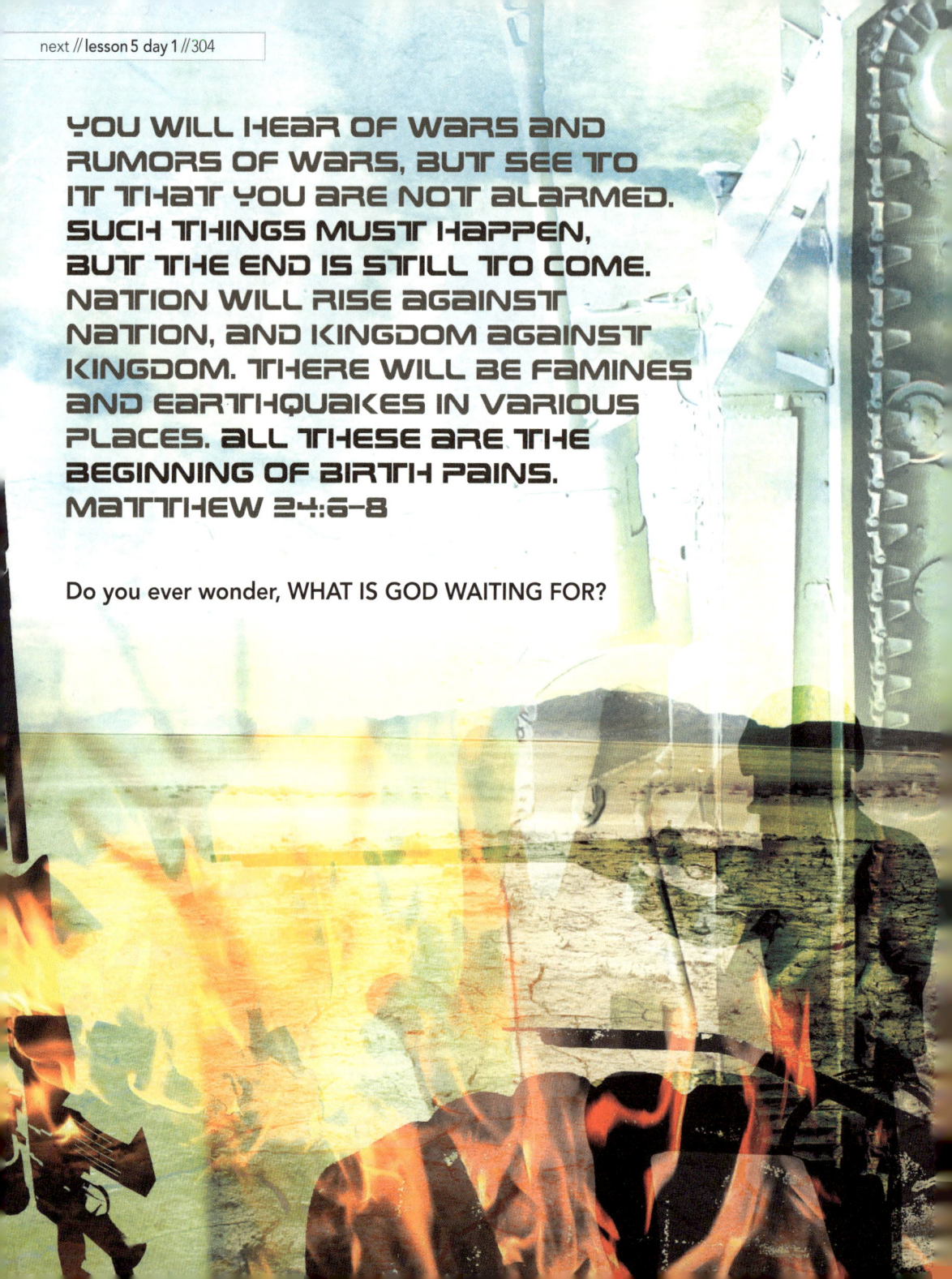

YOU WILL HEAR OF WARS AND RUMORS OF WARS, BUT SEE TO IT THAT YOU ARE NOT ALARMED. SUCH THINGS MUST HAPPEN, BUT THE END IS STILL TO COME. NATION WILL RISE AGAINST NATION, AND KINGDOM AGAINST KINGDOM. THERE WILL BE FAMINES AND EARTHQUAKES IN VARIOUS PLACES. ALL THESE ARE THE BEGINNING OF BIRTH PAINS.
MATTHEW 24:6-8

Do you ever wonder, WHAT IS GOD WAITING FOR?

THE END?

God's patience is for the sake of God's patients. He is the great physician and this world is sick. He desires to see more people healed, more people saved before the credits roll and the curtain closes on this old world. What are some situations you know of that are unhealthy? What stories wouldn't have a happy ending if they were to end today? Write out some ways you can be a part of God's work, tying up loose ends, helping mend some broken hearts, and seeing people healed and experience God's salvation in Christ. What if Jesus were literally waiting on you to do that one last thing before He returned? (Not that He is, but if He were, what might He want you to do?)

DEVOTION

What is the difference between a mystery and a suspense thriller?

In a mystery novel or film you already know what has been done – you are simply going back to see how everything played out. Sure, there are twists in the plot and surprises along the way, but the whole story is driven by the fact that something has already happened. You usually have a smart detective sifting through the clues and evidence to solve a mystery. On the other hand, you don't know what will happen next in a suspense thriller or even where the story may be headed. You're on the edge of your seat waiting to see if the good guys win or if evil prevails. There is usually a chase scene or fight sequence. The suspense comes from not knowing how it will all resolve. The story could still go either way.

What about you? Do you prefer mystery or suspense?

God's story is more like a mystery, except it is not fictional. We already know what happens in the end – the mystery is how everything plays out until then. We know it's true. God wins. We don't have to anxiously grip our seats in fear that evil will triumph. We can live in peace and enjoy taking part in God's story.

Read 2 Peter 3:11-13. Here Peter is encouraging other Christ-followers to live a life that reflects God's victory. He wants them to know that God is the ultimate champion. Therefore, God's people can live as people who have won the battle. He urges them to be found spotless and blameless and at peace with God. The day will come when we as Christ-followers will not struggle any longer. Until that day we should celebrate God's victory with our lifestyles. We don't have to live in suspense to see if good or evil will prevail. There is no contest. God wins—forever.

Based on Peter's instructions, how can you celebrate God's victory in the way you live your life?

DON'T GET CAUGHT OFF GUARD

NOW, BROTHERS, ABOUT TIMES AND DATES WE DO NOT NEED TO WRITE TO YOU, FOR YOU KNOW VERY WELL THAT THE DAY OF THE LORD WILL COME LIKE A THIEF IN THE NIGHT.

While people are saying, "Peace and safety," destruction will come on them suddenly, as labor pains on a pregnant woman, and they will not escape.

But you, brothers, are not in darkness so that this day should surprise you like a thief. You are all sons of the light and sons of the day. We do not belong to the night or to the darkness. So then, let us not be like others, who are asleep, but let us be alert and self-controlled.

1 Thessalonians 5:1–6

next // lesson 5 day 5 //308

GOING UP?

Sure, you may be ready to go on up to the big party in the sky, but God is holding the door, waiting for others to come too. There's room for more people. Who are we waiting on? Invite someone today to join you.

STUDY

Paul, the writer of 1 and 2 Corinthians, addressed the church at Corinth because they were experiencing divisions within themselves. Paul lived and worked in Corinth for over a year, establishing the church there. A fellow worker in the community named Apollos was gaining popularity and the church became divided over who to follow. Paul wasn't concerned about another man's ministry becoming popular, but he was concerned about people missing the point of being ministered to by turning church life into a popularity contest. Personality and celebrity factor shouldn't be the primary factor in church leadership. People needed to focus on the Christ in God's Word instead of the preacher delivering the message.

Paul urged them not to follow any one man but encouraged them to make Jesus their foundation. In this section of Scripture, Paul tells the Corinthians to make their work while they are on earth count for something eternal rather than something that will fade away. We see over and over in the Bible that this world will one day be burned in a holy fire. If that is true (and you know it is), are you spending your time collecting ashes or do the things you spend your time on have eternal significance?

Read 1 Corinthians 3:10-15

Paul used a carpenter's term, *foundation*, three times in this passage to make his point. He used it the first time to describe the support on which you would build a structure. He used this term the second time to refer to the prerequisite the church should have in order to grow, which was Jesus. The third time he used this word referred to an individual's life. Take a closer look at each time he used the word.

3:10- Paul said that he laid the foundation just like a carpenter would and now someone else has come behind him to continue building on it. That someone Paul was speaking of was Apollos. Paul was trying to teach the Corinthians that he and Apollos were not against each other. They were on the same team. Both of their missions were to glorify God and further His Kingdom.

3:11- Here Paul tells the Corinthians that unless they build their church on Christ, they will fail. It sounds obvious, but we often need reminded that church is not about an entertaining experience from professionals or Christian celebrities, it is about a relationship with Christ.

3:12- Next, Paul brings things down to a more personal level. Some people recognize that Jesus is the most important part of life but still rely on the things of the world. To these people he says that their work will one day be exposed by fire and if their work had eternal value it would show up in the end.

The things of eternal value that need to be built on your Christ-foundation are things like loving your neighbor, sharing Christ with your friends, helping someone with their Christian walk after they accept Christ (which is called discipleship). If you chose to spend your time on these things, your eternal reward will be great in heaven when Christ returns. However, if you choose to build your life around temporary pleasures, you are merely adding fuel to the eternal fire. You will be saved because Christ is your savior, but it will be as if you wasted your entire life and all you had to show for it was your initial salvation experience.

Paul urged people to move past their salvation experience and into a life lived as a servant for Christ. What a tragedy for the person who is baptized to never exit the baptismal pool and step into a new world of wonder and service to their Savior, Jesus Christ.

next // lesson 6 day 1 // 310

I TELL YOU THE TRUTH, UNTIL HEAVEN AND EARTH DISAPPEAR, NOT THE SMALLEST LETTER, NOT THE LEAST STROKE OF A PEN, WILL BY ANY MEANS DISAPPEAR FROM THE LAW UNTIL EVERYTHING IS ACCOMPLISHED. MATTHEW 5:18

The things of this world will fade, but every word of God will stand forever. What are you putting your trust in? Temporary things of this world? Or the eternal truth of God?

next // lesson 6 day 2 //311

STUDY

Read Matthew 25:14-30

In this particular parable Jesus tells about a master and his three servants to whom he gave a different amount of talents (a talent was worth more than a thousand dollars). One servant received five talents and turned his into ten talents. One servant received two talents and gained two more giving him four total talents. And the third servant received one talent but was too afraid to do anything with it, so he hid his one talent.

One day the master returned without warning and settled his accounts with the servants. To the servants that increased their total number of talents he said, "Well done good and faithful servant." But to the servant that hid his talent, he was very displeased and said, "You wicked and lazy servant!"

It's pretty obvious that we don't want to find ourselves in the shoes of the wicked and lazy servant, wasting our lives and the incomparable riches of the gospel.

Jesus was teaching the disciples several things here.

1. **We have a responsibility to use what we've been given to the best of our ability.** God has given you a gift whether it is music, athleticism, art, academics, a friendly personality, or whatever. The focus should not be on what you've been given, but how you're using your gifts to impact your world for Christ?

2. **Not using the gift God has entrusted to you is wicked and lazy.** Wow. Sounds pretty harsh, but those are Jesus' exact words. The greatest gift you have been given is the grace of God through faith in Christ. Are you sharing the gospel? Or are you hiding the truth about salvation and eternity, scared of what will happen if you try to tell someone?

3. **We do not know when Christ will return.** Until our Lord comes back, we should do everything we can to serve Him well.

Previously in Matthew 24:30-44, Jesus described the day of His return. Although He promised that there will be signs pointing to that day, Jesus warned that no one knows the day or the hour except the Father. We need to always be ready for Christ's return. Will we be found doing something faithful with what we've been given or will we be caught being lazy with what God has given to us?

What gifts has God given you? (Come on, it's okay to brag in something like this because we're talking about a gift. It's not like you did anything to earn it.)

How can you use these gifts for God?

Are there any gifts you have that you are not using for God?

DEVOTION

What is the difference between a pain pill and a vitamin?

Pain pills temporarily relieve problems. They numb areas and mask the pain. They just cover up what is really happening. People coming out of surgery or people who have recently been in an accident rely on pain pills to take their mind off of their suffering. It is dangerous to take pain pills too regularly, so they are just taken when problems arise or pain grows too intense to handle on one's own.

Vitamins, on the other hand, are more defensive. They help you fight off disease. If you take them regularly, you will be a healthier person. The vitamins help make your bones stronger, your heart healthier, your eyes sharper, and they give you more energy. Taking one here and one there doesn't really do you much good. They are a more long-term solution than a temporary fix.

Read Luke 9:18-27. In this passage, Jesus was teaching His disciples. Peter had just confessed that Jesus was the Christ. Even though Peter didn't fully understand everything that Jesus would suffer and accomplish, he believed that Jesus was the Messiah. In verse 22, Jesus offered some clarification as to what it meant to be the Christ. He said that He would have to die and be raised from the grave. In verses 23-27, Jesus described what it meant to be a disciple (since they also didn't fully understand what to expect in their own futures as a result of their relationship to Jesus.

Following Christ is something that is done daily, not just when you need a little Jesus to fix your problem or help you feel better. Honestly, most people tend to treat God like a pain pill. God did not send Jesus to die for your sins just so you could call on Him when you are hurting. God desires a daily relationship with you so that you will experience abundant life. (That doesn't mean it's an easy or comfortable life, as Jesus warned.)

Although this metaphor falls short in several ways, our relationship with God should be a way of life—much like a vitamin. Taking vitamins will not mask pain; it doesn't always prevent illness. It helps make you stronger when these times come. In the same way, a relationship with Jesus doesn't keep bad things from happening. Our daily walk with Christ helps us to deal with what does happen to us when things go bad.

How can you make sure you are ready for Christ's return?
What can you do to make sure others are ready as well?
How can you guard yourself from using God as a heavenly painkiller?

next // lesson 6 day 4 // 313

DAY PLANNER

Keep record of everything you do today OR think back and write down everything you already did today (depending on what time you are reading this).

If today were the last day of your life, was everything "worth it"? Was your time well spent? Is there anything that was a waste of precious time? Is there anything more you would've done for the sake of the next world instead of spending time on this life that will soon be over?

If you were going to prom or had a big date or big concert or big game, you would be getting ready. Everything in this life is preparation for the next life. This is your pregame, your prep time. How are you spending your time?

WHAT IF HE CAME BACK TODAY?

Would you be ready? Would the people you know and love be ready? Do you live like He could come back today? Or tomorrow? Or the next day?

What would you do or say differently today if you believed that Jesus could come back at any moment (like the Bible says)? Why don't you live that way all the time?

next // lesson 6 day 6 //315

GO!

Until the day He returns, you have been commissioned by Christ to live as His witness. You are a living testimony to the fact that this world and life as we now know it will someday come to an end. So go! Don't just stand around doing nothing. Go tell the world that Jesus is alive. He has risen and is coming back someday. That's the best news in history!

He said to them: "It is not for you to know the times or dates the Father has set by his own authority. But you will receive power when the Holy Spirit comes on you; and you will be my witnesses in Jerusalem, and in all Judea and Samaria, and to the ends of the earth."

After he said this, he was taken up before their very eyes, and a cloud hid him from their sight.

Acts 1:7-9

So here you are.

Your journey is over. You've arrived at the end of this book.

There's an interesting question you should probably consider. Ready? Here it goes:

Are you different now than you were before you started this book?

It's a fair question. After all, you've invested a great deal of your time in reading and working through this book.

Do you know more about your relationships with God and with other people than you did before you started?

Do you have a greater trust for God, knowing that He cares about today and holds your future?

Are you excited about seeing every part of life in relation to worship?

Do you feel more equipped to extend grace and mercy to those who might not know Christ?

Hopefully, you answered "yes" to all the questions above. Hopefully, you're already making a difference for Christ in this world.

The most important thing you should have gathered from your time spent in this book is that God loves you. He created you for relationship and wants you to know Him personally. God loves other people too, so He expects you to share what you know with them. After all, your time in this world is just the beginning of an eternal relationship.

Don't miss out on being connected to something (and someone) so much greater than anything (or anyone) in this world. Your Heavenly Father knows best. Trust Him. Give yourself wholeheartedly to loving God and loving people.

This is what life is all about.

What you do today has eternal significance. The love you experience and share today could change the course of someone else's life forever. Today matters. You matter. People matter. It's all linked.

linked
CONNECTIONS BETWEEN GOD, EACH OTHER, AND US

STILL THIRSTY FOR GOD'S WORD?

31 verses EVERY TEENAGER SHOULD KNOW

If you like this book, you'll love any of the *31 Verses* devotional journals!

linked
31 verses EVERY TEENAGER SHOULD KNOW

- POCKET-SIZED COLOR JOURNAL—70 PAGES OR LESS
- 31 SHORT, DAILY DEVOTIONALS
- SHORT DEVOTIONALS FOR EACH VERSE & JOURNALING SPACE
- STARTING AT $4.99

OTHER 31 Verses Devotional Journals

- IDENTITY
- THE WAY
- THE BIBLE
- CHRIST
- FLIP
- reverb
- Here & Now

31VERSES.COM

studentlife**bible**study

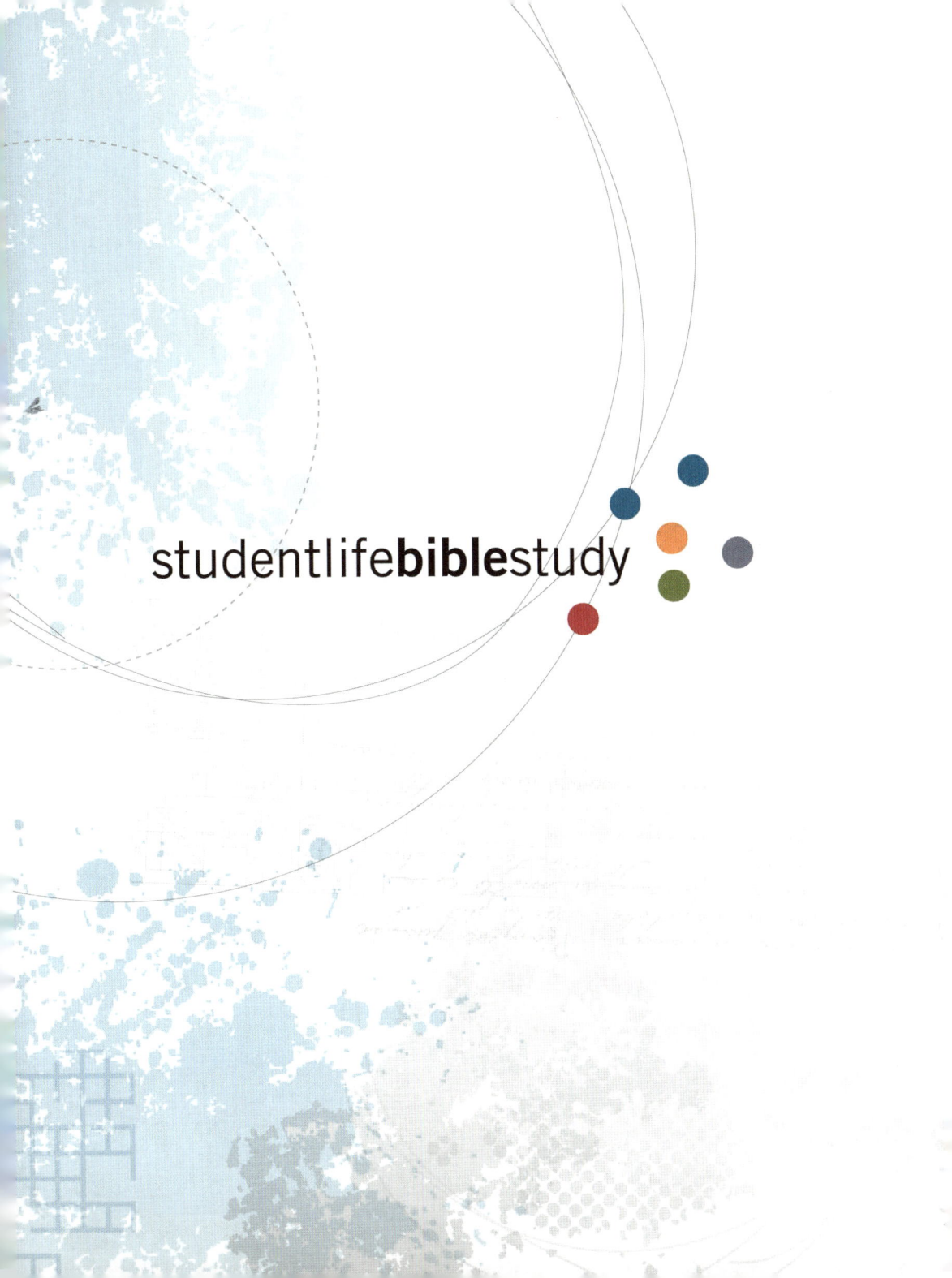